Why We Whisper

Why We Whisper

How Traditional Americans Can Stand Up to the Intimidation and Ridicule of Secular Progressive Elites

Senator Jim DeMint and
Professor J. David Woodard

ROWMAN & LITTLEFIELD PUBLISHERS, INC.
Lanham • Boulder • New York • Toronto • Plymouth, UK

ROWMAN & LITTLEFIELD PUBLISHERS, INC.

Published in the United States of America
by Rowman & Littlefield Publishers, Inc.
A wholly owned subsidiary of The Rowman & Littlefield Publishing Group, Inc.
4501 Forbes Boulevard, Suite 200, Lanham, Maryland 20706
www.rowmanlittlefield.com

Estover Road
Plymouth PL6 7PY
United Kingdom

British Library Cataloguing in Publication Information Available

Library of Congress Cataloging-in-Publication Data:
DeMint, Jim.
 Why we whisper : how traditional Americans can stand up to the intimidation and
ridicule of secular progressive elites / Jim DeMint and J. David Woodard.
     p. cm.
 Includes bibliographical references and index.
 ISBN-13: 978-0-7425-5252-4 (cloth : alk. paper)
 ISBN-10: 0-7425-5252-7 (cloth : alk. paper)
 1. Freedom of speech—United States. 2. United States. Constitution. 1st Amendment.
I. Woodard, J. David. II. Title.
 KF4772.D46 2008
 342.7308'53—dc22   2007020875

Printed in the United States of America

⊗™ The paper used in this publication meets the minimum requirements of American
National Standard for Information Sciences—Permanence of Paper for Printed Library
Materials, ANSI/NISO Z39.48-1992.

Contents

Preface   vii

1   Feeling the Heat   1

2   Who Is Right?   15

3   Who Decides What Is Right and Wrong?   29

4   The Culture Development Cycle: Shaping American Values   47

5   Power to Intimidate: The SLAPP Factor   63

6   Public Schools: Deconstructing American Values   79

7   America's Secular Cathedrals: Higher Ed or a Lower Way?   91

8   War of the Worldviews: Attacks and Counterattacks   113

9   America's Secular Culture: The Cost in Dollars and Sense   125

10 Contrasting Worldviews: Intolerance or Compassion?   151

11 Overcoming our Self-Imposed Silence, Regaining Our Voices,
    and Winning the Culture War   173

Notes   203

Bibliography   223

Index   235

About the Authors   243

Preface

On an October morning in 2006, Pastor James Woods found the door to the community room of West Ken Lark Park locked. For seven years Issues of Life Ministries had used the room for meetings. Then the city of Lauderhill annexed and assumed management of the park. The pastor was summarily told to vacate the premises, and no reason was given for the eviction.

Issues of Life church had to meet outside in the park. An attorney for the group declared, "This church had the same right to use city facilities as all other groups, yet the city evicted them without explanation."[1] The church found itself, literally, outside in the cold.

The removal of a church from a public facility by a government official is both a warning and a metaphor for the concerns of this book. More and more, the nation is involved in a debate over foundational values. Anyone who thinks that the country is not involved in a serious culture war, just because people aren't stepping over dead bodies in the streets, should pause to read the newspapers.

Americans today live in the greatest nation the world has ever known. Never before has a country been the producer, and beneficiary, of so much wealth and freedom. But this success is no accident. It came from a free people, described by Ronald Reagan in his second inaugural address as, "hopeful, big-hearted, idealistic, daring, decent and fair."[2] The economic, social, religious, political, and military systems of the United States are envied and copied around the globe. The entire world is dependent on the success of America for their protection, prosperity, and survival.

With great success comes even greater responsibility. Part of the American legacy is to pass our values to our posterity, as well as to future generations in other nations. We must leave America even greater and stronger than it was when we received it. To meet this responsibility, the next generation must understand what made our country great, what is working, what is not working, and how to improve all the ideas that contributed to past success. An eradication of this memory could result in the erosion of the American spirit. But a rediscovery of our founding principles and vision, a knowledge of the difference between isolated events and directional trends, and ultimately between problems and the real cause of problems can revitalize our culture and country. Our task is to be critical of ourselves with the goal of making our nation better.

No factor is more important in this task than our First Amendment right to freedom of speech. This right is the most treasured benefit of living in a free and democratic nation. But freedom of speech is more than a help, it is also a foundational principle that promotes and protects a healthy democracy. The American right to freedom of speech is both a means and an end to improving and strengthening the nation.

This book is about free speech in America, but not "freedom of speech" as it is often defined today. We are not speaking of the freedom to practice destructive behavior or to produce obscene material. This book is about freedom of speech as it was intended by the visionaries who designed the Constitution and the Bill of Rights. The First Amendment empowers Americans to join the public and political debate with their ideas and values, including those traditional ideas and values that have made America great. This fundamental freedom is under attack, and unless principled Americans fight back, our grandchildren and future generations all around the world will receive a greatly diminished inheritance.

All free societies aspire to some ideal of freedom of discussion, and for most of its history, the public debate of contentious issues has been a hallmark of American democracy. From its original design in the *Federalist Papers* before the Constitution was ratified, through countless public debates in county squares, to major national debates such as the historical Lincoln-Douglas debates, Americans have expressed their opinions and debated issues publicly in a spectacle of freedom before the entire world.

The founders knew that this civil and public expression of differences was democracy's substitute for violence. The Civil War stands as America's one great failure to resolve disputes through nonviolent debate, and freedom of speech has been the hallmark to protect and preserve democracy for more than two centuries. The civil rights movement in America is a recent reminder of how major societal differences can be resolved through nonviolent public expression.

Historically, freedom of speech is crucial in any democracy. Uninhibited and unrestrained discussion of issues is essential to conversation in an open society. In fact, we might say that democracy is—by definition—a conversation about freedom, about what is right or wrong, and about what is fair to all. Good government is a result of freedom debated. The demise of good government comes when this conversation is abbreviated, as we believe it has been.

The classic argument for making freedom of speech a fundamental right is based on the premise that it is protection against what John Stuart Mill called the "tyranny of prevailing opinion." In his influential and timeless essay, *On Liberty*, Mill argues "against the tendency of society to impose, by means other than civil penalties, its own ideas and practices as rules of conduct on those who dissent from them."[3] Mill was upset about the domination of nineteenth-century England by Christian ethics, morality, and lifestyle, especially as it related to his relationship with Harriet Taylor. While we sympathize with Mill's position, and with those today who wish to escape the imposition of societal mores, we are more concerned here about its opposite: a "tyranny of prevailing opinion" that *excludes* Christianity and traditional values from participation and discussion in the public square.

Our argument here is that, for a host of reasons, the values that were instrumental in forming the basis of our culture have been ignored, forgotten, or, worse, forbidden in public debate. As a result, in the words of Robert Bork, "Large chunks of the moral life of the United States, [along with] major features of its culture have disappeared altogether, and more are in the process of extinction."[4] We are concerned about the process that has caused this decline, and we believe that its continued operation, and ultimate replacement by a secular ethic, will prove fatal to our society.

We will show that through court rulings, bureaucratic pronouncements, and well-intentioned, but ultimately unhelpful laws, secular values have allied with government authority to dismantle the ideals of a moral and decent nation. A country once confident of its values and optimistic about its future is now pessimistic, nervous, and confused. Traditional American institutions like the Boy Scouts, churches, businesses, college campuses, and public schools are routinely targeted for attack and government regulation. As a result, morally responsible, patriotic Americans are forced to withdraw into the shadows of public opinion, where their freedoms of speech are reduced to whispers.

The positive influences and societal protections of tradition have been routinely ignored by the new secular elites who have been ensconced with government power and are now anxious to advance their agenda. We are discouraged with how those who seek to alter America have staked out their positions and, more significantly, how they are succeeding in their transformative campaign. We have watched as moral relativism and secularism have savaged education, law, religion, business, and traditional notions of proper behavior.

The younger generation grew up after the fall of the Berlin Wall and does not appreciate the demise of the antifreedom regime of the Soviet Union. In short, our children have grown up in a radically different moral environment than the one we experienced. The main difference being that we had parents, grandparents, teachers, pastors, neighbors, sports heroes, television shows, recording artists, and even journalists, who were outspoken in their convictions and reminded us that some things were wrong and we shouldn't do them. We had a community of support around commonly held values. Government was a kind of backstop to these principles because state and federal laws were supportive of the prevailing social morality. Beginning in the 1960s, that backstop collapsed, resulting in an open floodgate that is now drowning our society in morally reprehensible behavior and values.

The present generation has few of the advantages of shared community values that we experienced, and unless Americans respond quickly to this growing threat, our grandchildren will be saddled with crushing debt from social costs and an economic decline that inevitably accompanies moral deterioration. America's new value system insists that a belief in right and wrong is no more than a prejudice, but these new values have been a disaster. In the words of William Bennett, "Over the past three decades we have experienced substantial social regression [and] . . . today the forces of social decomposition are challenging—and in some instances, overtaking—the forces of social composition."[5]

Although America has amassed enormous debt in recent decades, the economic gains since the 1960s continue to mask the growing costs and long-term threat of our moral decline. America's population has increased 40 percent in less than half a century. The gross national product, which is the total dollar value of all final goods and services produced for consumption in society, has more than tripled, and we have experienced real growth in personal income. However, other statistics chronicle a social regression that reads like a criminal rap sheet. Again, using the 1960s as a benchmark, we have experienced a 560 percent increase in violent crime, a 400 percent increase in births outside marriage, a quadrupling of divorces, a tripling in the number of children living in single-parent homes, and a more than 200 percent increase in the teenage suicide rate. The United States leads the industrial nations in murder, rape, and other violent crimes, and is at the bottom in elementary and secondary achievement scores.[6] Americans are conditioned to view juvenile crime, illegitimacy, abortion, suicide, and drug addiction as mental problems instead of moral problems. The Roman Orator Cicero (106–43 BC), looked out at the society of his time and declared that the pursuit of material wealth and political power made a nation "barbarous, however great its mastery of nature." But he also declared that: "Where there's life, there's hope."[7]

We are just now awakening to the realization that our much maligned and fading values were not punishments but protection for all of us from our baser natural instincts. If government allows, protects, and even subsidizes destructive behavior, social problems will lead to the decline, and ultimately the fall, of the United States. The American people can no longer allow this cultural decline. We must expect and demand government to promote positive behavior that is aligned with our historical and cultural principles. Those in authority must not only encourage but listen to, embrace, and institutionalize the whispers of the muzzled majority of Americans, and rediscover the values that made the nation exceptional in the first place.

The present situation leads us to a final premise. What government has undone it can repair. Instead of hiding in the shadows and whispering complaints while government promotes destructive behavior, Americans must force it to act in the best interest of the common good. In short, we must exercise our freedom of speech! Our laws and social policies must discourage destructive behaviors such as promiscuity, divorce, illegitimacy, pornography, drug abuse, and gambling that, although labeled by the left as "victimless crimes," have in fact proven harmful to society and potentially ruinous to future generations. Government has played the leading role in the decline of our culture, and it must now play the pivotal part in reversing that degeneration.

Isolated examples of social improvement led by government are in evidence, and they will be discussed in the chapters that follow. Though few in number, we find instances where policy changes by government led to social regeneration. In 1996, Congress passed welfare reform, which served to encourage marriage and discourage illegitimacy. Tougher state divorce laws help hold families together. Strong child support laws have caused a reduction in illegitimate births in several states. These isolated examples are enough to show that modern-day social pathologies can be reversed.

This book outlines the causes, the consequences, and the solutions for America's serious and growing social problems. To open our exploration, we offer, in the first chapter, our personal anecdotes of the social muggings we have received merely for suggesting that government endorsements of destructive behaviors were detrimental to society. Our own experiences of losing our right to say that some things were wrong became the motivation for the research that resulted in this book. The "whispered" encouragement received from intimidated friends and supporters inspired the title. It is our hope that our personal experiences, along with the documentation in this book, will inspire other Americans to stand up, speak out, and reclaim our culture before it is too late.

We believe there is still time to push back against the challenge of social engineers and moral relativists, but we must act quickly. Like the proverbial frog that eventually meets its demise in the simmering pot, our society has moved at breakneck speed. Just yesterday we were relaxing school dress codes, and today police patrol school hallways looking for children with guns. We can no longer just stand by speechless.

We dedicate this book, with affection, to our grandchildren—in most cases yet unborn. They will bear the weight of our cultural decisions if we do not reduce the burden. We are reminded of that chilling statement in the Preamble of the Constitution that declares its intent to "secure the blessings of liberty to ourselves and our posterity." The greatest debt, as always, goes to our families, who inspired and encouraged us in this effort, especially to our wives: Debbie DeMint and Judy Woodard. Several Clemson University undergraduate students provided helpful comments and worked as research assistants. We remember: Tarin Holcomb, Jessica Edwards, and Philip Curtis. Emily Shuler was a thorough proofreader, critic, and friend who worked to polish the final draft.

To all these people and many unnamed others we owe our deepest thanks. Any mistakes, errors, or prejudices of interpretation are ours alone.

Jim DeMint
United States Senate
South Carolina

J. David Woodard
Clemson University
Clemson, South Carolina

Chapter One

Feeling the Heat

Speech is power. Speech is to persuade, to convert, to compel.

— Ralph Waldo Emerson

JIM DEMINT: THE FIRST DEBATE—OCTOBER 3, 2004

I was dead tired. After almost two years of campaigning for the U.S. Senate seat, my mind and body felt almost numb from running on adrenaline twenty-four hours a day, seven days a week. I was on my way from Columbia, South Carolina, to Charleston for the first televised debate with my Democratic opponent.

I thought back to the summer, when I was embroiled in the middle of a six-way Republican primary. The polls showed me a distant third, well behind the front-runner, former governor David Beasley, who was predicted to get over 50 percent of the vote in the first round of the primary. Second place in the polls with 18 percent was Charlie Condon, a former attorney general in South Carolina and a recent candidate for governor. I was stuck in third, barely ahead of a political newcomer, Thomas Ravenel. The Ravenel name was well known around the state because Thomas's father had been a congressman and a state senator—in fact, a bridge in Charleston was named for him. Thomas was a self-made multimillionaire who had vowed to put over $3 million of his own money in the race. No one really believed he would do it. Before it was over, he did.

Fifth in the polls was the mayor of Myrtle Beach, Mark McBride. While not well known outside of the city where he was elected, McBride was a young, energetic, handsome candidate with a popular "put America first" message. Sixth place was held by latecomer Orly Davis. Davis was unknown

1

and underfunded, but as the only woman in the field, she threatened to capture enough votes to change the outcome of a close primary.

Together we were headed for the most competitive and expensive Republican primary in South Carolina history. On June 14, 2004, Governor Beasley received 36 percent of the vote. I was a distant second at 24 percent, barely edging out Ravenel in third, who had come on strong the last two weeks and gained 23 percent of the vote. Fortunately for me, South Carolina election laws require that candidates receive 50 percent of the vote to win a primary election without a runoff. Now the race was between David Beasley and me, with the election scheduled two weeks later.

I knew what I had to do. Six years earlier, in 1998, I finished as runner-up to another candidate in my first congressional primary. That year I won the runoff and the general election in November. This runoff was a repeat of that one. To win, I had to double the number of votes Beasley received, and get the support from Republicans who had voted for other candidates in the primary. The *State* newspaper in Columbia virtually wrote me off, saying, "Jim DeMint is the guy you'd want to do your taxes. . . . David Beasley is the guy you'd want to be with when you blew your refund."[1] But something remarkable happened in those two weeks. Campaign contributions poured in, and we were able to outspend Beasley on television.

On election night I was uneasy. When the results came in, I won the Republican runoff 59 percent to 41 percent, almost a twenty-point spread. The newspapers were at a loss to explain the margin of victory, and they quickly turned to writing about the difficult general election contest I would have in the fall against my Democratic opponent.

Inez Tennebaum was in her second term as state superintendent of education, having won more votes in her reelection than any Republican running for a statewide office that year. She began the general election race with a fresh disposition and had significantly more money than I did. I was exhausted, and the $4 million I had raised had been spent to win the primary. Now I had to start again from scratch to contest the general election.

One consolation of spending money in the primary was that I began the general election campaign with the same name awareness as Superintendent Tennebaum. The polls even showed me with an early lead. My campaign team was well aware that any margin would likely evaporate once the Democrats started their television advertising. The Tennebaum campaign stumbled out of the gate, but she soon fired her campaign leadership team, and our polls showed me with an eight-point lead going into our first televised debate in October. The margin was less than it had been several weeks before because the Tennebaum campaign found something in my record, and they bore down relentlessly, like a hornet working in the spring.

The national Democratic Party began to air commercials saying that I was going to raise the sales tax 23 percent on everything we bought. The allegation seemed so preposterous that my campaign was slow to respond. We didn't think anyone would believe that one of the most conservative members of Congress would raise taxes by any margin, let alone by 23 percent. After millions of dollars worth of commercials aired saying I would raise taxes, my lead in the polls evaporated. For the first time, the Democrats saw that they had a good chance to win.

Tennebaum redesigned her whole campaign around the sales tax charge. Commercials showed her walking around grocery stores with a cart full of bags each labeled, "DeMint 23%." She visited nursing homes telling seniors that I would raise taxes on their prescription drugs. She told college students their books would cost 23 percent more. Her entire campaign was built on a lie, but in time the attack worked.

The origin of the charge lay in my desire to reform the tax code. For years, I had pushed tax reform in Congress, constantly encouraging the Republican leadership to begin the debate about how to fix a tax code that I believed was the biggest job killer in America. I cosponsored any bill that would replace the current system, including one plan to eliminate all federal income tax, payroll (FICA) taxes, capital gains taxes, corporate and business taxes, death taxes, and replace them all with a 23 percent national sales tax. I didn't think this proposal was perfect, but by cosponsoring this and other plans, I hoped to encourage the tax committee chairman to think differently about taxation and to be willing and open about debating different plans. I wanted to reform the tax code nearly any way I could.

Of course my Democratic opponent failed to mention that the 23 percent sales tax would replace *all* other federal taxes, and that I had supported other tax reform initiatives. But as I was learning that fall, the truth doesn't often get in the way of a good political campaign. The Democrats plowed millions into the effort to mislead and confuse South Carolina voters. The *State* newspaper, with the largest circulation in the state, appeared to be part of the staff for Tennebaum. They consistently referenced "my plan" to raise taxes 23 percent, and criticized me for wanting to raise taxes on the poor. By the night of the first televised debate at the College of Charleston, the main issue in the campaign was the 23 percent tax increase. I was on the defensive, and I knew it.

Tennebaum and I were seated at a small round table along with the debate moderator. Across the table sat my opponent, in the same bright red dress she wore in every television commercial and had pledged to wear every day of the campaign. The audience was diverse—it included both my own and Tennebaum's supporters, a large contingent of the college's faculty and staff, and a smattering of students. I could tell by the scowls that there were few DeMint devotees in the audience.

The questions went as I expected for most of the hour. Whatever query the moderator asked Tennebaum, she responded with how my sales tax increase was going to destroy the nation. She was well rehearsed, and brought every issue back to the 23 percent tax.

I felt like I was debating a parrot.

On important national issues like the war on terror, reforming Social Security, and the state of health care, she had almost no in-depth understanding of the problems. Even on education, which was supposedly her strength, she offered no new ideas, only a defense of her accomplishments while superintendent of education.

Then, just when I thought I had escaped the first debate without a major gaffe, the moderator read from a document, and asked me: "The state Republican platform says that practicing homosexuals should not be allowed to teach in our public schools. Do you agree with this statement?"

My full response was:

I think Americans have a right to live in the way they want, but if they try to redefine our institutions such as marriage, which is what's going on today . . . we cannot have the government doing that. A marriage is our most esteemed institution, and we need to protect it, and we need the folks that are teaching in schools to represent our . . . values. And I certainly think people should be able to live as they want, but I don't think the government should embrace [homosexuality], just as the military doesn't. If a person is a practicing homosexual, they should not be teaching in our schools.

Tennebaum responded:

Well, first of all, this is America and people should be able to live their life freely, and a person who's a homosexual that wants to teach in our public schools, they should be allowed to. And many wonderful teachers may or may not be gay. I don't think anyone asks them that, because they respect their privacy. But to say that a homosexual can't teach in a public school is really, really a bad thing, and it's just un-American.

One of my political weaknesses is that I always try to answer whatever question I am asked. More than that, I want to help people understand my answer. This is not smart in politics. I had another problem as well. As I prepared for the debate, I realized I was not only tired, but also sick. At this point, I just wanted the debate to end.

This question was a curveball, and I am fairly sure that if I had been at the top of my game, I would have answered that the question was not a federal issue and was not relevant to a U.S. Senate campaign. I should have let that curveball go by. Instead I took a big swing at it. I was confident that my answer was defensible, or at least worthy of debate. The Supreme Court had decided that public school teachers could not pray in class because of a child's inherent "emulation of teachers as role models." If the Court concluded that the special teacher-student relationship was strong enough to result in religious indoctrination from a simple prayer, surely there would be concern about students emulating openly homosexual teachers. I would soon discover, however, that the same logic used to remove prayer from the classroom did not apply to politically protected behaviors.

The question about gay teachers was just one of many that we took that night, and I had forgotten about it until I walked into the pressroom before leaving the college. The only question that I was asked was whether I thought the "don't ask, don't tell" policy of the military should apply to gays teaching in the public schools. I said I thought it should.

After the debate, I had dinner in Charleston with my campaign staff, and we were all in the mood to celebrate. In spite of the curveball I'd been thrown that night, I believed we were headed into the home stretch with all the momentum.

I could not have been more wrong!

The front page, top-of-the-fold headline in the *State* newspaper the next morning screamed: "DeMint Says Gays Can't Teach in Schools."[2] The article was scathing in its indictment of my prejudices. Newspapers across the state took advantage of the situation to use biased sources to push their editorial agenda. "I'm surprised that any candidate with three terms in Congress could be that politically awkward," said Jack Bass, a professor of humanities and social sciences at the College of Charleston. "His comments have definitely hurt him. It's become the principal issue in the race."[3] In Myrtle Beach, a letter to the editor declared that "DeMint's comments [were] not isolated. . . . The Republican Party is fomenting intolerance . . . [the] anti-gay stance shows how far to the right the Republican Party has lurched."[4]

The irony in this controversy was that the South Carolina Department of Education brochure, distributed under the supervision of Inez Tennebaum, included a "Code of Ethics of the Education Profession" section. The so-called "un-American" stance I took was fully in compliance with the "highest possible degree of ethical conduct," of the profession as advocated by the State Department of Education. What is more, my position was in conformity with South Carolina law. Under the "just cause" for removal of teachers, the Code (59-25-160, 1990) lists "immorality and conduct involving moral turpitude" as reasons for the revocation of a teaching certificate. I was about to learn that "immorality . . . and moral turpitude" were outdated concepts where teachers were concerned.

My opponents, and the press, finally had what they wanted from me: a mistake. Over the previous year the *State* had not bothered to send a reporter to most of my press conferences, but when this offered them the opportunity to radicalize my values by painting me as a gay-bashing homophobe, there was not enough ink to publish my remarks. In Washington, the *Hill* newspaper declared that my comments had turned "what looked like a sure win over Democrat Inez Tennebaum into a cliffhanger."[5]

Two days later I added more blood into the water. While meeting with an editorial writer for the *Aiken Standard*, I explained (it's always a mistake to explain) that my comments were not intended to single out gays. I would have given the same answer if the question had been about "an unwed pregnant teacher who was living with her boyfriend."[6] I didn't think any parent should be forced to put their child into a classroom with a teacher who was openly opposed to their values. As I saw it, the law had its roots in a well-intentioned desire to protect underage students from morally suspect lifestyles or questionable viewpoints. Moreover, it was the responsibility of the local school board—not a distant legislator or administrator—to determine what was or was not morally appropriate for a public school education.

The *Aiken Standard* must have e-mailed my comments to the Associated Press before I left their parking lot. The media liked Act Two even better than Act One, and a brush fire quickly became a forest fire. My campaign staff suggested I make a public apology, and it was clear that we needed to do something. The media was making "teachers" the only issue of the Senate race.

I built my campaign strategy around a positive, proactive message that included discussion of the real national issues of tax reform, Social Security reform, health insurance reform, and educational choice. But it had become painfully obvious that the press cared more about symbols than substance. None of these important national issues were being covered by the media, and the sensational was making headlines over the substantive.

I decided to make an apology, but I would not apologize for what I believed. We issued a press release in which I apologized for answering the question. The press release stated, in part, "I clearly said something as a Dad that I just shouldn't have said," and I went on to say that the issue was a local school board concern. I apologized for distracting from the debate by answering a question that had nothing to do with the U.S. Senate. "Whether DeMint was apologizing for Sunday's remark about gays, Tuesday's remark about unwed teachers, or both, wasn't clear from the statement," said the *Greenville News*, "[and] DeMint's campaign declined to clear the air."[7]

I had befuddled the media at their own game. Calls from the press wanted to know if I was apologizing to homosexuals or to unwed mothers. I chose not to respond. One letter to the editor said, "Jim DeMint is either a bigot, an idiot or a savvy campaigner," and another, "it is obvious Jim DeMint is a condescending, chauvinistic, good old boy who has obvious disregard for the very laws that are in place to protect the citizens of this country."[8] A University of South Carolina professor of education opined that he knew of no "data showing that homosexual teachers, single [or] pregnant and living [with a] boyfriend had a negative influence on students." A leading columnist in the *State* declared that my position was "un-American, bizarre and unconstitutional,"[9] although he was vague or simply ill-informed as to where the Constitution endorsed and protected gay teachers.

The press didn't like it, but the strategy worked. The issue eventually faded, and my opponent went back to telling voters I was going to raise their taxes 23 percent. The moderators in all the remaining debates attempted to trap me into explaining my apology, but I ignored their questions.

Although the issue lost traction in South Carolina, I had become a novelty in Washington. On CNN's *Crossfire*, Democratic political consultant James Carville declared, "In the right-wing city of stupidity, I have discovered a skyscraper by the name of Jim DeMint . . . whose IQ must be somewhere around freezing on the Celsius scale." He went on to say, "[DeMint] opposes abortion, even in cases of rape and incest, and then made a fool of himself by saying gays and single mothers shouldn't be allowed to teach in schools, this on top of proposing a 23-cent national sales tax that would throw millions into poverty." Tim Russert on *Meet the Press* interrupted me on the air, and bullied me about what had happened. I just kept repeating that it was "a local school board issue." It wasn't pretty, but we stopped the bleeding and went back to running the campaign the way we had planned.

My poll numbers continued to decline, and the *Charleston Post and Courier* showed the Senate race as a statistical dead heat. "The poll of 625 voters . . . showed DeMint leading Tennebaum . . . by a four-point margin that is within the poll's margin of error."[10] Our internal campaign polls indicated that the reason for the decline was related to the 23 percent attacks, not the homosexual or pregnant teacher issue.

While the media was blasting me about my school teacher comments, and my opponent continued to confuse voters about my tax policy, something profoundly encouraging was happening. In every meeting, after every speech or rally across the state, people would come up to me, lean real close and whisper, "stick with your values," "you're right," "don't apologize," or "don't let them back you down." Businessmen, teachers, parents, and young people gave whispered support. They sent e-mails and letters. But almost none of this appeared in the public record.

The whispers continued to grow, but there was virtually no public defense of my comments. As far as I know, there were no media sources, no pastors, and no state politicians that came to my defense. In short, there were hundreds of whispers, but no public support. People seemed willing to talk about almost anything in public forums, but on this issue they whispered.

No one wanted to be associated with the public pounding I was getting from the media, but I gained passionate private supporters because I was willing to say something they believed in but were afraid to say out loud. I had never seen such a large number of people so completely intimidated.

On election day 2004, I emerged victorious with 54 percent of the ballots cast. I found out later that my poll numbers actually went up when the press was most critical. Thankfully, the people of South Carolina spoke louder with their votes than the pundits did with their endless commentary.

ACADEMIC FREEDOM FOR ALL BUT CONSERVATIVES: DAVID WOODARD'S STORY

It began with a phone call in 1993. The caller identified himself as an attorney for the State of Colorado. He asked: "Would you be willing to testify in federal court about the political power of homosexual groups in American politics?" I hesitated, in those embryonic computer days, before Google and widespread use of the Internet, because it was not easy to get extensive information about the money and expenses of groups active in the political process. I knew something about the subject because I taught a course on parties and elections and had learned more as a political consultant for candidates for elective office.

Newspaper coverage of the 1992 presidential election estimated that homosexual groups like the Human Rights Campaign Fund had given some $3 million to the Clinton campaign. While I didn't know the specifics, anyone on a college campus knew that homosexual rights was *the* emergent issue. Gay and lesbian groups were organizing on campuses nationwide, and their proponents were outspoken in class discussions. In my class a student called me a "bigot" and walked out when I said in lecture that homosexual rights were far different from those sought by black Americans in the civil rights movement of the 1960s.

The attorney asked me if I knew about the Amendment Two controversy in Colorado. I had read in the *New York Times* about an amendment referendum, but didn't know the specifics. Before we hung up, I agreed to serve as an expert witness for the State and discuss the influence of homosexual groups in the political process.

In that one decision, I unexpectedly jeopardized my academic career and entered as a volunteer into the fiercest battle of the emergent culture wars.

About a week after the phone call, a box of material arrived and I began to read about the specifics of the case. The controversy was a classic one with citizens defending themselves against the intrusion of government on their personal lives. It began in February of 1991, when the state legislature opened hearings on an "Ethnic Harassment" bill. Buried in the legal jargon of the legislation was a provision that gave homosexual "orientation" legal standing equal to that afforded racial minorities. Adding "sexual preference" as a protected category, in the same way that discrimination was forbidden on the basis of age, race, and gender in the 1964 Civil Rights Act, had long been a goal of homosexual groups. Various cities in Colorado, such as Denver, Vail, and Aspen, had already expanded the entitlement claims of homosexuals and authorized substantial legal damages in cases of bias. A homeschooling mother at the hearing alerted family action groups in the state, and the battle was joined. If the bill became law, even verbal criticism of homosexuals could have been punishable as a felony offense.

After working to defeat the legislation, a group calling itself Colorado for Family Values (CFV) was formed to amend the state constitution to prevent special class considerations for homosexuals.

Most social revolutions begin quietly, modestly, with little or no media attention. That is what happened in Colorado. CFV decided to amend the state constitution to forbid special consideration for homosexuals. The Colorado for Family Values group was poorly funded and made up mostly of volunteers. They faced the daunting task of collecting nearly 50,000 signatures to put the proposal on the November ballot. Those charged with soliciting signatures at tables in front of stores and in malls found that few people understood what was happening, and most didn't want their convictions made public by signing a petition. However, when shown the title, which read: "no protected status based on homosexual, lesbian, or bisexual orientation," hundreds, and then thousands, signed without hesitation.

Prominent state politicians either opposed the petition drive or chose not to comment on it. Governor Roy Romer (D), Congresswoman Patricia Schroeder (D), and Senator Ben Nighthorse Campbell (R), all spoke out against passage of the proposal. Resistance came from a number of liberal Denver pastors, rabbis, and representatives of the state's elite media. Some radio stations refused to run advertising by Colorado for Family Values. Polls showed Amendment Two failing badly, and opponents of the measure were confident because they had raised more than twice as much money as CFV — critical sums for an extensive media blitz in the weeks before the vote.

CFV approached popular University of Colorado football coach Bill McCartney for help. He was nationally known for his Christian convictions, especially his work with Promise Keepers, a Christian men's organization that encouraged men to be faithful husbands. McCartney went before the press and declared that a stand against homosexuality was "inherent in the Christian faith." In the subsequent month, supporters of the Amendment Two ballot initiative gathered 84,445 signatures. The backers received help from Christian radio stations and the unexpected support of six popular African American civil rights activists, who urged minorities to vote for the issue. Even with this support, the underfunded and politically inexperienced CFV was written off as a fringe group by pundits and election experts. The conventional wisdom was that it had little chance of success.

On election night in 1992, Amendment Two passed by a comfortable margin: 53.3 percent to 46.7 percent. Even though Bill Clinton carried the state that election night, favorable votes for Amendment Two outnumbered votes cast for Clinton by more than 13 percent.

The outcome brought a firestorm of criticism. Gay and lesbian groups immediately labeled Colorado the "Hate State," and called for a boycott of it during the lucrative ski season. The entertainer Barbara Streisand and record mogul David Geffen, along with a host of other prominent Hollywood elite, cancelled their annual holiday vacations to places like Vail and Aspen. The Atlanta City Council, the New York City government, and officials in five other cities banned travel to the state. Prominent spokespersons for various groups called press conferences around the country to decry the vote.

Within a week of the vote, a lawsuit was filed in Denver District Court challenging the result. To win the case, homosexuals had to prove that same-sex attraction was an immutable, inborn trait, and that they had a history of discrimination by heterosexuals that resulted in their being politically powerless.

Virtually none of their evidence was convincing. I appeared as an expert State witness to debunk the claims. No record of a genetic or "immutable" trait was available, and it could not be proven, though some argued that a "gay gene" was inherited at birth. As a group, homosexuals were among the most economically successful people in the country, with an average household income some 66 percent higher than comparable straight groups. When it came to politics, gay, lesbian, and bisexual groups were a well-organized and powerful lobbying force. In the year of the lawsuit, the top six gay groups raised more than $12.5 million for political purposes. That year the Human Rights Campaign Fund (HRCF), as the leading homosexual political action group, ranked in the top 50 of more than 4,700 political action groups.

The Amendment Two case in Colorado ultimately went to the U.S. Supreme Court. On appeal, the federal courts sustained the homosexual plaintiff's contention that Amendment Two should be set aside because the State had no compelling interest in such a law. At the same time, the judges ruled that homosexuals as a group did *not* meet the criteria for a "suspect class" under federal law.

The court ruling had no effect on campus. The gay and lesbian movement was actually emboldened by the decision, and their cause gained the enthusiastic support of academic administrators and faculty. "Gay Pride" parades, "Coming Out" days, and curriculum innovations to "study" (no one would dare say advocate) "gay, lesbian, and bisexual" causes proliferated on campuses. Student services and housing resident advisors indoctrinated incoming freshmen about their "prejudices" against opposing homosexuality as a lifestyle. Campus groups regularly used student fees to sponsor speakers who favored the passage of "hate crimes" legislation, and advocated gay marriage.

The guise of social science was invoked to do "research" on the plight of students not accepted by others because of their sexual practices. Conferences were called, journal articles published, and panels held to "investigate" the new social prejudices. The Internet fairly crackled with academic findings. In such an atmosphere, academic freedom became a myth, and "value-free" inquiry an illusion. Students came to my office to ask about required speech topics like: "Homosexual Rights and Civil Rights Today" and "Hate Speech on Campus." Sympathetic faculty put stickers with the words "Safe Zone" outside their office to let homosexual students know they were "safe" to talk to them about their problems. Anyone without a sticker was, by self-admission, "unsafe."

I appeared as the expert witness in Cincinnati the next year and began to write about this issue. My theme was usually the same: based on the court rulings, the campaign by homosexual groups for inclusion as a protected class was for "special" rights, not "equal rights." When the issue of gay marriage or special class distinctions was placed on the ballot, it failed every time, even in California.

On campus it was another story. To be a conservative on a college campus today, I discovered, was like being a believer in capitalism in Stalin's Russia. Instinctively, you knew that everything the Politburo was doing went against the grain of human experience, but you were silenced and powerless to stop it. The campaign for gay rights and gay marriage became the single most important issue among many campus administrators and faculty. To publicly oppose these positions, was the equivalent of being sent to the university Gulag. A colleague told me to "cool it on the gay stuff" before anyone found out. I ignored him. Later, when I applied for an on-campus administrative position, I was told by a colleague that I was "ideologically incompatible" with the department involved, and with the general values of the university.

Once identified as a pariah, the label remained. I returned to my office several times to find the word "homophobe" scribbled on a note for my door. I came back from class one day to find all the announcements from around my door removed, the same note now written across it in permanent marker. When I wrote an article in a campus newspaper arguing that homosexual marriage had high social costs, citing the rising divorce and out-of-wedlock births in countries like Denmark and Sweden, a student wrote me an e-mail saying I should not be on the faculty, since my article "blatantly attacks an entire group of people with harsh generalizations."

The worst experiences were with the newspaper "interviews." Virtually every major metropolitan area has a free arts and entertainment paper, or a gay "Blade," that is critical of anyone opposed to homosexuality. Reporters would regularly call me at home or at the office for a comment, and then vigorously chastise me for opposing their "rights." Of course, after a while, I purchased "caller id" and was no longer subject to the verbal hostilities. However, the criticism on campus remained and took many forms. I found it unhelpful to ever stand for election in any faculty referendum, be it to the athletic council or the faculty Senate. One of my colleagues said I was "misguided" in my beliefs. I found myself out of favor, and against "academic freedom," when I questioned the pedagogical value of a Spanish teacher showing "Fahrenheit 9/11" to her class just days before the 2004 presidential election.

In private, I was hearing the same whispers as Jim DeMint. Isolated faculty and students would call (telephones can't be traced like e-mails) to offer encouragement. Some stopped to say: "I'm glad someone is standing up to them," and "don't back down." Secretaries, parents of students, and staff around campus whispered. Students came in, closed the door to my office, and expressed their disdain for assigned topics in speech and English classes. The one thing they all had in common is that they were all scared, and they spoke in whispers.

The incongruity between what was happening on campus and in the rest of the country puzzled me. For example, on November 7, 2006, South Carolina became the twentieth state to say that marriage was *only* between a man and a woman. Why, I wondered, were we whispering when the rest of the state, and the majority of Americans at the ballot box, were speaking so loudly? On campus you would never know the votes across the country were taking place.

My academic career hit a dead end when I assumed that academic freedom extended to debating the truths of sexual rights. However, I did receive a consolation prize of sorts from my political consulting work. I was a close advisor to four congressional candidates, two of whom are now in the United States Senate. I worked with Senators Lindsey Graham and Jim DeMint and Congressmen Bob Inglis and Gresham Barrett on position papers and public policies. My convictions may not be compatible with academics, but voters seem to like them well enough.

Chapter Two

Who Is Right?

"Free speech is the whole thing, the whole ball game. Free speech is life itself."

—Salman Rushdie

Was it wrong for a U.S. Senate candidate to say that openly homosexual people or unwed mothers should not be teaching in public schools? Was it wrong for a professor to testify in court in support of a state's case against special rights for homosexuals? Was it right for the media to come to the defense of homosexuals and unwed mothers without any discussion of the merits of the opposing position? Was it right for academia to break with its own culture of academic freedom by attaching a permanent stigma to one of its own who broke with the widely held opinions of the intelligentsia?

We begin to answer these questions by asking another. How does a society decide what is right and wrong?

History suggests that enduring communities have shared values that are passed to succeeding generations. An abiding American value holds that human beings cannot be treated mechanically. Every society can be evaluated by the standard of how it treats people. If a nation has a good record in this regard, and certainly American history does have blemishes amid accomplishments, then revolutionary value changes can have the effect of slicing the arteries of a culture.

Today there appear to be fewer and fewer standards that are commonly accepted by a majority of citizens and almost no agreement on what is valuable for the next generation. In fact, what is right and wrong in America has become a subject for debate. That debate is an ideologically driven and often strident conflict over the meaning of America. James Davidson Hunter's book

Culture Wars, published in 1991, introduced the phrase he used as his title that has since gained wide use. He states, "[It] can be traced ultimately and finally to the matter of moral authority . . . the basis by which people determine whether something is good or bad, right or wrong, acceptable or unacceptable."[1] This cultural erosion is much bigger and more serious than the seemingly isolated skirmishes over the differences of opinion about unconnected issues like prayer in public schools, abortion, whether laws should be expanded to protect the rights of homosexuals, the equality of the sexes, and the increasing acceptance and open distribution of pornography.

The culture war has profound implications for a host of public and private institutions. Hunter argued that a number of "hot button" defining issues — like those listed above — were really subsets of two definable positions.

He characterized the ideological polarity of the two different assumptions about moral authority either as: (1) defined by the spirit of the age, a spirit of rationalism and subjectivism (labeled "progressive modernism") or (2) a commitment to consistent, unchangeable measures of value, purpose, goodness and identity (labeled "orthodox traditionalism"). The progressive impulse challenged traditional sexual morality and focused on nontraditional family structures like serial marriages from easy divorce and same-gender relationships. In the conclusion of one study, the researcher noted that, "the individual self must be its own source of moral guidance." A woman interviewed for the study declared that "God is a sort of name that's been assigned to that particular kind of function for me, to make the most of my life."[2] In sum, the progressive impulse embraces the tendency to revise historic religious faiths into the prevailing assumptions of contemporary life.

By contrast, the orthodox and traditional impulses were committed to resisting the desertion of established morality. Orthodoxy identified objective and transcendent authorities (i.e., the Bible and historic statements of faith) as the sources of influence in the culture and society. While differences remain between Christians and Jews, they both share a commitment to a transcendent standard and agree that American society should be shaped by these tenets. "The cultural progressivism of the 1960s and 1970s, and the orthodox response of the 1970s and 1980s, drew the lines for a new form of American cultural conflict."[3]

This conflict is not an abstract academic debate. All of us develop a worldview early in life through which we filter aspects of our lives. A worldview is a philosophy of life that includes explanations for where we came from, why we are here, and the *shoulds* and *oughts* in life. A person's worldview is shaped by parents, teachers, religious leaders, friends, the media, and other social role models. It contains beliefs that establish values and moral principles that guide how that person lives. Not all of these personally held beliefs can be fully proven or demonstrated, which means all worldviews contain some aspect of subjective beliefs or faith.[4]

Each of us believes that our view of the world is right, and that those with differing views are wrong (or at least not as right). In many cultures around the world, those with the most power strive to impose—often by force—their worldview on others and to eliminate opposing views. Not so in America! One of the cherished notions about America is that our Constitution, history, and laws actually encourage debate and consideration of ideas. This freedom of expression was established as one of America's highest priorities in the First Amendment to our Constitution. While there are many different worldviews in America, they are allowed to percolate and compete in open dialogue.

We agree with Hunter, and others, that these worldviews fall into two major camps: the "orthodox," "traditional," or "Judeo-Christian" in one, and the "progressive," "secular," or "modernist" in the other. Virtually all of the major public policy debates today are the result of the significant and substantive differences that come from these opposing philosophies. It is a reality that there is a culture war underway in America. And it is between those that believe in traditional moral values and those that believe in moral relativism. To join the battle one must first understand and appreciate the beliefs and values of these two worldviews.

ORTHODOXY: THE TRADITIONAL JUDEO/CHRISTIAN WORLDVIEW

Western culture, with its roots in reason (from the ancient Greeks) and a Supreme Being (from Judeo-Christian beliefs), holds that human beings, though marked by original sin that makes them both fallible and sinful, have a great capacity for good if disciplined and restrained by religious and societal conventions. Adherents believe that there is an objective moral law grounded in God's law and God's plan for humanity. Traditionalists believe that their purpose in life is to serve God and to love one another. The "golden rule" is central to Judeo-Christian ethics: *do unto others as you would have them do unto you* (Matthew 7:30).[5] As a result of being created in God's image, each human being is unique and is endowed with immeasurable worth. The guiding text for this worldview is the Bible, along with a host of cultural expressions like Washington's "Farewell Address," Lincoln's "Gettysburg Address," and Martin Luther King Jr.'s "Letter from a Birmingham Jail," all derived from it. The civic culture is an intermingling of public prayer and respect for scriptural principles and values that come from this legacy.

The American philosophy of humanity can be traced to the Puritan Protestantism at the founding of the American republic. As religious historian George Marsden notes, "Evangelism . . . had much to do with the shaping of American culture."[6] Even with the influx of Catholic and Jewish immigrants from Ireland, Italy, and Western Europe in the second half of the nineteenth century, the three major faith traditions—Protestant, Catholic, and Jewish—shared a commitment to transcendent, timeless sources of moral authority that regulated human behavior.

Not surprisingly, proponents of this moral foundation believe that religious truths and values matter in public, political, and moral debates and should be considered when shaping public policy. For example, the Pledge of Allegiance phrase "under God" and the pledge "In God We Trust" on dollar bills are both rooted in this legacy. Traditionalists are committed to the separation of church and state in the sense that no particular denomination or religious philosophy should have the government promote its specific doctrine.[7] However, they do not agree that policies promoting the common good, and based on these values, should be eliminated from the public debate simply because they are connected to religious precepts.

Orthodox-traditionalists believe that America's founders shared their worldview and that the separation of powers ordained by the Constitution was based on the corruptible tendencies of human nature, a view held by Judeo-Christian religious adherents. They also contend that the American political system is distinctly different from that of all other countries because it is based on the belief that our rights come from God, not from government. Our rights, therefore, cannot be taken away by government.

More importantly, traditionalists believe that there are moral absolutes (known as natural laws), with benefits to society that have been confirmed by centuries of practice. The theologian Thomas Aquinas held that because man was endowed with reason, he participated more perfectly than all other natural beings in the order of divine providence. "Although they do not have the written law, they have the natural law, whereby each of them understands and is conscious of good and evil."[8] These absolutes include sexual purity until marriage, fidelity in traditional marriage, strong families, honesty, service to God and fellow man, the protection of life and human dignity, personal responsibility, and a strong work ethic where people are rewarded for their efforts. Proponents of this worldview insist that these "values" are not optional, but instead they are essential to the success and long-term survival of America.

SECULARISM: THE PROGRESSIVE WORLDVIEW

The traditional Judeo-Christian worldview dominated the private and public landscapes in America until the mid-twentieth century. As the morally liberal and largely secular baby boom generation challenged traditional values and sought greater freedom for the acceptance of alternative beliefs, a conflict that had previously been limited primarily to religious leaders became widely popularized.

Secularism was originally the purview of a few atheists and academic elites, but it spread quickly in the decade of the sixties. Brendan Sweetman provides an excellent definition of progressivism or secularism:

> Secularism, broadly understood, is the view that all of reality is physical, consisting of some configuration of matter and energy, and that everything that exists either currently has a scientific explanation or will have a scientific explanation in the future. The universe is regarded as a random occurrence, as is the appearance and nature of life on earth. Thus, secularism is not simply the negative claim that there is no God or that there is no soul; rather, these claims are supposed to follow from its positive theses. Like other worldviews, especially religious ones, secularism contains beliefs about the nature of reality, the nature of the human person and the nature of morality. And many of these beliefs have political implications.[9]

The secular perspective first surfaced in popular culture in the 1960s, when proponents of "value-free" academic research argued for a revised set of values declaring older ones as racist, sexist, and authoritarian. Secular revisionists derided the "establishment" values of the past. They argued for a new set of ethics based on two extremist principles. The first, radical egalitarianism, advances the notion that there should be an equality of *outcomes* rather than *opportunities*, which does not mean we should all be on an equal playing field. Rather, it means that we all succeed or no one succeeds, and that all success and its rewards are the same. The second, radical individualism, suggests an expression of personal gratification without societal or government interference. What began as "do your own thing" in the 1960s became an obsession with personal peace and economic affluence in the 1990s. The state is jealous of any God and continually seeks to limit belief and allegiance to anybody or anything but itself. In the second half of the twentieth century secularism became *the* dominant worldview in the public sector. We'll explain why in the next chapter. Sweetman uses the work of Christian Smith to detail the goals of "the secular revolution:"

> The revolution occurred in seven main areas: (1) religion and science: science was promoted by secularists as the way of enlightenment, knowledge and progress, and religion was seen as backward, oppressive and superstitious; (2) higher education: many institutions of higher education, as the historian George Marsden[10] has shown, were transformed from religious institutions into secular ones; (3) mass primary and secondary education: schools were transformed from offering their mainline Protestant program into offering a "neutral," nonsectarian, secular education curriculum, from which religion is excluded; (4)

public culture and philosophy: mainline Protestant custodianship of public culture, with its emphasis on Christian America and moral integration, was sup-
planted with liberal political theory, with its emphasis on pluralism, relativism
and procedural justice, while again excluding religion; (5) law: the view that religion had no place in public and social policy decisions, often made by the
courts, was vigorously promoted, and a "wall of separation" between religion
and politics was gradually established by the judiciary; (6) the religious view of
the self: the understanding of the self as a spiritual and moral being concerned
with caring for the soul in which the churches would play a major role was replaced by a naturalistic, psychologized model of human personhood, over which
therapists and psychologists are the authorities; and (7) print and broadcast media: the media marginalized religion and adopted a (supposedly) religiously neutral approach to news and opinion.[11]

The term "progressive" has been added (or substituted for) the secular
worldview as a way to redefine the movement from one that is against religion to one that accommodates religious language in order to promote secular values. The largely liberal Protestant culture sought to reconcile the claims
of community and individuality by downplaying the authority of the Bible
and accommodating social change under the banner of "tolerance," "multiculturalism," and "fairness."

The term, "progressive," has turned out to be a misnomer. The consequences of secular philosophy have caused a costly *regression* in our culture.
Secular-progressives promote a type of liberalism that has led to unrestrained
individual freedom at the expense of the common good. Gone is the conviction, which underlies the founding of the nation, that the community needs a
social contract to bind its members to one another to avoid the chaos of unrestrained freedom. The moral relativism advocated by this worldview, as
well as secular-progressives' efforts to exclude proven morals and values
from public debate, have resulted in an explosion of destructive behaviors.

THE CHALLENGE TO FREE SPEECH

As secularism gained a foothold in the late twentieth century, traditionalists
failed to understand that secularists were interested in more than simply
bringing their worldview into the public debate. Rather, and more profoundly,
they were intent on *excluding* traditionalist participation in leading the country. Now we have such secularists as Chris Hedges of the *Nation* magazine
who, in an unapologetic and unprecedented maneuver, calls for legally restraining conservative, traditionalist speech.[12] There is an unbreakable connection between politics and moral judgments, and between moral judgments

and religious beliefs. The great peril of the American culture is that it would eviscerate the vitality of public life by excluding transcendent moral referents. As prominent Catholic writer Richard John Neuhaus has written:

> What is relatively new is the naked public square. The naked public square is the result of political doctrine and practice that would exclude religion and religiously grounded values from the conduct of public business. The doctrine is that America is a secular society. It finds dogmatic expression in the ideology of secularism.[13]

A decided minority of secularists have capitalized on the progressive impulse to change American culture. The traditionalists were slow to understand that the secularists had an intense disdain for traditional authority. Sam Harris, author of the book *Letter to a Christian Nation*, makes the point that religion is now, and has always been, a serious impediment to science and human progress. He makes his intentions clear in saying he wants to "arm secularists in our society, who believe that religion should be kept out of public policy, against their opponents on the Christian Right. . . . I have set out to demolish the intellectual and moral pretensions of Christianity in its most committed form."[14] While Harris's derision is directed primarily at Christians, his attacks apply generally to all those who hold a traditional Judeo-Christian worldview.

The progressives range from those vaguely religious to the openly agnostic or atheistic. What unites them is a deep impulse about the welfare of the community and the nation. Harris points to a recent Gallup poll that found only 12 percent of Americans believe that life on earth evolved through a natural process without the guidance of a deity. He finds this troubling and even dangerous, concluding that America stands alone in these beliefs among the nations of the world "like a lumbering, bellicose, dim-witted giant . . . the combination of great power and great stupidity is simply terrifying."[15]

Secularists hold that Christianity is an ancient myth, a fantastic story for which there is only contradictory evidence. They are emphatic that embryonic stem cell research, the teaching of creationism, the offering of public prayers, public display of the Ten Commandments, and the mention of God in public school classrooms are venues for the battle between these two worldviews. Secularists work to marginalize the traditional worldview by arguing that public policy and public debate should not represent any worldview. Neuhaus responds that there is no such thing as a neutral public policy position. "The truly naked square us at best a transitional phenomenon . . . a vacuum begging to be filled. . . . When the democratically affirmed institutions that generate and transmit values are excluded, the vacuum will be filled by . . . the state."

Secularists believe that Americans should be free to believe whatever religion they choose, but that all religion should be private and have no influence on public policy. The problem with this assertion is that government impacts every area of our lives, from parenting to personal behavior, churches, business management, education, societal values, and all aspects of judicial and political decision making. If religion has no place in these areas of our lives, it has no relevance anywhere in our lives.

In the mind of the progressive, freedom of speech does not apply to religious speech. This desire to exclude religious speech includes speech about values and morals that can be connected with religion or a heritage rooted in faith. Secularists contend that such religious beliefs are "irrational or are not quite rational enough to take seriously, because they are dangerous, sectarian, and against the U.S. Constitution, or because the public-square debate should be a 'neutral' debate."[17]

Secularists disqualify religious or values-oriented speech by contending that reliance on religious arguments is based on faith, not fact, and that such beliefs are not rational. They foster and encourage public hostility to religion by contending that they only want "neutral" values in public view. When the Reverend Franklin Graham ended his prayer at George W. Bush's 2001 inaugural with the words, "In Jesus' name," Barry Lynn of Americans United for the Separation of Church and State dubbed the prayer "inappropriate and insensitive." Progressives fail to recognize that their worldview also relies on faith, and that many religious-based arguments can be supported by better historical facts and arguments than those offered by the evolutionary side.

THE ARGUMENTS OF THE PROGRESSIVE WORLDVIEW

Science, according to the typical secularist, proves that the universe, the earth, all matter, and life are the result of evolution. They hold that the existence of God cannot be rationally proven. Therefore it is irrational for anyone to interject religion into the public debate. Consequently, they believe that all scientific pursuits, all public or state-supported education, and all public policy should be conducted with the assumption that there is no God or guiding religious precept.

This values-less approach is readily apparent in the stem cell debate, for instance, where progressives argue that acquiring embryonic stem cells is good science. We assert, as do our fellow traditionalists, that the use and subsequent destruction of embryos for scientific research is ethically unacceptable. The orthodox contend that the Bible and the Judeo-Christian tradition forbid the casual destruction of human life, especially for speculative scientific ventures. "When you debate an issue as if God does not exist, you are essentially debating as if secularism is presumptive, as if religion is inferior, and as if secularism is true."[18]

For the sake of fairness (an attribute not reciprocated by our adversaries), let's briefly consider the rationality of these secular arguments. When Darwin created the theory of evolution in the nineteenth century, he believed that the cell was the basic building block of life, and that matter consisted of a relatively small number of basic elements. Relative to today, he knew very little about the size and complexity of the universe. As a leading critic has written, "In short, highly sophisticated molecular machines control every cellular process [and] the details of life are finely calibrated, and the machinery of life enormously complex."[19] Doubtless life is too complicated to have evolved by accident. Today a strong case can be made for this idea, and science has proved that energy, matter, and all forms of life are too complicated and well organized to have happened by chance. Unfortunately, Darwin is not around to recant, and his myopic followers are zealous to pursue his secular worldview in the face of all evidence to the contrary.

We now know that matter consists of a complex array of atoms and molecules. Each atom has an organized system of protons, neutrons, and electrons that have in storage enough energy to destroy an entire city. Even inorganic matter like a handful of dirt contains millions of molecular structures that are far too complex and organized to have simply appeared accidentally, magically out of nothing. On to the galactic perspective, modern day telescopes have revealed that this intricate and organized matter exists throughout a universe and extends millions of light years to huge galaxies that could not have even been imagined in Darwin's time.

Darwin would be dumbfounded to see the discovery of the genetic structure of cells and the intricately designed DNA blueprints that exist in every form of life, from the simplest plant cells to human beings. The more scientists understand the complexity of life, the more unlikely it becomes that life could have happened unintentionally. Biologists generally agree that in order for complex human life to have evolved accidentally, all organs and systems would have had to develop concurrently. The probability that this happened is so infinitely small that it is virtually unthinkable.

The accidental occurrence of the universe—all matter, all energy, and all varieties of life—is a physiological and statistical impossibility. It could not have happened! Any plausible scientific application of physics, biology, and statistical probability would rationally rule out evolution. Science does not prove the foundational premise of secularism, it disproves it. It is irrational to believe otherwise.

When it comes to public policy, adherents to the secular-progressive philosophy are more unreasonable than their scientific counterparts. They deny the laws of human nature. They reject the historical evidence that all people have a natural innate tendency toward behavior that is destructive to themselves and society. The original obligation in social-contract theory was to seek mutual human well-being in community instead of in a state of nature. The traditional belief was that social institutions like family, community, church, civic organizations, and government are essential in providing the discipline and structure to restrain the destructive tendencies of human nature and to develop positive behavior patterns.

Secularists believe that people are inherently good—that people will always do the right thing—and that human failures are, ironically, the result of inequalities, oppression, and injustice. This belief fosters advocacy of public policies by secularists that focus on government programming rather than individual responsibility. In this view, the purpose of government is to encourage "restorative justice" rather than punishment for crimes. Restorative justice promotes income redistribution (without shame or respect from the haves to the have nots), welfare (everyone is entitled to more than a safety net), education, and medical collectives. It is an approach to governance that abhors alternatives, debate, dissent, or even parental choice. Overall, the secular-progressive worldview advocates larger government, centralization of power, and blind obedience that threatens individual freedom and thought.

The most irrational and destructive of secular-progressive philosophies is the fanatical, near gleeful removal of moral standards from the culture at large. Central to the definition of a civilization is its ability to know the difference between a higher and a lower way, and the inevitable advantage of the former. But the adversary culture has turned this commonsense realization rooted in the Judeo-Christian tradition into something outdated for modern times.[20] Their belief is that all behavior is right as long as it doesn't harm another person. This philosophy has led to the promotion of abortion, same-sex marriage, premarital sex, single-parent families, no-fault divorce, legalized gambling, ubiquitous pornography, the legalization of drugs, and an expanding welfare state to promote this behavior. The problem with this view, as we will document in this book, is that these behaviors have proven to be destructive to individuals and society throughout history, and have dramatically increased the size and cost of government.

THE ARGUMENTS OF THE TRADITIONAL
JUDEO-CHRISTIAN WORLDVIEW

Secularists may maintain that a traditional worldview is irrational and not scientifically provable, but there is ample historical evidence that the traditional worldview results in the best outcomes for individuals and society. Irrefutable evidence demonstrates that stable societies with human beings enjoying personal freedom are produced when traditional views and policies are followed, and they should not be ignored simply because such views have religion as part of their foundation. The existence of religious content in a public policy position should neither qualify nor disqualify the argument. The quality of an argument about public policy can be judged by simple maxims: How does it treat people? Are they safe from enemies, both foreign and domestic? Will future generations enjoy freedom? Any policy can be judged based on its anticipated and measurable impact on the quality of life for individuals and the success of society as a whole.

Bill O'Reilly makes this important point in his book *Culture Warrior*, "I don't believe this culture war will be won in the religious arena. . . . The most powerful nonreligious argument against the [secular-progressive] agenda is that it is simply better public policy for the United States to stay close to the vision of the Founders, which includes independence from big government, hard work, personal responsibility, and looking out for your neighbor."[21] Government-approved, church- and state-sanctioned precepts should not dictate public policy. However, traditionalists have every *right* to believe that America's founders wanted religious principles to be involved in public discourse and debate. On the very day that Congress approved the wording of the First Amendment, which guaranteed freedom of speech and the prohibition against establishing a government religion, it also requested that President George Washington establish a day of public thanksgiving and *prayer*.[22]

Secularists cannot prove that God does not exist. Granted, traditionalists cannot empirically prove that He does. What traditionalists can prove is that traditional practices and religious principles have resulted in historically superior cultural influences when compared to the secular public policies ascendant in the past several decades. As O'Reilly asserts, "The traditionalist understands that true feeling for others requires a helping hand that leads to problem solving—not the collapse of standards that would make it easier for people to destroy themselves and others."[23]

Research validates the traditionalist belief that values that encourage abstinence until marriage, strong traditional marriages and families, respect for God and country, strong work ethic and personal responsibility, and integrity and character result in better citizens, a stronger economy, and a superior quality of life. When a nation shuns or denies the superiority of cultural achievements and substitutes morally relative, feel-good-for-today values in their place, the result is cultural dissolution. Human society, like nature, abhors a vacuum and will eventually establish a standard of acceptable behavior. The erosion of civilized standards by secular intellectuals, including an unhealthy number of federal judges and university professors, began as a demand for personal freedom without consequences. In every area of public life, the result of this unvanquished freedom has been the public acceptance of the lowest standards of human conduct, untrammeled by the fear of social or legal sanction. Secular values result in cultural deterioration.

THE SILENCED MAJORITY

About 92 percent of Americans say they believe in God, and approximately 88 percent believe that God created or guided the creation of the world and everything in it.[24] Why has the media refused to report these numbers? The majority of Americans has been told by the entertainment media, the news media, and the college professoriate that what they believe is a personal matter and should be kept out of public discourse. They have accepted that all political debates and contemporary discussion must be based exclusively on the secular-progressive worldview.

> It is now almost the default view in modern Western culture, the culture of democratic pluralism, that one's religion should be a private matter and should make no contribution to public debates on political, moral or social questions. . . . [S]ome religious believers may feel a little bit marginalized from the political discussion, especially in contemporary American society, feeling perhaps as if they do not quite belong in that discussion, as if there is something "wrong" with their views. . . . [I]t is not easy to see what is supposed to be wrong with an appeal to religious arguments, but there is an unmistakable presumption that there is something wrong with them, that one should in general keep quiet about one's religious views in political discussions.[25]

Americans are experiencing a type of national schizophrenia because their strongly held beliefs no longer have any application in public life. Secularism is the default. Freedom of speech has become "selective" speech that excludes religion and values-based discussion. Many Americans are constantly conflicted as they try to hold two opposing worldviews at the same time: traditional views in their private life and secular views in public.

Brendan Sweetman explains:

> A recent Gallup poll showed that religious believers today experience an intense religious hunger, but they seem in general not to be sure about what they believe and why. Many believe in God, but admit that this belief is not the first thing they appeal to in many aspects of their lives. They also say that their religious beliefs have little impact on their own lives or in society. One reason for these attitudes is the increasing secularization of society. The practical effect of the in-

fluence of secularism on traditional religion and the influence of groups like Americans United for the Separation of Church and State is to produce an influential group of (liberal) religious believers who further advance the secularist cause by watering down their religious beliefs and by calling for the elimination of religion from politics.[26]

Traditionalists are being mocked for their beliefs. They are being trivialized and marginalized. They are being told not to "impose" their beliefs on others. They are continually reminded that there is a separation of church and state—as if the principle means that people with religious beliefs are prohibited from speaking their minds and from public participation. The secularist strategy is to silence—or at least confuse—traditionalists, which as we've seen, is the overwhelming majority of Americans. Traditionalists don't know what hit them. They don't know how basic beliefs could have changed so quickly, and they feel powerless to defend their traditional views. They are too intimidated to speak out, so their complaints are reduced to whispers. Most stand aghast at behavior that has become the norm in America, but they cannot say that anything is wrong without appealing to their religious convictions. They know that their religious arguments are excluded and have no credibility in a public debate.

The great majority of principled Americans have been silenced. They know that something is wrong, but they are afraid to speak out. They whisper because they no longer believe that free speech applies to what they believe, or to them for holding such beliefs! This has made them less sure of what they believe and less confident that their worldview is right. They want to know who is right, and more important, who decides what is right and wrong.

Chapter Three

Who Decides
What Is Right and Wrong?

No one can bar the road to truth, and to advocate the cause I am prepared to accept even death.

—Alexander Solzhenitsyn

Contrasting definitions of moral truth held by sympathizers with the traditional and progressive worldviews lead to different definitions of right and wrong. The issues associated with this division have gradually separated the culture into opposite factions. Over the past thirty years, the distinctions that split conservative Catholics, Protestants, and Jews from one another began to shrink as they found themselves in agreement when it came to various issues like abortion, gay marriage, and pornography. At the same time, the secular sympathizers manipulated academic and government authority to cloak their own ideas with respectability. Their success meant that the traditional Judeo-Christian worldview came in for criticism and eventual abandonment as the guiding philosophy for American public policy decisions.

It is unlikely that many Americans saw this issue very clearly. No formal vote was taken, and we cannot point to any specific date when the nation decided to replace traditional views with a secular philosophy. The process was gradual through court decisions, government mandates, the rise of the secular media, and the abandonment of traditional values by academics. Average Americans assumed that since they were holding to historic views, the cultural deterioration in America was the result of uncontrollable factors that happen naturally in a modern society. Few realized that the traditional worldview was removed from American public life by neglect. The secular revolution achieved many of its goals before most Americans ever knew they were in a fight.

HOW THE TRADITIONAL JUDEO-CHRISTIAN
WORLDVIEW SHAPED AMERICA

In the last days of treaty negotiations after the American Revolution, the British negotiators made a proposal that would impair New England's fishing rights off the coast of Newfoundland. John Adams rose from his chair, smoldering with indignation, "If Heaven in the Creation have a right," he said, "it is ours as much as yours."[1] The ideal of fishing privileges, as well as political rights, coming from God, and the prominence of the Christian religion—whether it is defined as affiliation, belief, or practice—in defining them, has been with the nation from inception. It is impossible to walk through historic areas of the nation without confronting the profound role the Christian religion played in the nation's development. In America, more than any other advanced industrial society, faith defined political right and wrong.

Judge Charles Pickering discusses this legacy in his book *Supreme Chaos*:

> Sculpted around the chamber of the U.S. House of Representatives are the profiles of history's lawmakers, and in the very center—the only one with his full face—Moses. The law bringer Moses, who according to Jewish, Christian, and Muslim religions brought the Ten Commandments down from Mt. Sinai, can also be found above the entrance to the Supreme Court, where he stands holding the Ten Commandments, flanked on each side by other law givers. Inside the Supreme Court, above the justices, is another depiction of the Ten Commandments.
>
> Engraved on the east face of the metal cap of the Washington Monument are the Latin words Laus Deo, which means "Praise be to God." On the stairway of the Washington Monument are carved in memorial stones various biblical passages including "Bring up a child in the way he should go and when he is old, he will not depart from it" (Proverbs 22:6). There are references to God at the Lincoln Memorial, the National Archives, Senate and House office buildings, the Jefferson memorial, and the Library of Congress.[2]

From the beginning, the American governmental experiment was distinguished by a view of biblical infallibility, the divinity of Christ, the necessity of a conversion experience for salvation, and a commitment to evangelization. The early cultural values were Protestant. Later, despite religious differences, there was a fundamental agreement among the three major faiths—Protestant, Catholic, and Jewish—to the same transcendent source of moral authority. These values stamped the culture from the beginning and made the United States unique among developed nations.

When apologists for the secular-progressive worldview contend that the Constitution dictates that "religious" practices and philosophy be separated from public policy, they are flying in the face of the historical facts and faith that made America exceptional. The framers of the Constitution quoted the Bible more frequently in their deliberations than any other source. At one crucial time of debate, called by Georgia delegate William Few, "an awful and critical moment," Benjamin Franklin rose to declare that, "the longer I live, the more convincing proofs I see of this truth—that God governs in the affairs of men."[3]

When debating education policy, one of the first and most important pieces of federal legislation was the Northwest Ordinance, which proclaimed, "Religion, Morality, and Knowledge being necessary to good Government and the happiness of mankind, schools, and the means of education shall forever be encouraged."[4] The call for prayer by Benjamin Franklin at the Constitutional Convention of 1787, and the fact that both Houses of Congress and the Supreme Court continue to this day to open every session with prayer are legacies of this cultural belief.

The traditions of individual freedom and limited government were successful only because of the restraining religious principles inculcated into the hearts of citizens. Because citizens controlled themselves or were regulated by churches, community values, and accepted norms, the national government was constrained. The presence of these principles was verified in 1835 by one of America's earliest observers. Alexis de Tocqueville, a French nobleman, wanted to know what made democracy work in America and why American democracy would be the model for Europe. His conclusion: "Religion in America takes no direct part in the government of society, but it must be regarded as the first of the political institutions. . . . Thus, while the law permits the Americans to do what they please, religion prevents them from conceiving, and forbids them to commit, what is rash or unjust."[5]

The religious roots of our country are no longer taught in our public schools. Despite this intentional historic ruse, Americans are beginning to see the results of the "separation" of these two cultural forces. Judge Pickering reiterated Tocqueville's warning in saying:

> confusion and ultimately tyranny would result from the destruction of religion in America: Tocqueville wrote that, "When a people's religion is destroyed doubt invades the highest faculties of the mind and half paralyzes all the rest." People find they have nothing to rely on but continually changing personal opinions: "When there is not authority in religion or in politics, men are soon frightened by the limitless independence with which they are faced. They are worried and worn out by the constant restlessness of everything. With everything on the move in the realm of the mind, they want the material order at least to be firm and stable, and as they cannot accept their ancient beliefs again, they hand themselves over to a master."[6]

Take religion out of the public square and the "restlessness of everything" is a daily reality. In our own time this fear is being realized. It explains why anxiety and depression are two of the most prevalent health issues in America today. According to the National Institute of Mental Health (NIMH), in any given one-year period, 9.5 percent of the population, or about 20.9 million American adults, suffer from a depressive illness.[7] Individuals today are confronted with two aspects of existence that do not change: the vast universe in its form, and their own unique sense of right and wrong. Religion gives answers to these questions, but a meaningless, impersonal universe has no answers for right and wrong. If everything is a matter of change and energy, then we are left with only relative morality and knowledge. The rise of this worldview explains why so many Americans give the government control over their lives. Without a personal value system to face the trials of the twenty-first century, they look to a supposedly benevolent helper.

TRADITIONS THAT SHAPED THE AMERICAN CHARACTER

The traditionalist worldview had both a confidence in God and a fear of human frailty. This belief is that truth is grounded in the character and existence of God, and what has been given to humans by creation and revelation. The traditional worldview left little room for government, but it had much room for humans to develop and exercise their gifts and creativity.

For example, these traditional religious principles and values yielded a people with the character and courage to tame the wild and dangerous American frontier. This is not to suggest that all early Americans adhered to religious principles, but the worldview was regnant. Certainly there was lawlessness, destruction, and unbelief, but the consensus standards held by society as a whole created an expectation of "goodness" and "exceptionalism" that restrained individual behavior and shaped societal laws.

American individualism and volunteerism were expressions of this belief, and were paramount at the nation's beginning. This legacy of colonial independence and self-determination lay at the very heart of the American Revolution in its struggle against monarchial and aristocratic authority. When Americans went West, the ideals of personal autonomy became legends. The settlement of the western frontier and the admission of new states were the independent products of individuals who relied on God first and expected little from the federal government. Soon, this so-called "rugged individualism" became part of the mythical culture of the country.

Americans created many of their own heroes, who embodied individual responsibility and strength. Paul Bunyan was a fictional creation of northern logging camps. He symbolized the hearty tree-harvesting accomplishments, and subsequent settlement, by men in the Northwest Territories. "Pecos Bill" was a legendary cowboy in the southwest who personified the hardened virtues of strength, courage, ingenuity, and superhuman feats of horsemanship necessary to survive in the region. Later, television and the movies during the 1950s and 1960s recreated cowboy heroes in white hats: Gene Autry, Roy Rogers and Dale Evans, and the Lone Ranger. The cowboy heroes were followed by the private detectives, all epitomizing the ideals of individual character and personal accomplishments of American life. And the good guys always won.

As America began the second half of the twentieth century, traditional values were the implied consensus values in homes, schools, churches, businesses, and government. These values were reflected in the media with family shows such as *Father Knows Best, Leave It to Beaver, Ozzie and Harriet, Andy Griffith,* and *Bonanza,* whose themes all reaffirmed the accepted morals. Hollywood practiced restraint and produced movies that reflected societal consensus about right and wrong, as well as America's virtuous stands in war and peace. Sports heroes did not smoke in public, and it was unthinkable that any celebrity would curse during an interview.

What changed so dramatically? What transformed American patriots into critics of their own country? Until recently, if anyone asked Americans what was the greatest danger facing their country, they would typically point to something external. The great fears and calamities during the last half of the twentieth century were: the expansion of the Soviet Union and the fear of a nuclear confrontation in the 1960s, the loss of the Vietnam War and the energy crisis in the 1970s, and the growing menace of radical Islamic fundamentalism throughout the final decades.

Today the outward problems remain, particularly the growing threat from terrorism. More and more people, however, have come to see that our greatest wounds are now self-inflicted. Broken families, subpar public schools, violent crime, moral decline, a growing despair and disrespect for culture, and the pessimistic view about the inability to reverse these trends have become the new cultural villains. As Vaclav Havel, the former Czech president, said in 1987, "western culture is threatened more by itself than by [Soviet-made] SS20 rockets."[8]

As the twentieth century came to an end, it was evident that these self-made problems had worsened. Yet few today seem to connect this cultural deterioration with government's adoption and promotion of a secular-progressive worldview. One who does, Dinesh D'Souza, argues that the left is the primary reason for Islamic anti-Americanism as well as the anti-Americanism of other traditional countries around the world. "The left is waging an aggressive global campaign to undermine the traditional patriarchal family and to promote secular values in non-Western cultures."[9] As America subverted its own traditions and values, it lost its moral compass. Centuries of tradition—basic concepts of right and wrong—disappeared seemingly almost overnight.

In the years before World War II, individuals and the private sector had the freedom to decide what was right and wrong without much government interference. While the government served as the referee, societal values and morality were settled by an ongoing competition between the voices of a free people. Individuals, speaking through countless churches and voluntary organizations, ultimately determined society's moral standards. With the close of the twentieth century, however, government and its paternalistic views were the primary determinants of right and wrong. It doesn't take a village, as some secular-progressives would want us to believe. What they really hold in their hearts and minds is that it takes a distant, centralized, statist, collectivist government.

When did the shift from individuality to collectivism begin? Few Americans today realize that the administration of Woodrow Wilson (1913–1920) was one of the great watershed events of American history. Until this time the country frolicked in a laissez-faire society that was by no means unrestrained, but where limitations were imposed by their belief in a God-ordained moral code rather than a government devised by man. When Wilson arrived in Washington, the country had just adopted the Sixteenth Amendment, which authorized a federal income tax and placed in the hands of Washington politicians the fiduciary power to restructure society.

Woodrow Wilson came to the conclusion that the national government should curb the power of the unfettered economy. It was Wilson who introduced America to big, benevolent government with the Federal Reserve System, the Federal Trade Commission, the Federal Farm Loan Act, and a Treasury Secretary—William McAdoo—who shifted power from New York to Washington.

In spite of these changes, prior to the 1950s, the federal and state governments were generally supportive of the traditionalist worldview. Government did not directly promote any specific church or denomination. Rather, it was organized to follow the consensus views of the wide majority of Americans to prevail in private and public settings. In more recent years, distinctions between private and public were minimized. For example, a Christmas manger scene at a county square was just as expected as the same scene in front of a church. No high school football game would have started without a prayer for the players' safety. "Public" meant community-owned or by community standards, not government controlled.

Public schools and teachers were allowed the flexibility to pray before meals and to integrate theories of creation by God into biology lessons. Schools were not allowed to teach evolution because those teachings conflicted with the beliefs of the overwhelming majority of families. The teaching of character and discipline was unquestioned, with much of the content for these lessons grounded in generally accepted religious principles. Students who violated behavioral standards were disciplined, suspended, or even expelled without the recourse of lawsuits.

These traditional views were naturally integrated into all aspects of American life. Government didn't force these views on the people. Instead, they allowed citizens the freedom to shape their own lives and to participate in shaping the values of their communities. Businesses could hire and fire based on the character and behavioral preferences of the owners. Community organizations with religious missions regularly partnered with local governments to provide humanitarian services. Elected officials were expected to believe in God and to uphold traditional principles of honesty and decency in office. State and local governments passed laws that enforced traditional standards without the interference of the federal government. Pastors, priests, and rabbis were often the most visible leaders in communities.

Traditional values faded as the federal government grew. In 1930, spending by the federal government amounted to only about 3 percent of the gross national product, and most of the money collected went to pay for past wars. The army and navy were the largest line items in the budget each year, but the post office was probably the most familiar federal presence in the day-to-day lives of citizens. Only a small minority of Americans, about 10 percent, paid income taxes. The cost of the national government was such that a person could have an income of $10,000, enough to live in a comfortable house with servants, and pay only $154 in federal taxes in 1930.[10]

Seventy-five years later, the situation is much different. While the United States has the largest and most technologically powerful economy in the world, that growth has come at a price. The influence of the federal and state governments means that virtually everyone files an income tax form. Over three-quarters of Americans pay more in payroll taxes, such as Social Security and Medicare, than income taxes. State and local taxes take another chunk of the GNP. When these costs are added up, government spending approaches 40 percent of the GNP.[11]

The reach of the federal budget into the economy is one easily understood measure that explains the influence of government on citizens. It is instructive only because of the old adage about the "golden rule": "He who has the gold makes the rules." Today, government has the money and makes most of the important decisions. This book is mostly about the effect government has on the personal behavior of citizens, but the economic principle is the same as the social one. Any analysis begins with an understanding of government intrusion and pervasiveness. The federal government is the largest and most important actor influencing individual finances in the nation. Its reach is deeper than dollars. The rulings of courts and administration agencies affect every job in the country, every student and every family. Government sets the tone for how all of us work and live.

HOW SECULARISTS USED THE GOVERNMENT TO OUST TRADITIONAL VIEWS

Even though secularists represented only a small, elite fraction of the American populace before 1950, they were free to bring their ideas to the public square. While public stigma and rejection were often the response to their views, the government did not forbid the free expression of those who held a secular worldview. It was represented by a small but increasingly vocal and militant minority in academia, the media, and Hollywood, which gave them platforms that were far more influential than their numbers justified.

Secular progressives were a small minority in America, and their views would never prevail in the court of public opinion. They could not pass legislation that supported their worldview by using the traditional democratic process. However, secularists ultimately discovered that they could achieve their goals by manipulating opinion through the media, academia, and the law school faculty; by denigrating traditional values through the arts; and—especially—by using cases in federal and state courts. This could not have happened under the traditional understanding of the judicial process. Courts were once a kind of neutral umpire. The Constitution was seen as the repository of timeless wisdom and the keeper of a consistent political order, predictability, and gradualism, while the will of the justices was subordinate to legal precedence. The Court drew its legitimacy from generations of deference accorded the law, and no individual was able to override that legacy. This was known as the "rule of law." In the words of Alexander Bickel, a former professor at Yale Law School:

> In discharging their limited office, the courts must be astute not to trench upon the proper powers of the other departments of government, nor to confine their discretion. . . . [E]very action of the other departments embodies an implicit decision on their part that it was within their constitutional power to act as they did. The judiciary must accord the utmost respect to this determination, even though it be a tacit one.[12]

The result was a conservative understanding of the judiciary's limited function. Several notable—if not notorious—Supreme Court rulings since the 1950s, however, significantly changed this traditional understanding. Federal, district, and circuit court judges responded to these rulings by continuing to realign and pervert the intent of the Constitution. Para-government groups such as the ACLU, labor unions, and radical civil rights groups have used these precedents to intimidate and silence the voices of reason, sending our culture into a downward spiral.

The first major success by secularists was to use the courts to separate religion from public life. The First Amendment "establishment of religion" clause was intended to keep the federal government from *establishing* a national state church or state religion. This protection by the First Amendment served its purpose for more than 150 years after the adoption of the U.S. Constitution. Some states had churches supported with local taxes, and all were allowed access to the public square. The federal government allowed states to regulate the interaction of church and state. A generally constructive coexistence was in place between religious principles and the operation of government.

As late as 1947, the Supreme Court continued to defer to the states on religious issues. In *Everson v. Board of Education*, the Court ruled that the state of New Jersey *could* fund schools (including parochial schools) for the cost of public transportation to school. Although state money was used to directly assist students attending religious schools, the Court ruled that this amounted to equal treatment of *all* students and thus did not impose religion on *anyone*. Speaking for the majority opinion, Justice Hugo Black said that the New Jersey policy was general because it applied to public and private school students and did not single out those attending religious schools. Justice Black added that the funding of busing was similar to the public payment of policemen and firemen who protected both public and parochial school students. If the Court, and even Justice Black, had remained consistent, this precedent could easily be applied today to education scholarships that could be used for students to attend public, independent, or religious schools.

However, in the 1962 *Engel v. Vitale* case, the Supreme Court ruled against a New York school board that required every class to start each school day with the following statement:

"Almighty God, we acknowledge our dependence upon Thee, and we beg Thy blessing upon us, our parents, our teachers and our Country."[13]

New York State officials developed this declaration as part of their "Statement on Moral and Spiritual Training in the Schools." At that time, schools commonly accepted their role in character education.

It is a stretch to call this statement a prayer or a religious activity. The statement is a far cry from establishing or even favoring a religion. Any casual student of American history would find this statement perfectly consistent with the founders' writings, the Declaration of Independence, and numerous court rulings before 1962. Unfortunately, the Court did more than ban prayer from public schools. It implicitly banned everything else that was included in the statement: respect and honor for parents, teachers, and country. Public acknowledgment of God was inextricably linked to adolescent behavior, classroom discipline, and good citizenship. When the Supreme Court banned the teaching of respect for God, it effectively rejected the traditionalist worldview and replaced it with the secular-progressive worldview.

This decision unleashed a flood of political attacks, social ostracism, and legal challenges against any and all moral teaching in public schools or tacit support—no matter how minor or tangential—of faith-based groups or activities by any level of government. By 1970 America was embroiled in a "sexual revolution," antigovernment demonstrations, an explosion of unwed births, increasing crime, expanding dependency on government, and economic decline—referred to by President Jimmy Carter as "malaise." By the 1990s, Americans witnessed moral debauchery in the White House, widespread corporate corruption, serious declines in student achievement, and continuing increases in unwed births and sexually transmitted diseases. The ACLU and other self-appointed guardians attacked traditional organizations like the Boy Scouts, veterans' celebrations, saying the Pledge of Allegiance, public Christmas displays, and traditional American values.

The secular activists found a vehicle to force compliance in the general culture through court rulings. The unelected judicial branch could overrule policy decisions of duly elected representatives. The result was perhaps the single most important Supreme Court case in American history, the *Brown v. Board of Education* decision of 1954. The new philosophy held that the Constitution was "living" and written in broad terms. It should be interpreted in light of the changing needs of society. A phrase from the case *Trop v. Dulles* (1958) captures best the approach of the "living constitution" theorists.

> [T]he words of the [Eighth] Amendment are not precise, and . . . their scope is not static. The Amendment must draw its meaning from the evolving standards of decency that mark the progress of a maturing society.[14]

In the 1960s, the Court came to be seen, and the justices came to see themselves, as the voice guiding the maturing society. The result was that the law was no longer bound by original meaning or *stare decisis*. Instead, courts became the mouthpiece for evolving social ideals of the new legal elite. "Many university courses in constitutional law now . . . begin with *Brown*, the line of instruction being that the Supreme Court, and other courts, were compelled, in light of *Brown*, to take note of social protest, such as demonstrations and riots—especially when they were ignored by Congress—in shaping decisions."[15] In short, the progressive worldview interpretation now had a powerful advocate.

This transformation of law provided the legal force for tectonic societal changes. On the one side of the emerging "culture war" was a majority—albeit weakened—of the population, comfortable with traditional American values, practices, and institutions. On the other side, was a small minority consisting of the secular "knowledge class," who attended elite schools; worked in the prestige professions; and inhabited the halls of academe, mainline churches, and the literary intelligentsia. As social observer David Brooks has written, "[I]n America today it's genius and gentility that enables you to join the elect. . . . [S]umma cum laude embraces summa cum laude."[16] The self-anointed elite saw themselves in an adversarial relationship with the rest of society. And they now had the nearly unfettered support of one of the branches of government as they waged war on historic values and assumptions.

The 1990s witnessed the blossoming of a new type of social life that began in the 1960s. That unrelenting and distorting critique by radicals was of America's traditional values and economic principles, dismissing them as a "myth of objective consciousness" and nothing more than a mask for establishment power.[17] A new economic order had emerged from the advancing secular worldview, euphemistically called postmodern or postindustrial or a consumer society by the media, with terms like "globalization" and multicultural capitalism replacing the American identity and the historically proven American way. The postmodern ethos, which is now ingrained in the secular-progressive worldview, was centerless—and nationless—if not meaningless. There were no longer common standards to which people appealed in their efforts to measure, judge, or value ideas, opinions, or lifestyle choices. Gone was allegiance to a common sense of authority, or a commonly regarded and respected wielder of legitimate power. Science was elevated as a divine source, as partisans rejected any notion of overarching truth and reduced all ideas to social constructions of class, gender, and ethnicity.

The secular philosopher Michael Foucault offered a name for the unfocused, secular ideal: "heterotopia."[18] The term was the opposite of *utopia*, which was the design of a modern society where peace, justice, and love would reign. Now there were no universally agreed upon values or desired outcomes. The secular expression of "heterotopia" was pluralism, which celebrated diversity, absent of foundational values. Secular-progressive cultural expressions undermined the concept of a powerful, originating ideal by destroying the ideology of absolute truth and replacing it with multiple choice questions.

This was the worldview that infected law. The postmodern, secular-progressive theory of jurisprudence emphasized relative values, a world of heterogeneity with a multiplicity of different concepts of the world. The prevalent ideal held that jurisprudence should guarantee a multicultural experience for every citizen. Different concepts of the world and life were equally valid (regardless of their historical contributions), and the theory of postmodern law declared them all equally legitimate. Critics of the new secular legal philosophy maintained that "postmodern philosophy [fell] short of a positive jurisprudence," but its ideals remained popular in legal circles nonetheless.[19] The proponents of the secular-progressive worldview refused to consider the societal impact of their new philosophy.

Judges, and especially the justices of the Supreme Court, were usually products of elite law schools, the same institutions heavily influenced by secular, postmodern theory. Many saw themselves as members, if not masters, of a new cultural class. Over the past half century they had chosen to make themselves the final authority on the most basic issues of social policy. The effects of this process became apparent after the *Brown* decision of 1954. When confronted with the injustice of Jim Crow segregation on the one hand, and long-standing constitutional interpretations limiting judicial relief on the other, the Court felt boxed in by its own precedents. In the *Brown* decision, the Court declared "that if the Constitution as it stood was unable to provide necessary relief, the Constitution would have to yield."[20] And yield it did. The result was a new source of extraconstitutional authority: elitist, circular arguments that could be selectively employed to justify and advance a judge's desire for social reform. Instead of requiring Congress to fix bad laws or permitting citizens to amend the Constitution, the Court became America's Supreme Legislature.

Once freed from the burden of constitutional texts and tradition, urgent progressive causes were placed on the docket. Their arrival was facilitated by a host of para-government groups (like the ACLU, environmentalists, unions, same-sex advocates, etc.), anxious to remake society in their own image. The old canon learned from high school and college texts about the legislative branch making the laws, the executive seeing to their enforcement, and the judiciary ruling on their legality was replaced by a new institution. The rise of modern judicial review made courts, not elected legislators or executives, supreme on matters of public policy. Over the next forty years, activists used the courts to achieve social and political change that would have been impossible in legislatures. The new process had one procedural advantage: there was no appeal.

The historical democratic process of making compromises and working bills through a legislative process, then overseeing their enforcement in executive agencies was replaced by a new procedure. The laws were immediately appealed to a judicial elite. No wonder, then, that Supreme Court nominations took on a high drama. In 1987, they also reached a low point when Judge Robert Bork, a District of Columbia federal appeals judge, was rejected by the U.S. Senate. The controversies over Bork, and later Clarence Thomas, were both cultural benchmarks. Depending on the nominee, the Court and the country could either continue or stymie the slide into the abyss of secularism.

What was new was the nature and importance of legal decisions, which now made law and the interpretation of the Constitution the vehicles for novel and radical fashion.

For example, following in the wake of the *Brown v. Board* decision, secular groups initiated lawsuits that culminated in a Supreme Court ruling about school busing in Charlotte, North Carolina. The decision held that a long history of state-sponsored racial segregation had to yield to a new racial integration formula for students in every public school. The *Swann* decision was binding on a large number of communities, most of whom had no history of segregation approaching that of the City of Charlotte and the County of Mecklenburg. While Congress can hold hearings, gather information, and make compromises before making a law, the courts can only rule on a specific set of facts.

The busing decision set off an avalanche of more litigation where dozens of local school boards had to defend themselves against plaintiffs arguing that a particular school placement plan violated federal statutes. Everyone was left to guess what the correct procedure was and await a host of appeals to define the new mandates nationwide.[21] Without question, racial segregation needed to be addressed by state legislatures and the Congress. However, judicial usurpation of legislative authority created years of costly confusion, diminished America's democratic heritage, and degraded the value of representative government.

The "living constitution" reached its nadir with the definition of a new "right of privacy" discovered in 1965. Estelle Griswold, executive director of Planned Parenthood, was fined $100 for violating a Connecticut law prohibiting the use of any instrument for the purpose of contraception. Although the Bill of Rights does not mention "privacy," Justice William O. Douglas, writing for the majority, took it upon himself to discover the existence of such a right in what he called the "penumbras" of other constitutional protections. In dissent, Justice Potter Stewart said, "I think this is an uncommonly silly law . . . [that] is obviously unenforceable [but] we are asked to hold that it violates the United States Constitution. . . . And that I cannot do."[22]

The *Griswold* decision set loose a score of later decisions based on the dubious theory that an individual in private became a law unto himself. This so-called right to privacy was extended to procreative sexual acts and to cover abortion. Additionally, the reasoning was stretched to the breaking point to declare sodomy laws unconstitutional, and to give presumed legitimacy to gay marriage. All this was done by advocacy groups using the courts to enhance a political agenda with a nonexistent "right" in defiance of public opinion and elected legislatures. What is more important, it was done with only the most tenuous connection to the text of the Constitution and to judicial precedent. Once advocacy groups had the imprimatur of the U.S. government, they went on the attack.

HOW GOVERNMENT DECISIONS STRIPPED PRINCIPLED AMERICANS OF THEIR FREEDOM OF SPEECH

The federal system now works much like a television courtroom drama where the judge excludes essential evidence because of a technical error in how the evidence was obtained. It doesn't matter if the evidence is true and helpful in finding the right verdict. Once the judge says the evidence is "not admissible," the jury is not allowed to see it. This is how the government at all levels now addresses traditional ideals rooted in the Judeo-Christian worldview that are brought to the public square: they are excluded. No sober-minded lawyer will argue that prayers have a place in public schools, that the Bible should be taught as literature, or that ethnic studies should be eliminated and diversity replaced as an important social value. Historic views of right and wrong are not admissible in the development of public policy because they have a religious connection that disqualifies them from the discussion.

According to several state courts, traditional marriage cannot be protected even with the overwhelming support of the American people, because it represents a religious prejudice. Other courts have ruled that the theory of intelligent design cannot even be presented in schools along with the theory of evolution because it assumes the existence of a creator (even though, as demonstrated in chapter 2, the complexity of life demands a designer and accidental evolution is a statistical impossibility). Schools cannot teach that it is wrong to have premarital sex because that teaching agrees with many religious teachings, but it is okay to teach underage students about condom use and the values of gay sex! Anyone who says abortion or euthanasia is wrong will find themselves fighting with a government agency that says it's more a topic for discussion. Businesses cannot fire employees who leave their families for an extramarital affair because government forbids discrimination based on marital status. As we will see in this book, even churches have found themselves at odds with the courts for disciplining their members. Even simple values of financial accountability and paying debts are betrayed by a government ethic of entitlements and borrowing. Right after the 2004 election, the national debt reached its legal limit of $7.4 trillion, and Congress had to raise the ceiling by another $800 billion. When you add discretionary earmarks to the public budget, you are telling a new generation of American children that it is responsible to spend what you don't have. Americans have lost their right to say that destructive behavior is wrong, because our government has said that traditional ideas of right and wrong are not admissible in the pubic debate.

THE NEW SECULAR ORDER

In an ideal world, Americans might still have the right to celebrate their freedom of speech, and to decide for themselves what is right and wrong. But the real world is profoundly different from the ideal one. Today it is government that guides and defines what is acceptable behavior. By government, we mean the cumulative effect of laws and legislative decisions, bureaucratic procedures, court decisions, and executive rulings that constitute ruling authority. Sometimes these effects are at cross-purposes, but the important thing about them is that they cannot be resisted. Today, the authority and complexity of government effectively constrains the individual.

Politicians and judges have, with mostly good intentions, changed public attitudes, destroyed constructive values, and promoted destructive behavior by citizens. The traditional social values of the past embraced a higher, self-regulating morality than the pervasive government mandates and rules that permeate society today. Before government became involved, social regulation was much different. For generations, Americans prospered through an informal cultural consensus of respect for inherited values, institutions, and laws. People were kept from a rootless hedonism by religion, morality, community standards, and a "shame culture" that embarrassed or excluded those with persistent "bad" behavior. Also, the laws protected these values, and those who espoused them.

Government was smaller and less obtrusive, and when it interfered, it was to establish minimal standards. For example, employers were free to hire and fire employees at will. Landlords evicted tenants who were too noisy without apology or fear of reprisal. Children born out of wedlock were cared for by family, church, or volunteer agencies unregulated and unsubsidized by government. Laws governing employee/employer relations, landlord/tenant agreements, and "illegitimate" (the designation was dropped in government statistics as of 1950) births were minimal. The government statutes that did exist represented the lowest acceptable standards of the society, while higher principles were maintained by voluntary compliance to ethical standards and a respect for religious principles as an expression of societal esteem.

Government was less involved in the day-to-day interaction between people because citizens, employers, and workers held to principles higher than those defined in law. For example, companies were held to societal standards in matters of employee protection. Laws did not interfere with society's voluntary higher ethical standards or with organizations that "discriminated" against those who violated these ethical standards. Support for such values was not seen as prejudice, while compliance with higher standards was seen as a valuable asset to society as a whole.

Of course, we do not maintain that the past was perfect. Today, critics are quick to point to government-sanctioned racial separations in the past, the limited opportunities for women, and a "status quo" mentality in business as evidence of earlier social oppression. These injustices, however, did not happen without government support. Critics of voluntary standards should be reminded that racial and gender discrimination often had the tacit, if not direct, support and management of government. It was both local and state laws that allowed and enforced nefarious segregation in schools, public accommodation, and employment.

What is not mentioned by the critics is that a consensus on marriage and sexual mores, support for schools and teachers, and respect for authority figures resulted in a culture that lessened individual dependence on government, expanded personal opportunity, kept taxes low, and maintained a safer, less violent society.

What is rarely explored in the legal community and the secular world is the permissibility to discriminate in order to correct past discrimination. We despise the legacy of Jim Crow so much that it is ironically a function of today's government to discriminate. If the United States was a conformist and traditional society in the 1950s, that allegiance was to generally socially helpful values. What is more, the campaign to correct past discrimination was waged in a Judeo-Christian context that emphasized forgiveness and redemption.

We are confident, and government statistics support us in this belief, that this informal cultural consensus about right and wrong was in place, and that these standards were above those of the government edict. The quality of life was maintained by an adherence to community, agreed upon values of fidelity in marriage, a belief that children were raised best in homes with both biological parents, and "fairness" in business practices.

In sum, the American culture of individual rights and a free market capitalism needed traditional values to authoritatively restrain and direct the expanding freedoms in a post–World War II nation. But in the 1960s, the government forcibly lowered societal standards, which freed artists and intellectuals to mock the traditional beliefs that guided the community in its social lives and economic pursuits. In 1965, the Beatles released their *Rubber Soul* album in which the song "Nowhere Man" critiqued the establishment of values by declaring that the middle class "doesn't have a point of view," that it is without purpose or direction.[23] If the spiritual values of America's social and economic structures were eroded, then the individual was cut free to indulge in whatever passions he or she could imagine. Unfortunately, the 1960s marked the decade when these unrestrained base appetites received government sanction and protection.

THE GOVERNMENT REDEFINITION
OF "RIGHT" AND "WRONG"

Through court decisions, new laws, bureaucratic mandates, and executive rulings, the official policy of the country shifted from supporting stable social values into making them illegal. In a steady drumbeat of political pandering to victims groups, bureaucratic practices, and judicial rulings, federal and state governments began to encourage divorce, out-of-wedlock births, then abortion, homosexuality, pornography, and, most recently, equal rights for illegal immigrants. The government has effectively reversed the values that made the nation exceptional in the first place, and replaced them with a new set of their own making. Honest dissent is scorned and criticized. God and belief in God were banned from public assemblies, the Bible was outlawed from study in the public school curriculum, then from campuses, and children were taught that they were evolutionary accidents. Every ethical decision became situational. Marriage was denigrated, and government programs subsidized and encouraged illegitimate births as regrettable, but acceptable, behavior. It all goes by the label "moral relativism."

A nation's moral life is the foundation of its culture, and as the values of right and wrong began to change, so too, did the culture. It did not take long for the unthinkable things to become the norm, and then be held up as a new standard. In the emerging era of new values, costly and destructive actions were enfranchised as rights in society. Abortion, no-fault divorce, illegitimate births, pornography, promiscuous sex, and homosexuality were espoused as deserving of public support to repair past prejudices against disadvantaged groups, rather than behavior detrimental to society.

Once the government says something is right, it is impossible for individual citizens to say that it is wrong. In the late twentieth century, the authority of political power became wedded to the secular-progressive worldview, a philosophy that replaced absolute truths with grand abstract narratives and unfounded pronouncements. This new worldview asserts that since there is no public truth, the only thing that matters is private truth. As Americans lost their right to disagree with secular-progress beliefs, they were forced to bear the costs, often extreme, of the new standards of behavior. These resulting costs of our deteriorating culture are now borne by Americans who cannot complain without being berated and being labeled racist, sexist, homophobic, intolerant, and ignorant.

The average American who believes in traditional values is confused and worn out from the fight. Who can stand against the government? Schools and universities have now ingrained secular teachings and antireligion philosophies into several generations of Americans. Few private citizens have the resources to even defend themselves against para-government groups if they choose to speak out. Most of us have just decided to stay in the shadows and whisper. But as Bill O'Reilly said in the first sentence of his book, *Culture Warrior*, "At times you have to fight."[24] And we can win! If only a small minority of Americans can hijack our government and subvert our culture, then certainly the large majority of Americans can take it back. If we are indeed a government of the people, by the people, for the people, then we must fight to reclaim our birthright, our culture, and our government.

Chapter Four

The Culture Development Cycle: Shaping American Values

> Give me the liberty to know, to utter, and to argue freely according to conscience.
>
> —John Milton

The government is not solely at fault for America's cultural decline, but it has been the catalyst and power behind much of the deterioration of our society since the 1960s. The cultural character of a nation is developed by many factors in the public and private sectors, but as the reach of government in America has extended into all areas of life, so too has its ability to shape the culture. The ever-expanding reach of government has multiplied the destructive impact of a secular worldview. Today, as the only part of society that can back its decisions with unquestioned authority, government has become the primary sculptor of a valueless, secular American culture.

As we discussed in previous chapters, the government's first major move toward secularizing the culture was to exclude religion, then traditional values and conventional behavior from public policy debate. The ripple effect of these decisions quickly removed many historical behavioral restraints in society, lowered the moral authority of parents and other authority figures such as teachers, and diminished America's ability to distinguish right from wrong. Court decisions sowed confusion in both the private and public sectors, often contradicting existing laws as well as the nation's foundational documents.

For example, the Supreme Court has ruled that the government may not "teach or practice religion" or exert "subtle coercive pressure" on students by prayers or religious instruction. As Thomas West, a professor of politics at the University of Dallas, explains: "by the logic of today's view of religious liberty, it is unconstitutional to teach the Declaration of Independence in public

school. The Declaration contains four distinct references to God: he is the author of the 'laws of . . . God,' the 'Creator' who 'endowed' us with our in-
alienable rights, 'the Supreme Judge of the world,' and 'Divine Providence.'[1]
How can public schools teach about the Declaration and not mention God?
Government's attempt to say it is neutral toward religion means that the foundational ideas of the republic are ignored. The contradiction between the
Founders' traditional values, and today's official positions of government results in a confused understanding of both. Religious restrictions in the public
schools spill over into recreational and extracurricular programs, and at all
levels of government, people whisper because they cannot openly discuss the
moral foundations of American government.

THE MYTH OF GOVERNMENT
NEUTRALITY TOWARD RELIGION

As government's adoption and promotion of the secular-progressive worldview evolved into a habit, an increasing number of conservatives and liberals
came to believe that the principle of religious liberty demanded that the government be neutral or indifferent toward religion. Today's so-called neutrality
toward religion "is grounded in moral relativism, [and] leads people on the
left to demand the expulsion from American public life . . . of the few remnants of traditional morality and religious expression."[2] This view has encouraged traditionalists to reject the revised America that appeared to be at
war with their heartfelt beliefs and convictions. It would be like learning tomorrow morning that you were adopted, and everything you believed to be
true about yourself was wrong. Americans with traditional views now find
themselves torn between a love for their country and a government denial of
what they believe about right and wrong.

"This is a false dilemma," claims West, "The prevailing interpretation of
religious liberty is wrong." It is also confusing. The existing state of governing legal standards is both greatly in flux and riddled with major defects and
inconsistencies. For many people, the things they loved about their country,
like its moral convictions and compassion, are now suddenly, and inexplica-
bly, inappropriate topics for public discussion. To make matters worse, it is
your country that is telling people that this is now wrong. So bad is the condition that many citizens no longer know the difference between "neutrality"
and "advocacy." In their confusion they remain silent. West reminds traditionalists that a country "neutral" toward religious values "is not fit for human habitation."[3]

Atheism and humanism, beliefs that attach prime importance to human
rather than divine ideals, are promoted when government says it is neutral to-

ward religion. In fact, the public endorsement of atheism rebuffs the established religious tradition and is, in fact, a nonneutral policy. There is no religious neutrality, no neutral law, no neutral education, and no neutral civil government. If progressives can convince the judges and other government officials that there is such a thing as "neutral" policies, then it follows that only secularism will be supported by the state. Such an outcome will erode, and then push into oblivion, religious liberty in the United States.

Federal judges, in their manic attempt to keep up with ever-changing standards, have sown confusion around the issue of religious practice and traditional values for several decades. One court says public school dollars can be used for religious schools (Cleveland's school voucher program of 2002 in *Zelman v. Simmons-Harris*), while another court (the Florida Supreme Court in 2006) rules that tax dollars can't go to private schools. Congress bans late-term abortions, only to have a federal judge rule that the law is unconstitutional. Several states amend their constitutions to support valid marriage as being between one man and one woman, and a court in another state "legalizes" same-sex marriages. Cultural confusion is a problem in America because when there is doubt about what is legal, there is doubt about what is right and wrong, and the default position among many of the powers that shape our culture is to adopt a lower standard. When that happens the question becomes: what law prevails? Do we leave it to federal judges who have the power to write their predispositions into decisions, or do we rely on proven cultural traditions?

Despite the claims of neutrality by some federal judges and liberal advocates for progressive views, federal and state governments today are anything but neutral about religion. As traditional religious values and standards have been systematically excluded from public policy development, the government has adopted a secular worldview with an antireligious, anti-Judeo-Christian bias. This antireligious sentiment has blurred the public's perception of right and wrong, and since social values are often connected with religious principles, it has become increasingly difficult for the government to develop policies that serve the common good by promoting ethical behavior. Thomas West summarizes America's dilemma and offers a recommendation:

> Since we no longer distinguish between liberty and license, we no longer understand the Founders' conception of liberty, including religious liberty. For them, the freedom to follow one's religion should be protected, in Washington's words, as an "inherent natural right." No one may be harmed or punished for his mode of worship. But religious liberty is not religious license. Government may and should promote religious practices and convictions that accord with reason, which favors individual responsibility and political liberty.[4]

Unfortunately, secularists are determined to purge all remnants of religion-based traditions, morals, and values from public policies. The American Civil Liberties Union is engaged in a crusade to define as the establishment of religion any mention of God in the public square. The official dogma, evident in public television's airing of *Cosmos* by Carl Sagan, is that the impersonal cosmos is all there is, or ever will be. The result has been a reversal of public policies that have protected the American people for generations.

ARGUING WITH A TRAFFIC LIGHT

The New Hampshire Constitution of 1784, like many of America's founding documents, encouraged citizens to act in a way that would benefit the greater good of society: "When men enter into a state of society, they surrender up some of their natural rights to that society, in order in insure the protection of others."[5] A simple example of giving up personal freedom for the good of society is the traffic light. The government puts traffic lights where cars and people intersect to keep citizens from hurting each other. Without traffic lights, Americans would be freer, but there would be chaos, confusion, and many injuries. Obeying traffic lights is not voluntary. We either obey, or we will be arrested and fined. Traffic lights are a social and legal contract between the government and the people. Government is not neutral when it comes to traffic lights. It mandates individuals to restrict their freedom, under a penalty of a fine or criminal prosecution, in order for all of us to have safer, more efficient roads.

In this example, individuals create a greater freedom for society as a whole when they restrict their personal freedom by agreeing to stop at red lights. Everyone gains the freedom to travel on roads throughout the country with greater safety. However, unless everyone complies with the laws, the system won't work. In this context, running a red light is wrong because it is dangerous and destructive to the person violating the law and to society at large. Consequently, if any citizen—politician, pastor, professor, or parent—says that running a traffic light is wrong, there is no dispute because everyone knows that it is reckless and harmful to disobey the law. Societal views about right and wrong in regard to traffic lights have been shaped by the government.

But consider this not-so-far-fetched scenario: What if some members of Congress became concerned that the fines for running red lights were unfairly burdensome to the poor? Or what if a judge came to the same decision and ruled to the same effect. Envision a new federal program created to pay the fines for people who earn, say, up to twice the poverty level as well as the medical expenses for the poor who were injured after running a red light. The program even pays unemployment benefits for low income workers who lose their jobs because of injuries or because they have their driver's licenses suspended after repeated offenses.

Not surprisingly, the number of people running red lights begins to increase dramatically, as do injuries and deaths. The spending for the new federal program expands as well, while the cost of auto insurance skyrockets for everyone. The problem becomes so severe that the Department of Education implements a new driver education program in all public schools that teaches students how to "safely" run red lights.

As these federal programs expand, research confirms that they serve mainly to encourage students to run red lights, and it finds that a majority of students no longer believe that it is wrong to run red lights. Conflicting laws change society's views of right and wrong. One teacher is even fired for embarrassing a student in class who ran a red light. A newspaper reports how a trucking company lost a lawsuit to a truck driver who was fired because he had perfected the technique of running red lights in his eighteen-wheeler. Responsible drivers who stop for red lights are often harassed by those who must wait behind them. Oddly enough, during this whole imaginary incident, it remained "illegal" to run a red light. A candidate for Congress is roundly criticized by the media for favoring strong enforcement of red lights, while the opposing candidate calls him intolerant for suggesting it is wrong to run red lights, and asserts he is prejudiced against poor people.

Does this sound preposterous? Hardly! Look around the country with wide-open eyes.

This has been the pattern of government at all levels of society for decades now, beginning in the 1960s. Politicians and judges have, with good intentions, changed public attitudes, destroyed constructive values, and promoted destructive behavior by citizens. Our government has turned right and wrong upside down by subsidizing and supporting immoral and sometimes illegal behavior. Change the hypothetical from traffic laws to drinking and driving, premarital sexual relations, or teachers and coaches having "relationships" with students and athletes. What was once unthinkable is now commonplace.

THE CULTURE DEVELOPMENT CYCLE

America's culture is shaped by immigrant settlement patterns, ethnic beliefs, family habits, court rulings, laws, the media, and many other elements created by both government and the private sector. These factors do not act independently to influence the values and mores of our culture. Culture is shaped by a cycle that constantly accommodates, transforms, and often amplifies multiple voices in society. It is important to understand that the American culture is shaped by a continuous "cycle," because this continuous feedback system compounds and magnifies seemingly insignificant behaviors into societal events.

For example, the Columbine High School shooters, Eric Harris and Dylan Klebold, played the violent video game Quake and listened to Marilyn Manson's songs before going on a rampage. Children who watch female pop icons like Britney Spears copy their fashions and mimic their behavior. A story in *TV Guide* tells how some shows target teens by suggesting suicide is painless and even sexy.[6]

The cultural process creates a system of social precedent. Like legal precedents that use previous court decisions to guide the next one, both the private and public sectors are sensitive to a social precedent based on cultural trends backed up by government decisions. In the early 1990s, the late Senator Patrick Moynihan famously said that one of the problems with society was that we were "defining deviancy down." In other words, the American public was more and more tolerant of intolerable behavior. Each time the government makes a decision, beliefs and behaviors are influenced throughout the culture.

From America's founding until the mid 1900s, traditional values and beliefs held by Americans were supported by government. Cultural factors—including families, churches, media, and government—reflected consistent values and traditions that made America the envy of the world. These values were reinforced by a culture cycle that regularly confirmed beliefs and standards of behavior with consistent feedback from all areas of society.

Americans realized from the beginning that democracy was sustainable only if individuals regulated their own behavior. The founding fathers, many of them the very embodiment of character and Christian convictions, considered the welding of liberty with virtue to be the first priority of government. George Washington said that "virtue or morality is a necessary spring of popular government." Benjamin Franklin, himself a man with questionable private behaviors, still recognized that "only a virtuous people are capable of freedom." John Adams opined that "liberty can no more exist without virtue and independence than the body can live and move without a soul." The emphasis of America's founders was on the importance of a free people holding tightly to moral principles. We could easily fill up an entire book with quotes of their warnings that such principles not be abandoned.[7]

Generations of earlier Americans learned and understood the value of virtue as it related to citizenship. A textbook on American political parties, first written in 1943, declared that Americans owed their success to the "philosophy of common sense that permeated its thinking for so long," and to John Witherspoon who educated James Madison.[8] Witherspoon's Princeton curriculum took for granted the cultivation of piety, wisdom, and prudence, in a "school of duty" where men learned the ancient Christian virtues of respect for the permanent things.[9] These values guided Madison, as the "Father of the Constitution" and John Adams, who wrote a letter to his cousin, Samuel Adams in 1790 declaring, "human appetites, passions, prejudices, and self-love will never be conquered by benevolence and knowledge alone, when introduced by human means."[10]

The consistency of American traditions, values and laws allowed citizens the freedom to discuss their religious convictions and to insist that government actions support the traditional ideals with proven benefit to society. Proposed laws and regulations had to meet the test of the values held by the public. The cultural cycle served as a living and active foundation for America's political, economic, and social systems. Like the human body's circulatory system, the culture development cycle constantly restored the good and removed the bad from society. "American public life was far more religious before the 1960s, when Americans thought their pro-religious policies were consistent with their principles. As we will see, they believed that what they did was not only compatible with religious liberty, but a necessary foundation of that liberty."[11]

In the 1960s, however, a number of court decisions created confusion and contradictions within America's culture development cycle. The immediate effect of these changes was to weaken societal moral restraints and to shake the confidence of those who held traditional views. With the infusion of the secular-progressive worldview into the culture development cycle, it didn't take long for such talk as that of Madison, Adams, and Witherspoon—which had shaped America's culture for generations—to be denigrated by secularists as "establishment" bunk.

As new ideas "cycled" through the culture with the power of government edict, studies of civics and American history were soon replaced with a secular, "values-free" social science. The social sciences came to mean the management of society by the educated elite who understood the nature of social structures and trends. The new worldview held that democracy was a "system" that could be managed by social science experts. In such a conception, the ideal of virtue was obsolete. Academia, which had long held latent secular views, was liberated to push an agenda of their own making under the guise of "science."

As a result, social science research has done little to help, and much to hasten, the pace of cultural deterioration. To understand how to improve society, a person must have some notion of the "good state." This was the classic education instilled in Madison and other leaders of the country, and well-understood for generations after the American Revolution. But in the 1960s, the traditional ideals of political philosophy were abandoned, so an entire generation remained uneducated in a notion of what was "good" in politics. Instead they were educated in the managerial techniques of the "what is" of politics. This was education in the grand tradition of Machiavelli, who sought power as its own end without any idea of the purpose for which government should be used. The social sciences became rationalistic and romantic at the same time, and while they proved unhelpful, there was still one field where American ideals remained in the intellectual forefront. America's free-market ideals were copied by others, and stood as the envy of the world.

In business and economics, a notion of what was good, or "quality," was fundamental to competition, and crucial to success. The dictionary offers about a dozen definitions of "quality," according to J. M. Juran, the father of "quality management" and the notion of what became known as the 80-20 principle, and we think two of them are important. "In the eyes of customers, the better the product features, the higher the quality . . . [and] the fewer the deficiencies, the better the quality."[12] If we conceive of government as a producer of services, and citizens as customers or consumers, then we can ask questions about the best kind of products. Suppose we looked at government policies that encouraged divorce and illegitimacy as "poor quality," and those that encouraged biological families to stay together as "higher quality."

"Quality begins with intent," writes management guru Edwards Deming, "which is fixed by management [and translated by others] into plans, specifications, tests, production." The cultural richness of any nation depends on its people's values, how it manages the consensus values of its people, and government's support of the application of these values. Government support is important since it sets the standards for the nation as a whole. The problem is that government has no idea about "quality." "In most government services, there is no market to capture; [instead] a governmental agency should deliver economically the service prescribed by law or regulation."[13] Are more abortions, higher out-of-wedlock births, and rising numbers of illegal immigrants an intent of government or a by-product of bad decisions? We believe these shortcomings can be improved by "intent," to quote Deming, and without it there will never be any "quality."

In such a "corporate" culture, the purpose of government would be to encourage better quality, or the "best" quality (in other words: create the best for the common good). One way of doing this would be to require clear goals, such as reducing out-of-wedlock births to one-quarter of all births (instead of one-third) by 2010. Another task is to establish the means required to meet these goals. According to Juran, managing for quality involves a "trilogy" of the three processes of planning, control, and improvement.[14] In short, we must believe that government can reverse the trend that America must have a growing acceptance of "wrong" behavior as a natural part of living in a modern, secular society. Without the focused intent of government to guide improvement, the private sector—especially television, Hollywood, the education establishment, and universities—will continue to drive the devolution of our culture. Until Americans begin to understand the root cause of our cultural decline, we will not be able to reverse it.

To help in understanding the processes that create our culture, we have developed a diagram of how the *Culture Development Cycle* functions (see figure 4.1). This figure provides a visual illustration of how beliefs and behaviors are shaped. Americans elect individuals at every level of government who make laws, select judges, and appoint bureaucrats, who, in turn, have authority over all aspects of our lives. Some may argue that government control is not as pervasive as we suggest. However, even a cursory analysis of "government reach" will reveal laws and regulations that directly impact parenting, schools, churches, community organizations, charities, health care, businesses, lawyers, other professionals, financial markets and investment, retirement plans . . . all in addition to the functions of government such as law enforcement, roads and transportation, public buildings and lands, and all public policy. The public sector—our government in all its complexity—regulates and directs the private sector. The collective private sector, in turn, shapes the opinions of the people who elect the government . . . a continuous feedback cycle.

The culture development cycle ultimately shapes the attitudes of voters when they elect political leaders who make policy and appoint judges and bureaucrats. The significance of the culture development cycle diagram is that it magnifies the potential impact of seemingly insignificant government decisions. Later chapters will detail how the ACLU has used the threat of a lawsuit to attack and intimidate Americans holding traditional views. These assaults have significantly reduced the freedom of speech of those who hold traditional views. The absence of traditional voices in our culture has created a moral freefall in values that has ultimately influenced how voters view candidates and issues. Depending on the decisions made by voters, and what they expect of government, the cycle can improve or diminish future values.

The description of groups in the political process pictured in figure 4.1 is familiar to anyone knowledgeable about American politics. Citizens have a long-standing reputation for joining groups, but in recent decades a number of organizations have been formed specifically to work on social issues. The groups shown in table 4.1 organized in large part for cultural reasons.

Cultural Development Cycle®
Shaping Beliefs & Behavior in America

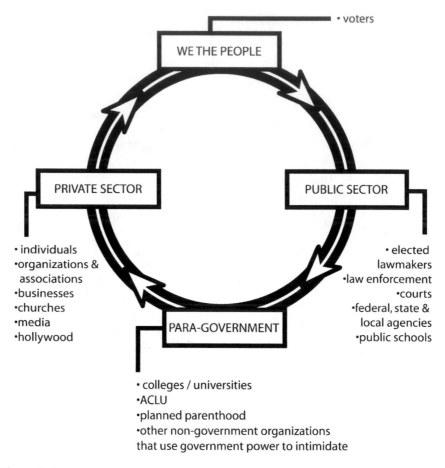

Figure 4-.1.

We choose to call these groups "para-government" because they have a close relationship to official power, and have often acted to change the ideals of government policy. The groups listed in table 4.1 are often opposite one another on significant cultural issues. We note that the "progressive" groups have the edge in organization, funding, and experience on these issues. The

Table 4.1.   Active Para-Government Groups with the Year of Their Founding

Progressive/Secular	Orthodox/Traditional
National Organization of Women (1966)	Eagle Forum (1972)
People for the American Way (1981)	Christian Coalition (1989)
American Civil Liberties Union (1920)	Alliance Defense Fund (1994)
National Abortion Rights Action League (1969)	Operation Rescue (1980s)

traditionalists were slow to realize that their values were threatened by a concerted alliance of secular-progressives.

In addition to the groups listed in table 4.1, colleges and universities could be included in the para-government category because even private universities receive significant funding through scholarships and research grants. As a result, most institutions of higher education have become major proponents of the secular-progressive worldview that has been adopted by the government.

Other para-government influences include quasi-interest groups who have a close relationship with government through personnel exchanges and previous political advances. They know how to use its mandates and rulings to influence legislators, public officials, and judges and secure funding from winning lawsuits. The American Civil Liberties Union has been the most destructive para-government group because it has been the most aggressive in attacking traditional Judeo-Christian views while actively working to impose secular views throughout the culture. For all intents and purposes, says Russell Kirk, the ACLU has been able to "harass out of existence" public expressions of faith.[15] The Alliance Defense Fund is a Christian organization that provides legal defense and advocacy for religious freedom, the sanctity of human life, and traditional family values. It is one example of a para-government group that attempts to enlist government support for traditional views, but it is only a recent recruit in the culture war conflicts. The battles between these and other para-government groups will be discussed in subsequent chapters.

The decisions government makes about what is legal—what is right and wrong—are absorbed and often amplified by multiple sources in both the public and private sectors. Court rulings and changes in laws since 1960, for example, have had a dramatic impact on movies and the entertainment industry. As government adopted a secular worldview and excluded religious and traditional views from the public square, television producers and the movie industry quickly threw off all restraint and began producing violent and sexually explicit entertainment. Court rulings also made most forms of pornography, regardless of how degenerate, legal. The ACLU assured any group that it would defend it in court, and this "message" to the public has significantly reduced moral standards, increasing acts of violence and aberrant sexual behavior throughout American society.

We believe the government can, and has, shaped positive beliefs and behaviors, as well as destructive ones, in the past. Laws against racial discrimination eventually reversed public opinions and created strong public stigma toward those who displayed any form of racism. Laws against littering, drunk driving, pollution, and smoking in public places have not only changed behavior, they have also changed beliefs. Americans, in large part, now believe that these behaviors are wrong. The government, in these cases, improved the culture.

Unfortunately, the reverse is also true. Because of changes in laws and court rulings, Americans are now hesitant to say "it is wrong" to have sex before marriage or outside of marriage, to have a child without being married, to have an abortion, and to have sex with someone of the same gender. One example of how government decisions empower para-government groups and establish social precedents occurred in the fall of 1993, when a seemingly isolated incident in a town forty miles northwest of Houston, Texas, made national news. That fall, four of Hempstead High School's sixteen cheerleaders turned up pregnant in the early months of the school year. All four girls were removed from the cheerleading squad. At a meeting of the cheerleaders' parents and school officials, the mother of one of the four girls announced that her daughter had had an abortion for medical reasons. The girl was allowed back on the sidelines for the Friday night football game. The parents of the still-pregnant cheerleaders were outraged and contended that the student who had had an abortion should be in the stands with the pregnant cheerleaders.

The conservative community, with local school rules forbidding extracurricular activities by students who are pregnant, was thrown into turmoil. The school policy was clear about pregnancy but said nothing about students who had abortions. Like many other districts, Hempstead had not had to wrestle with the question of pregnant cheerleaders, or those who had had abortions, because these students typically bowed quietly out of high-profile positions. When the school board voted to oust the three remaining pregnant students from the cheerleading squad, the controversy became a magnet for para-government groups and the national press.

Representatives of the National Organization of Women (NOW) and the American Civil Liberties Union (ACLU) soon became involved. They attended a school board meeting in October of 1993, where they distributed material citing federal laws and court rulings upholding the rights of pregnant or parenting students to participate in public school extracurricular activities.

Parents and school board members, who favored the policy of dismissal from the cheerleading squad, found themselves staring down the barrel of an expensive federal lawsuit in a small community just barely meeting its education budget. Discretion became the better part of valor in the confrontation, and the school board rethought its policy. All of the cheerleaders were allowed back on the squad. Behavior that was once wrong was now officially right, and the community lost its freedom to express traditional values. The lesson wasn't lost on other school districts who faced similar problems in the years to come.

In the postmodern, secular politics of the new millennium, "the political strategy is not to file a lawsuit, *it's to threaten to file a lawsuit*."[16] Legal posturing alone is usually enough to win a point. The ACLU regional director in the cheerleader controversy confirmed the strategy: "We've not been contacted by any of the cheerleaders about legal action, but the matter is of great concern to our organization."[17] Without an invitation, and with only a legal threat, the ACLU was able to force the school board to change its policy and dictate the outcome of the controversy.

The cheerleader case is but one example of the role played by the paragovernment groups in an unending cycle of culture war clashes in the United States. In the following chapters, we will expand this discussion to show how activist groups use the decisions and power of government to attack those who hold to higher values. This small, regional conflict reverberated through public schools and media outlets all around the nation. A policy of support of sexual abstinence in high school and against abortion was negated by a *threatened* lawsuit from an *uninvited* group.

The cheerleader incident, and cases similar to it, propelled the acceptance of new values around the culture development cycle. Subsidies for illegitimacy approved by the school system eventually stopped the practice of stigmatizing pregnant teens by placing them in alternative schools. Pregnant teens now attended class like everyone else. This act, along with dozens of others, helped to create a culture of illegitimacy in the country. The government made it "right" to have a child without being married, and "wrong" to direct stigma toward anyone who thought otherwise.

Today, the government has begun to stigmatize and intimidate Americans who live by, or even speak out on behalf of, Judeo-Christian cultural values. Standards in place for decades, and once universally accepted as necessary for a flourishing democracy, have been reduced to whispers. Who decides what is right and wrong? Unfortunately, it is now our growing and increasingly intrusive government. But fortunately, we are still a government of the people, and the people can change the government.

A HIGHER WAY

In spite of all the social statistics that confirm America's cultural decline and point to a similar root cause, few are willing to discuss changing the secular assumptions of government policies and programs. To paraphrase eighteenth-century political philosopher Edmund Burke, all that is necessary for barbarism to triumph is for civilized people to do nothing. In the past four decades, civilized people have done worse than that, they have been co-opted into endorsing and paying for behavior they disdain and know to be socially destructive. What's more, they have been intimidated into not saying anything about the situation. The fear of being labeled an advocate of traditional or "old-fashioned" values, of not respecting the "separation of church and state," or of being part of the "religious right" has led to cultural destruction in the name of tolerance and freedom.

Central to the very definition of a civilization is its ability to know the distinction between a higher and a lower way, and the inevitable advantage of the former. Accepted proverbs such as: "marriage is good for children and parents, divorce and births outside of marriage are harmful to both," have become obsolete. If government does anything, it should at least encourage biological families to stay together.

In the past it has often used its authority to encourage constructive and healthy behavior. For example, consider the interstate express lanes that are reserved for cars with two or more passengers. Such a provision is a good example of the government "discriminating" to encourage behavior that is helpful to society as a whole. When people carpool, there is less congestion on the highways and everyone benefits. Even drivers with no passengers, who are not allowed to use the express lane, benefit with less traffic from those who make the commitments necessary to receive the privilege. In this context, most would agree that it is wrong for a driver without any passengers to use the express lane.

Think what would happen if government thought it prudent to subsidize good social behavior by rewarding couples who stayed married with tax breaks when they retired, providing incentives to parents who raised children in two-parent married homes with their biological parents. Recall the traffic light example. Suppose people were rewarded for stopping at red lights (or at least not rewarded for running them) and allowed to ride in the express lane if they followed the rules.

When government denies the superiority of cultural achievements, and substitutes vulgar values in their place, the result is unvarnished cultural dissolution. Government actions have created a vacuum of values within America's culture development cycle. Human society, like nature, abhors a vacuum, and will eventually fill the void with a lower standard of acceptable behavior.

How people conduct themselves in their personal lives is not just a private decision. To use the terms of economics, private behavior has an effect on others. Private sexual acts between consenting teenagers has a consequence on everyone if it means that taxpayers must pay the day-care bill for their children in public schools, or if citizens become victims of violent crime at the hands of fatherless youth. The example of government sanction and support for destructive behavior like out-of-wedlock births, divorce, and abortion could be duplicated for a host of related social problems and will be discussed in later chapters.

The culture cycle offers America the opportunity and pathway to restore commonsense traditions and values to our society. But Americans must first change our government and its policies before positive changes can occur. Policies that benefit society can no longer be excluded simply because they are consistent with religious beliefs. Americans can win the culture war . . . if we are willing to raise our voices and stop whispering.

Chapter Five

Power to Intimidate:
The SLAPP Factor

My definition of a free society is a society where it is safe to be unpopular.

—Adlai E. Stevenson

So far, we have seen that government action created new definitions of "right" and "wrong," and then became the principal advocate to trigger profound changes throughout America's culture. Para-government groups, such as the ACLU and Planned Parenthood, funded in part with taxpayer dollars and cloaked with the banner of government "endorsement," quickly went on the attack against citizens, schools, businesses, and churches.[1] The bastions of traditional morality were put on the defensive. The news media and the entertainment industry joined in the cultural dismemberment and adopted the new morality now allied to government policies.

Today, traditionalists lament the liberal media, the excesses of Hollywood, left-leaning universities, and the deterioration of societal norms. But these societal changes were no accident, and unless we understand the causes, the American people will be powerless to reverse the decline of the culture. What we see now throughout the public and private sectors is a reflection of the official policy of the United States government. Either explicitly or implicitly, the official position of the federal government is that there is no God, that moral behavior cannot be required, that aberrant individuals must be coddled not punished, that marriage is nothing special, that homosexuality is no different from heterosexuality, that childbearing outside of marriage is no different from that in wedlock, that the killing of unborn babies is acceptable, that pornography is a right, and that the government will fund and support those schools that accept and teach this new morality. Perhaps most important, Americans have no right to say that any of this is wrong.

How is it that these changes took place? How is it that laws and behavior, acceptable for two hundred years, suddenly became unacceptable? The secularists used our judicial system to redefine "right" and "wrong" and to intimidate people and organizations that held traditional Judeo-Christian views. For eighty years, the ACLU has been the nation's leading religious censor, waging a war on America's core values. It is quick to "defend drug use or other religious practices skirting the edge of the law [but] is strangely silent . . . when the civil rights and liberties of Christian and Jewish organizations are in question."[2] "We now live in a country where traditional Christian and Jewish faith and religion—civilizing forces in any society—are openly mocked and increasingly pushed to the margins."[3]

Dennis Prager, a well-known conservative columnist and radio host, provided an excellent description of the nontraditional view of the law and how secular activists use the law to accomplish their goals:

> Generally speaking, the Left and the secularists venerate, if not worship, law. . . . To the Left, legality matters most, while to the Right, legality matters far less than morality. The religious have a belief in a God-based moral law, and the Left believes in man-made law as the moral law. . . . The Left is intoxicated with law-making. [It] functions as a religion.[4]

Secularists believe that if something is legal, or not illegal, that it is a "right." However, if existing law disagrees with their worldview, they work to change the law or have it overturned. This is, of course, their right. But this mind-set has a disdain for the will of the people and focuses on the judiciary and obscure legal theories to justify actions. Reformers on the left opposed to Judeo-Christian values cannot get their way through the democratic legislative process, so they often turn to the courts to impose their views on the public.

The American Civil Liberties Union has been extraordinarily successful in using a small group of dedicated lawyers, and the courts, to undermine Judeo-Christian practices. One of its first successes was the so-called "Scopes Monkey Trial" in Tennessee in the 1920s. Clarence Darrow, an attorney defending Scopes, engaged in what would become the standard-issue ACLU rhetoric: "Today it is the public school teachers, tomorrow the private. The next day the preachers and the lecturers, the magazines, the books, the newspapers."[5] To hear the secularists tell it, the whole culture was sliding down the slippery slope into the grip of a zealous theocracy. The argument that opposition to the secular agenda of the ACLU would lead to an authoritarian state was—and remains—propaganda disguised as legal argument. It appealed to people's emotions and fears, and attacked traditional believers as "sixteenth-century bigots." As a result it can now be said that there are two walls separating church and state in America: The original wall protecting religious liberty by forbidding a state church, and a second secularized one defined by the ACLU that segregates religion from government and the public square.

THE SLAPP FACTOR

Before we assess the numerous government and media attacks against America's moral structure, it is necessary to understand the legal premise that provides the power behind the secular worldview in the culture development cycle and allows secular attacks against those who hold traditional views. The legal community calls it SLAPP, an acronym that means "Strategic Lawsuits Against Public Participation." The SLAPP strategy uses the legal system to intimidate unwanted opinions by "slapping" people with lawsuits that create a media frenzy, and often result in the vilification of those who take a stand for traditional moral behavior. Even if the position is successfully defended in court, the adverse media attention can turn a victory into a defeat. A collateral aspect of the strategy is to *threaten* a lawsuit, and oftentimes intimidation is a more effective strategy than actually suing.

> A SLAPP suit is a merit-less action filed by a plaintiff whose primary goal is not to win the case but rather to silence or intimidate citizens or public officials who have participated in proceedings regarding public policy decision making.[6]

The SLAPP strategy was initially used by real estate developers in the 1960s to intimidate environmentalists who complained about their projects.[7] The strategy was codified by the federal government's Department of Housing and Urban Development in 1989 by including provisions in the Fair Housing Act that made it easier for group home advocates to sue residents and municipalities who filed complaints about the locations of these homes.

> Because HUD decided to interpret the anti-discrimination provisions of the Fair Housing Act as superseding the free speech and citizen petition provisions of the First Amendment, an individual or group opposing or criticizing a proposed group home—even in private conversation—risked being enmeshed in litigation that, subsidized by the limitless resources of the federal government, could drag on for years.[8]

SLAPP has been used for years by corporations and groups to intimidate individuals or groups who speak out against their policies or activities. But the most damaging use of SLAPP has been by the para-government groups like the ACLU, Planned Parenthood, National Abortion Rights League, National Organization for Women, Human Rights Campaign Fund, and others who have used lawsuits, the threat of lawsuits, and a sympathetic media to silence the voices of moral reason in America.

"Thousands of SLAPPs have been filed in the last two decades, tens of thousands of Americans have been SLAPPed, and still more have been muted or silenced by the threat," write law professors George Pring and Penelope Canan in their 1996 book, *SLAPPs: Getting Sued for Speaking Out*.[9] New York Supreme Court Judge J. Nicholas Colabella commented on these lawsuits in 1997, "The longer the litigation can be stretched out . . . the closer the SLAPP filer moves to success. Those who lack the financial resources and emotional stamina to play out the 'game' face the difficult choice of defaulting despite meritorious defenses or being brought to their knees to settle. . . . Short of a gun to the head, a greater threat to First Amendment expression can scarcely be imagined."[10] One researcher commented on the effect of SLAPP lawsuits: "What cannot be emphasized more strongly is the outright fear expressed by the victims of these SLAPP suits . . . the individuals who refused (who are afraid) to sign another petition, go to another public meeting, [or] send another letter to their government representative, etc."[11] The effect of the SLAPP lawsuits was to silence those who would speak out in opposition to secular advocacy groups, ultimately reducing their voices to whispers.

Here is a stereotypical example of how a SLAPP action works. We use documentation from the Boy Scouts, because their experience is so typical. This hypothetical case is a combination of the experiences many have had across the country and takes place against the backdrop of an activist judiciary from which there is virtually no appeal. The scene opens with a local school-sponsored Boy Scout troop meeting in a public school after school hours. A local ACLU attorney gets a complaint (or finds someone to complain) by a parent who is an atheist and doesn't like the Boy Scouts' requirement to say "God" in their pledge. Even though the parent's child is not a member of the Boy Scouts, the parent still finds it offensive that a "religious" organization is allowed to be associated with a public school. The ACLU attorney telephones the school principal and threatens to sue if the school continues to sponsor the Boy Scout troop. If the principal refuses, the ACLU sends a letter to the principal and the school district that threatens a suit. The letter is also sent to the local media with a press statement that is intended to embarrass the principal and the school district. The local newspaper, as well as television and radio stations, dutifully report the story about how the school has been accused of violating the constitutional separation of church and state. The story will quote the accusations of the ACLU attorney and the parent of the boy whose rights have been violated by the Boy Scouts. The school and the school district are advised by their attorneys not to comment.

The ACLU lawyers know that the principal, school district officials, school board, and Boy Scout leaders will all be stunned, confused, afraid, and embarrassed when they see their names along with accusations in the media. This type of media intimidation makes an average citizen feel like a criminal, and the ACLU lawyers love it. They have "SLAPPed" the school, the Boy Scouts and everyone associated with them. The school district now faces a tough decision. They can spend hundreds of thousands of dollars and countless hours and endure many more media attacks defending themselves, or ask the Boy Scouts to get another sponsor. The school knows that they are likely to win the court case, but they also know that even if they win there will be adverse publicity, and the law does not allow them to recoup the costs and emotional strain of defending themselves. Regardless of the outcome, they lose.

The easier decision for the school board is to ask the Scouts to leave the school. If this is the school's decision, there will be no expensive lawsuits, no embarrassing press articles, no angry school board members . . . no pain. This is why most SLAPP cases never go to court. But every SLAPP case rings "round the world," around the culture development cycle. Every public school in America will know about the case. They will either know that one school lost hundreds of thousands of dollars defending themselves, or that the school backed down and gave in. Many other schools will then ban the Boy Scouts without even getting a call from the ACLU.

The resulting victory, when the Boy Scouts decide to leave the school, is broadcast into a complex, media-driven reality where viewers read and hear about the outcome without knowing the specifics of the controversy. The coverage means that the loudest, best financed and most rehearsed voices get their messages across more effectively and more often. In short, the SLAPP Factor works. It works to intimidate those who are against pornography, abortion, homosexuality, unwed births, easy divorce, gambling, and other behaviors that diminish society. It also works to intimidate those who support a respect for God, moral principles, strong character, traditional marriage, values in the school curriculum, and other behaviors that make for a stronger nation. All it takes is one SLAPP court case, or even the *threat* of a court case, to fuel hundreds of attacks on individuals and organizations through the media for years to come.

The news media operates on a system of precedent within the culture development cycle, much like the courts. If one newspaper or television outlet inveighs against an individual or organization for taking a moral stand, other media feel justified to take the same position in another part of the country. It only takes one accusation in one city to justify attacks anywhere. This "precedent" system has so engrained itself in America's culture development cycle that lawsuits are often not even necessary for the SLAPP Factor to silence those who believe that moral behaviors are useful to our nation. Their complaints are reduced to whispers.

The SLAPP Factor Chart (figure 5.1) demonstrates how public intimidation by the government and its surrogates pushes the cultural cycle toward destructive behavior and silences those who would speak out for the values that strengthen the national character. On the left side of the chart, lawsuits, court decisions, and lax enforcement have actually encouraged behavior that is *against* the law and removed the stigma from those that verbally support destructive, and often illegal, behavior. The "Perceived Range" represents the public perception that it is acceptable to say and do things today that have tra-

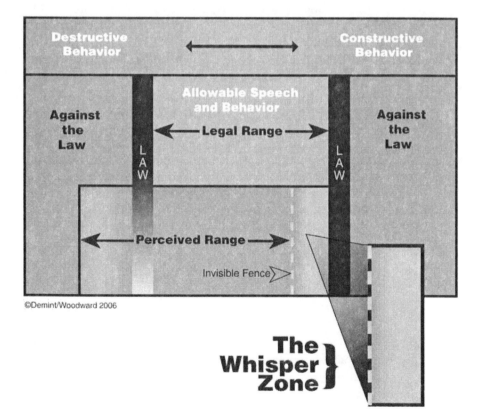

Figure 5.1.

ditionally been considered immoral or even illegal.

As demonstrated in the last chapter, because of a few court decisions, support from universities, and the mainstream and far left (which, of course, could be seen as redundant) news and entertainment media, many Americans believe that pornography, late-term abortions, cohabitation, unwed births, premarital sex, and drug use are "right," even though some state and federal laws still say they are "wrong."

On the right side of the chart, court decisions and media intimidation have made people afraid to speak out and take action that they know is good and well within the law ("Legal Range"). Reverence for God, prayer, after school Bible studies on school property, character traits, traditional marriage and family, sexual abstinence before marriage—all have been made virtually obsolete in today's postmodern culture—even though these things are known to be beneficial to society as a whole.

Since many positive behaviors such as public prayer and discrimination that traditionally battle destructive behaviors have been declared illegal, other legal beneficial activities have been subjected to lawsuits and media attacks. Much that is good in America has been "SLAPPed" to the left where beneficial behaviors go into social oblivion. Many constructive behaviors and speech are now in "The Whisper Zone." Traditional ideas of right and wrong have either been declared illegal or have been pushed out of public life into the corners of private life where they are only mentioned in whispers.

The accumulated effect of SLAPP lawsuits and media intimidation has had a dramatic effect on public opinion. A Gallup Poll in 2003 found that 58 percent of the respondents in a national survey said sex between unmarried men and women was "morally acceptable." Two-thirds of those surveyed said divorce was "morally acceptable," and having a baby outside of marriage was agreeable to a majority, 51 percent.[12] The same poll in the 1970s found that none of these behaviors (premarital sex, divorce, or out-of-wedlock births) were supported by a majority of Americans.[13]

Although there were laws against cohabitation in many states, federal welfare ruling since the 1960s encouraged such behavior by disallowing welfare payments to mothers and children if the mother was married. Federal support of illegitimacy eventually SLAPPed acceptable behavior about marriage and childbirth to the unlawful side of the chart. Lawsuits were unnecessary because federal law actually pushed the culture away from marriage and childbirth within wedlock. Illegitimacy became "right," and marriage "optional." Today a person can be figuratively SLAPPed in the media for even using the word "illegitimacy." Many states have changed their laws and lowered their standards to comply with the evolving standard created by the intimidation from para-government groups and the resulting government standard.

The SLAPP Factor works on people like an invisible electric fence works on dogs. Electric fences are effective because the dog wears a collar that shocks every time it crosses the invisible fence line. The dog's owner teaches the dog to stay in the yard by taking the dog all around the designated area and letting the dog feel the shock wherever the fence is buried. It just takes a few shocks for the dog to stay away from the invisible borders. The smarter the dog, the further it stays from fence. And since dogs are never exactly sure where the shock will take place, most never get within ten or fifteen feet of the fence.

This "shock" factor was apparent in an incident at a high school in Vancouver, Washington. In March 2007, a dozen students attending Heritage High School were suspended for praying at school. The students were members of The Church of Truth, a congregation of predominately Russian-speaking immigrants who settled in the United States for the opportunity to freely express their religious beliefs. Administrators said the participants did not follow the rules about organizing a student group.[14]

But there is more than meets the eye here. The individuals met at 7:00 a.m. and were confronted by an administrator when an alleged Satanist student complained to the school office. Clearly the administrators would rather suspend the students than try to guide them into some ACLU-sanctioned club that might meet court scrutiny. Rather than support the students, it was easier to just remove them from campus.

The shock of being SLAPPed has the same effect on people. It keeps people from standing up and speaking out for what they know is right, and against what they know is wrong. They are intimidated even when they have a legal right to do what they are doing. If they have not been personally SLAPPed (shocked), they have seen, heard, or read about others getting SLAPPed. Americans, just like the administrators at Heritage High School in Washington, now avoid taking a position on what is right or wrong, and for good reason. The result is that most people who would otherwise speak out for what they believe is good and right keep a distance from what they can legally say and do, as is indicated on the SLAPP Factor chart. On the other side, however, those who want the freedom to behave in ways that are destructive to society feel little threat or intimidation from the law, media, or public opinion. While the good whisper, the bad roar.

SLAPP ATTACKS ON SCOUTS' HONOR

There are numerous examples of government sponsored attacks on the moral and cultural traditions of the country, a sampling of which will be documented in subsequent chapters. Here, the Boy Scouts of America is introduced as an organization that has been SLAPPed repeatedly and shamelessly for their adherence to traditional values. The Scouts merit a more detailed discussion because they are an example of how laws and court rulings are used to attack America's most wholesome and constructive institutions.

The Boy Scouts of America was founded by Chicago publisher William Boyce on February 8, 1910. The group received a charter from the U.S. Congress in 1916, and the President of the United States serves as their honorary chairman.[15] Currently, there are 5 million boys and 1.2 million adults involved in Scouting. To that number can be added the tens of millions of former Scouts who count their scouting years as having played an essential, positive role in shaping their lives. Scouting teaches leadership values that prepare young people for a lifetime of service and decision making. One website lists the following as some of Scouting's accomplished alumni.[16]

89 percent of the initial Astronaut Corps
89 percent of Senior Class Presidents
85 percent of Student Council Presidents
85 percent of FBI Agents
72 percent of Rhodes Scholars
70 percent of Naval Academy graduates
68 percent of U.S. Military graduates
63 percent of U.S. Air Force Academy graduates

The Boy Scouts' success was no accident; it rested on clear values that focused on character development through accountability to God, country, and fellow citizens. The Traditional Scout Law, shown below, may seem outdated by today's secular standards, but it has made a measurable difference in the lives of millions of Americans and helped to build a stronger nation:

Traditional Scout Law[17]

1. A Scout's honor is to be trusted.
2. A Scout is loyal.
3. A Scout's duty is to be useful and to help others.
4. A Scout is a friend to all, and a brother to every other Scout.
5. A Scout is courteous.
6. A Scout is a friend to animals.
7. A Scout obeys orders.
8. A Scout smiles and whistles under all difficulties.
9. A Scout is thrifty.
10. A Scout is clean in thought, word, and deed.

The Boy Scout Oath is another statement of time-tested beliefs and represents the best of American values, but it is this oath that has led to the attacks against the Scout organization.[18]

Boy Scout Oath

On my honor I will do my best to do my duty to God and my country, and to obey the Scout Law, to help other people at all times, to keep myself physically strong, mentally awake, and morally straight.

These ideals represented a "higher way" for most Americans and were seen as in conformity with the laws and traditions of the country. The award of the rank "Eagle Scout" was a privilege accompanied by a "Court of Honor" where parents, community leaders, and other scouts gathered to recognize the accomplishment. In the 1990s, this leadership tradition came in for criticism and legal attacks. Today, it is difficult for most Americans to understand why these ideals must be "separate" from public life, but that is precisely what para-government groups have been trying to make happen.

The assault on the Boy Scouts came from two major decisions by government. First, the growing conviction in legal circles, backed by court rulings, that there must be a separation of church and state in America. While the "separation of church and state" was not mentioned in the Constitution or in any of our founding documents, the First Amendment does make it clear that the federal government should not establish or promote a particular state church or religious denomination. But when the Supreme Court fabricated a "wall of separation" to ban public prayer and religious songs and readings from the public schools in 1962, the culture development cycle began to morph this decision far beyond its original intent. While the high Court action began with a ban of prayer in schools, it soon became a ban on God in public forums, and then it became an implicit ban on religiously based moral principles. For example, in 1992 plaintiffs filed suit in Oregon to prevent state officials from requiring clients to attend Alcoholic Anonymous meetings alleging that they required participants to "turn to God to overcome addiction." The next target was the Boy Scout Law and Oath.

Second, changes in laws and court decisions that began to promote the rights of homosexuals had a direct impact on the Boy Scouts. Until the 1960s, every state had a law criminalizing homosexual behavior. But because of the hard work of homosexual activists, thirty-seven states subsequently repealed these laws.[19] In 2003, the Supreme Court ruled six to three that sodomy laws (laws that make homosexual behavior illegal) were unconstitutional.[20] This ruling made the stance of the Boy Scouts the target of para-government groups, but the assault on the scouts began long before this ruling.

Since 1975, the Boy Scouts of America have had to defend themselves in more than thirty SLAPP-style lawsuits attacking their values.[21] Most of these suits challenged the Boy Scouts' right to set standards for membership: specifically the standards that required members to be male, have a belief in God, and not be openly homosexual.[22] The Boy Scouts won every one of these cases, either at trial or on appeal, but they did not recoup the millions of dollars they had to spend to defend themselves and their values. Neither did they receive any compensation for the millions of dollars in lost contributions and public support due to the hundreds of malicious and misleading news articles that appeared all across the country. For example, the *New York Times* coverage was typical with a first sentence lead that read, "To the dismay of gay rights groups and civil libertarians," the Supreme Court of the United States found for the Boy Scouts in a five to four decision.[23] At the same time, the *Seattle Times* quoted a local scout leader who said, "some members do not agree with the policy, but continue to support scouting."[24]

The most well-known of these court cases was decided in June of 2000. James Dale, a former Eagle Scout who was also an AIDS activist, had openly declared his homosexuality. As a result he was denied appointment as an assistant scoutmaster.[25] Dale filed suit under a New Jersey law that prohibited discrimination on the basis of sexual orientation in places of public accommodation. The case was ultimately decided by the Supreme Court. It ruled that Boy Scouts, and all private organizations, had the constitutionally protected right under the First Amendment of freedom of association to set their own membership standards. Initially, this decision appeared to be a great victory for the Boy Scouts and traditional values, but state and local governments, aided and abetted by the American Civil Liberties Union, simply changed their strategies and continued the attacks, saying that the organization was still in violation of local ordinances against discrimination.

It is important to understand the context of the Boy Scout policy not to admit homosexuals. Not only was homosexuality illegal and considered morally abhorrent when the Boy Scouts was founded, but throughout their history they had been faced with many cases of homosexual leaders who had committed sexual acts with teenage Scouts.[26] The Boy Scouts made it clear that they would not tolerate these abuses. Parents had traditionally placed their trust in the Boy Scout organization to protect their children, and it was a trust the Scouts took seriously.

Homosexual apologists used academic studies, along with statements from groups such as the American Psychological Association (the same organization that said it is only child abuse if the child felt bad about the relationship), to make their case that homosexuals are no more likely to be pedophiles or abuse children than heterosexuals.[27] Ultimately, their arguments were unconvincing, and the assertion of homosexual innocence has been proven invalid by other studies, which suggest that, while no more than 2 percent of male adults are homosexual, approximately 35 percent of pedophiles are homosexual.[28] The National Association for Research and Therapy of Homosexuality stated:

> Gay advocates correctly state that most child molesters are heterosexual males. But this is a misleading statement. In proportion to their numbers (about one out of thirty-six men), homosexual males are more likely to engage in sex with minors; in fact, they appear to be three times more likely than straight men to engage in adult-child sexual relations.[29]

Even these statistics seriously underestimate the potential dangers poised to the Boy Scouts by homosexuals. Not only are homosexual men more prone to sexually molest boys, they are prone to seek out organizations, like the Boy Scouts, where they have more intimate exposure to boys.[30] Historically, the Boy Scouts have had a serious problem with sexual offenses by male leaders against Scouts, "so serious that prevention has become a major preoccupation, with constant leader screening and training, the 'two-deep leadership' requirement, and programs for Scouts to identify warning signs of inappropriate advances by adults."[31] Leaders of the Boy Scouts understand that adults interested in molesting young boys are prone to enlist in voluntary positions, such as those taken by coaches, teachers, scoutmasters, and priests. "The Scouting organization simply refuses to allow what the Catholic Church has allowed—"gay networks or subcultures are using the priesthood as cover for their sexual acting out, believing that their only responsibility to the Church is a certain discretion."[32]

The irony of press coverage of these two controversies, the Catholic Church scandal and the Boy Scouts, is revealing. The press was unrelenting in its criticism of the Catholic Church when sexual abuse charges against priests were made public in the 1990s. The charges sent shock waves through various archdioceses and across the nation, prompting church officials to adopt new policies and pay exorbitant settlements. Reporters found that the church approved a number of gay men into seminaries, and tolerated known sex offenders in the priesthood.[33] The question was repeatedly asked: Why did the church look the other way and not report the crimes to the police, or at least eject the offenders from the priesthood and into jail? Why did the church not "take steps" to protect young children?

The answers became clear when stories on the Boy Scout controversy were examined. The media condemned the Catholic Church for ignoring predatory homosexuals, but were never critical of homosexuals. Simultaneously, they condemned the Boy Scouts of America for *not* allowing homosexuals to serve as leaders in their organization. The only logical conclusion, given the coverage, is that journalists will readily condemn traditional organizations such as the church and the Boy Scouts, but they will not dare to offer a critical analysis of the behavior that causes the problems they abhor. In sum, the traditional organizations have to change, not the "problem people" within them. The media are obvious active supporters of the gay rights movement, and they refuse to discuss the dark side of homosexuality. If reported, the facts about AIDS, pedophilia, child pornography, and violent behavior would be enough to cause parents to rally to the defense of the Boy Scouts. Instead, the public reads about Scouting's "bigotry" and the Catholic Church's "abuse" of children.

A study released by the Roman Catholic archdiocese of Dublin, Ireland, reported that 102 priests in the country were suspected of sexually or physically abusing some 350 children since 1940.[34] While the abuses within the Catholic church continued around the world, and the cause was obviously connected to homosexuality in the priesthood, the world remained too intimidated to even suggest that there could be something "wrong" with homosexual behavior. Instead, the discussion was reduced to a whisper. The Catholic Church shares some blame for this situation, because people have been far too deferential to priests. They grew up learning that it was not permissible to question or challenge the Catholic Church.

The Boy Scouts paid a high price for their convictions about homosexuality. In April of 2001, a report by the *Chronicle of Philanthropy* estimated that more than 50 of the 400 largest United Way organizations had either dropped the Boy Scouts from their rosters, limited donations, or changed their pledge forms to allow people to prohibit donations from being used to support scouting. That same month, Oscar-winning filmmaker Steven Spielberg stepped down from an advisory board of the Boy Scouts, saying he could no longer associate with a group that engaged in "discrimination."[35] The Chase Manhattan Bank, Levi-Strauss and Co., and Textron, Inc. bowed to public pressure and cut their support to the Boy Scouts. Wells Fargo severed ties in the early 1990s, and asked the United Way to steer its U.S. contribution of $400,000 away from the Boy Scouts. "The Boys Scouts are as American as apple pie, but this was an easy decision to make," said Tom Unger, a Wells Fargo spokesman. "We really have to, as a company, return to what our core vision and values are, and that is to not discriminate."[36] It was evidently acceptable to discriminate against anyone who held traditional values. Many United Way organizations asked to exclude the Boy Scouts of America from their corporate gift-giving.[37] In 2002, Carrier Corporation stopped funding the Boy Scouts.

A press release from the Communications Workers of America union, dated April, 2001 declared:

> It is with sadness that we now take action to sever ties between CWA and the Boy Scouts of America until such time as its leaders reverse their policy of excluding gays from membership or volunteer activities in scouting. This policy by the Boy Scouts organization is an appalling step backward at a time when other American institutions—churches, corporations, school systems, even the military—are moving in a more enlightened direction to banish discrimination against people because of their sexual orientation. Teaching intolerance is a very poor lesson for our youth—one that we must challenge. We urge the Boy Scouts of America leaders to reconsider and drop this policy. In the meantime CWA calls upon its local unions and members to refrain from supporting or participating in activities of the Boy Scouts.[38]

One wonders what the typical blue-collar union member felt about the CWA decision. The list of corporate, union, and fraternal donors abandoning scouting could fill a book. Clearly, even though the Boy Scouts *won* in the legal process, they *lost* much in the court of public opinion.

Around the country, governments terminated their support for the Boy Scouts. Even though almost any group could use public facilities, the city governments of Chicago, San Francisco, and San Jose told local chapters that troops could no longer use parks, schools, and municipal sites.[39] The Los Angeles Unified School District began a process to limit Boy Scout recruiting activity on campuses, and required troops that used school facilities to sign statements renouncing the national antigay policy.[40] The Minneapolis school board voted unanimously to end sponsorship of Boy Scout troops and to prohibit them from recruiting new members in the public schools.[41]

These new government policies are themselves discriminatory, and they send a frightening message to churches, community groups, and voluntary organizations who use school facilities for their meetings. If schools continue to give in to the secular left under the threat of lawsuits, it is yet another example of the effectiveness of the SLAPP strategy. Isn't it better for school systems to deny access to *every* group? This is the impending result that will change life for each citizen in years to come.

The evaporation of support for the Boy Scouts took place after a Supreme Court victory. One can only imagine what would have happened had the Scouts not won in court. The Boy Scout policy to exclude homosexuals cannot be viewed as discrimination or intolerance. Instead, it must be acknowledged for what it is: a reasonable and fair way to protect the boys and young men associated with the organization. Despite this fact, the para-government groups continue to work to overturn the Boy Scout exclusion of homosexuals. These groups include: the ACLU, NAACP, NOW, NEA (a national teachers' union), American Association of School Administrators, American Jewish Congress, the General Board of Church and Society of the United Methodist Church, the American Bar Association, the American Psychological Association, major American cities, and attorneys general from ten different states.

After the Supreme Court decision in 2000, the ACLU simply changed its strategy from arguments of "discrimination based on sexual orientation" to those of "separation of church and state" (the Boy Scouts have "God" in their pledge). They redirected their attack to public schools that chartered the Scouts. Schools were threatened, taken to court, and faced the prospect of spending hundreds of thousands of dollars defending themselves. Whether they won or lost in court, they lost.

Cities have been sued for allowing the Boy Scouts to use local parks. In 2004 the city of San Diego ended a three-and-a-half year legal battle by canceling its park lease with the Boy Scouts and paying the ACLU $790,000 in legal fees.[42] This is one of the ways the ACLU acquires taxpayer dollars to fund subsequent attacks. The message from any settlement was clear, and cities across the country understood it well: if you fight for the Boy Scouts, it will cost you.

The final insult for the Boy Scouts came in November 2004 when the U.S. Department of Defense terminated decades of tradition by ending their sponsorship of the Boy Scouts on military bases for their annual jamborees. This was the ultimate irony, since the military itself has a "don't ask, don't tell" policy of discrimination. But the decision to disallow the Boy Scout jamboree was another example of a traditional American institution—in this case the military—bowing to politically correct pressure. Even though Congress responded with the Support Our Scouts Act of 2005, this bill did nothing to reestablish official sponsorship by the military of Boy Scout events. It simply said that the government couldn't discriminate *against* the Boy Scouts.[43]

In February of 2005, the ACLU sent a letter to the Boy Scouts threatening legal action against public schools and other governmental agencies that chartered Boy Scout groups. The ACLU charged that sponsorship of the Boy Scouts amounted to religious discrimination and violated the separation of church and state. To save thousands of schools, cities, and states from further lawsuits, the Scouts finally voluntarily withdrew their charters from schools and all public entities.[44] The Scouts still had the same rights as any other community-based group to meet in schools and public places, but they could no longer be sponsored by any organization receiving taxpayer funds. Even though two-thirds of Americans support the Boy Scouts, they are now officially separated from public life in America.[45]

The Boy Scout controversy left an impression on other voluntary groups. "The Girl Scouts of America, the YMCA, 4-H Clubs, Boys and Girls Clubs of America, and Jewish community groups would not exclude gays because the Scouts had to pay millions in legal fees to defend themselves, while losing millions of dollars of public support."[46] The issue showed how government power could be used in an attempt by secularists to stigmatize one of America's most honored organizations, and silence one of the country's most valuable assets. For most of the nation's history, a Boy Scout uniform was synonymous with character and accomplishment. Today, the Boy Scout uniform and Scouts' honor continue to represent the best of the American spirit. Because the Boy Scouts of America stood up and fought for what they believed, they have displayed courage as an organization that deserves the trust and respect of all principled Americans.

Despite the onslaught of government sponsored attacks, intimidation and ruinous publicity, the Boy Scouts have stayed true to their values. They did not cower, they did not whisper. Although they were forced to retreat from schools, as well as many public and private associations, they continued to fight for their right to set their own standards. Because of many misguided judges and cowardly politicians, many poor children, particularly minority boys in public schools who desperately need a positive male role model, will find it more difficult to join a Boy Scout troop. Because of many weak-kneed business sponsors, politically correct United Way agencies, and secular national organizations, the Boy Scouts will have more difficulty raising money. But the Boy Scouts will prevail because they will fight for their principles. They have endured much, and lost much, but the biggest losers are all Americans.

America's future has been diminished, but the Boy Scouts have proven that if we are willing to fight, we can win the culture war. In 2010, the Boy Scouts will celebrate their centennial with nearly 5 million youth members and over 1 million adult volunteers. Every citizen that loves America should thank the Boy Scouts for fighting for our values. We cannot continue to allow our own government to attack this great organization and America's great traditions, because a nation that demeans honor and character cannot be surprised when their citizens have neither.

Chapter Six

Public Schools:
Deconstructing American Values

There is no real teacher who in practice does not believe in the existence
of the soul, or in a magic that acts on it through speech.

—Allan Bloom

In April of 2005, in Lexington, Massachusetts, a parent was arrested and
jailed for trespassing after refusing to leave his six-year-old son's elementary
school. David Parker wanted a commitment from the school to comply with
state law and notify parents before teachers discussed homosexuality or trans-
gender issues with his children. The school contended that the state statute requiring parental notice of instruction on human sexuality did not extend to library books, so they called the police and had Parker removed.[1]

David Parker and other parents were indignant with Joseph Estabrook Elementary School because its "diversity" curriculum showed kindergarten
classes pictures of families headed by gay and lesbian couples. Then a second-
grade teacher at Estabrook read a book endorsing gay marriage to her students. *King and King* is a story about a prince named Bertie who "never cared
much for princesses." When he meets another prince named Lee, the two
princes fall in love and get married. "The wedding was very special," reads
the text. The queen mother elevates the princes to kings, and the book ends
with a picture of Bertie and Lee exchanging a passionate kiss.[2]

Massachusetts is the only state with court-ordered legalized gay marriage,
which means that homosexuality is both "right" and "a right." One teacher repeatedly said, "It's the law in Massachusetts and we're going to teach it." The
law also means that parents have no right to say that homosexuality is
"wrong," except in private. But outraged parents did speak out. Robin Wirth-
lin, another parent, told a reporter, "My son is only seven years old. By presenting this kind of issue at such a young age, they're trying to indoctrinate

our children. They're intentionally presenting this as a norm, and it's not a value that our family supports."[3]

The school and its teachers were not involved in a sinister plot of their own making. No, they were dutifully carrying out the policies of a "value-free" sex education curriculum established by their state and federal governments. As the Lexington Superintendent of Schools told the *Boston Globe*:

> We couldn't run a public school system if every parent who feels some topic is objectionable to them for moral or religious reasons decides their child should be removed. Lexington is committed to teaching children about the world they live in, and in Massachusetts same-sex marriage is legal.[4]

In the secular world, there are no moral absolutes, but what is legal is absolute unless it goes against the beliefs of the secular community. Legal means "right," and what is legally "right" trumps what is morally "wrong." That is why secularists are diligent in their efforts to manipulate judges and politicians to reverse all laws based on traditional American standards and to replace them with a legal framework that excludes moral judgments. Educational professionals maintain that such teaching is in line with their historic purpose. States have been described as "laboratories of democracy," meaning that people of diverse beliefs and backgrounds are taught to live together effectively. Teachers of a secular mind-set believe that part of their mandate is to purge traditional values from the curriculum. As Kris Mineau, president of the conservative Massachusetts Family Institute, warns:

> We have always maintained that the very first level of impact would be in the public school system, where children would be taught morals that are counter to the morals that parents want them to be taught. Taxpayer money should never be used to put children at odds with their parents. . . . If I have children in my family, same-sex marriage immediately affects me.[5]

PUBLIC SCHOOLS: THE TIP OF THE SPEAR FOR THE SECULAR ASSAULT

Historically, the situation in Massachusetts' schools is not the experience of most families who volunteer for the classroom. Active parents who get involved with their children's school usually appreciate the teachers and believe that their school is providing a good education for their children. Teachers and principals are often friends and neighbors who share the same traditional values of the parents. The problem with public schools is not with the teachers or administrators. The problem is that public schools are government schools that are, by law, required to teach every subject from a secular worldview and to exclude anything that is representative of traditional history or values.

Public schools do not generally teach against traditional views or criticize religion. They just leave it out. Every subject is taught with the assumption that there is no God. There are no moral lessons that draw on the authority of God's laws. "Right" and "wrong" are seldom used as guides for behavior. These omissions are subtle and not evident on every visit to a school. There is certainly nothing about the exclusion of traditional views that would, on the surface, appear harmful to students. But parents should consider what has been lost.

History lessons have been revised to exclude or diminish the impact of religion on civilization and its great leaders. Students learn that many wars were fought over religious issues, but they have no context with which to understand these conflicts. They do not learn that most of the great men and women in history were motivated by a religious mission, or that faith played a part in exploration and discovery. The problem is that they do not know what Daniel J. Boorstin, the former Librarian of Congress, called "a history of heroes of the imagination." He has persuasively written that "Western religions begin with a notion that One—One God, One Book, One Son, One Church, One Nation under God—is better than many. . . . Man would himself be no mere object or victim or instrument of gods but part of the process of creation."[6]

Students in public schools do not know this. They do not learn that the great explorers like Christopher Columbus risked their lives because they believed they were serving God. They do not learn that most of history's great scientists and scientific organizations, like Isaac Newton and the Royal Society, were on a mission to learn more about God by discovering the mysteries of His creation. Because their education has no basis in faith, the students have no passion for learning.

Copernicus, Galileo, and Kepler—all devout Christians—were the first to prove that the sun was the center of the solar system and explain planetary motion. Descartes, often called the father of geometry and algebra, and Pascal, who documented some of the first laws of physics, believed that the order of math and physics was the result of God's design. Isaac Newton, often considered history's greatest scientist and mathematician, was equally well known for his Christian passion and writings about the Bible. Even many of this generation's greatest scientists, such as Charles Towns, a 1964 Nobel Prize winner in physics for his development of early laser technology, are well known for their integration of religious and scientific thought.

Louis Pasteur was the scientist known for developing the process of pasteurization for milk, as well as making major contributions to medicine by confirming the germ theory of disease and creating the first vaccines. Pasteur viewed his work as part of his service to God and once said, "I have the faith of a Breton peasant and by the time I die I hope to have the faith of a Breton peasant's wife."[7] Ludwig van Beethoven, the great composer, and Michelangelo, the famous painter, sculptor, and architect, dedicated their work to the glory of God.[8] American children will never know these important historical facts because their teachers cannot tell them.

Maybe it is the scattered curriculum that results in such poor academic performance. In a test of fourth graders, 60 percent did not know that the Pilgrims and Puritans came to America to practice religious freedom. The same percentage did not know that Missions were the center of religious discovery and activity in the Spanish colonies. Needless to say, because the faith and religious component is not taught, almost no students understand how America came into being, and why its citizens were different from their European ancestors.

Secularists argue that the religious convictions of great men and women have no relevance to their work and should not be included when their contributions are taught in government schools. The progressive worldview holds that science and religion are in opposition; while history's most influential people believed both are pursuits of the same truth. Any objective analysis of history will prove that the secular argument is illogical and factually incorrect. Religious conviction often provided the inspiration and motivation for mankind's most important achievements. The world's most renowned scientists built their research methodologies on the belief that God had created an ordered universe with predictable laws that could be discovered and used to improve quality of life.

Today students are being taught that their own thoughts and lives should be divided into separate compartments—with "walls of separation" between their hearts and minds. What is true in one compartment is not true in another. This is completely opposite from the beliefs of the great people of history and the beliefs that made America exceptional. Rational, integrated thinking and action depend on a holistic perspective that believes truth is truth. The laws of physics and math are the same in private and public life. History is the same in school or in church. Religious truth is consistent with scientific truth, but it is never taught.

When schools teach history as fiction—including the theory of evolution— they create a worldview for our youth that is the exact opposite of the traditional worldview that inspired their forefathers. If God didn't create the world and all life, then human existence is an accident and has no eternal purpose. Everything that happens in life is random chance, and there is no hope of life beyond the grave. When people begin to think this way, there is no place for the freedom of people as humans, they are merely statistics. If humanity and nature is all there is in the world, then whatever *is* is right, and no standard exists to hold government accountable.

Under this worldview it is rational to say, "eat, drink, and be merry, for tomorrow you will die." Children are not stupid, and while most schools do not explicitly teach this worldview, the message is crystal clear: "God has no relevance in anything you need to know for your life." What is not said, but implied, is that when the memory of a Judeo-Christian consensus on values is forgotten, a manipulating authoritarianism will take its place.

Parents have been led to believe that they can teach their values at home and church, while schools can be "value-neutral" when educating their children. Some diligent parents may succeed, but for most this is wishful thinking. The average parent spends little time in meaningful conversation with their children, and most families spend only an hour or two a week in church. Certainly schools are not to blame if parents, the most important traditional institution, fail to teach moral values. Children spend more than thirty hours a week in school and average twenty-eight hours of watching television.[9] Because of this constant emersion in the secular worldview and the forced compartmentalization of their lives, God now has the same status for many children as Santa Claus and the Easter Bunny: they pretend He's real at home, but in the real world, they have to live as if He is not.

Government schools have control of most of America's children for 900 hours a year from kindergarten through high school.[10] Schools teach students about sex without telling them it is "wrong" to have sex before marriage. Translation: premarital sex is "okay." Schools will teach students about childbirth without telling them it is "wrong" to have children before they are married. Translation: unwed childbirth is "right." They teach students about abortion, homosexuality, and a wide range of moral issues without addressing the question of whether these behaviors are "right" or "wrong." Translation: it is not appropriate to make moral judgments or to say that anything is "wrong." In sum, public schools have become the training camps for the secular-progressive worldview.

GOVERNMENT DECISIONS AND
RESULTING ACADEMIC PERFORMANCE

Until the 1960s, prevailing family and community values determined what values were taught in public schools. While there was nothing that approached religious indoctrination, there was a nominal integration of the traditional worldview and the moral purpose behind political action in America.

The government accommodated societal views, values, morals, and traditions, but did not require specific teachings.

The control of schools is crucial in any democracy where the preparation of young people for their future responsibilities involves the health of the republic. If social and educational purposes are dictated by government, then the political efficacy of students means they are likely to hand power over to others rather than take responsibility themselves. That is why the failure of American students to know their nation's history is so tragic—it portends future problems. The results of competition between American students and the rest of the world have consistently shown an appalling difference when it came to math and science, but now studies are finding a pathetic lack of knowledge among students of their own country's past.

National history and civics assessments show that most fourth grade students cannot identify the opening passages of the Constitution and the Declaration of Independence. Most high school students cannot explain the checks-and-balances theory behind the three branches of government.[11] "When thirteen-year-olds were asked the purpose of the Monroe Doctrine . . . 70 percent failed."[12]

There is plenty of data to suggest that young Americans are poorly informed about National and world events. A 2003 study by the National Conference of State Legislatures found that 64 percent of fifteen- to twenty-six year-olds knew the name of the latest American Idol, but only 10 percent could identify the speaker of the U.S. House of Representatives.[13] Here is a fact we all know: these results mean that subsequent generations will accept without protest that their freedoms and liberties were the benevolent gift of a generous government, not the result of free people living their lives before God. The longest-lasting constitution in the world begins with the words, "We the people . . . " and it is the people who will have to keep it alive. "I think we are sadly failing our children," said historian David McCullough before a government committee, "and have been for a long time."[14]

The historical gift of America was that it gave freedom to citizens by allowing local intermediary institutions, such as church, synagogue, and community, to regulate behavior. If there are no absolutes in religion to check the chaos and hedonism of humans, then there is only one other alternative left. In the words of the late theologian Francis Schaeffer, "If there are no absolutes by which to judge society, the society is absolute."[15] What we are witnessing today in public schools is the complete displacement of a worldview that gave individuals freedom, with one that makes them prisoners to secular beliefs.

In 1962, the United States government, through federal courts, began the transition from voluntary community standards to the secular worldview in public schools. The *Engel v. Vitale* Supreme Court case held by a six-to-one margin that teachers could not open classes with a prayer. The next year, in 1963, the *School District of Abington Township v. Schempp* decision (eight to one) held that a state could not require the recitation of the Lord's Prayer and the reading of scripture in public school classrooms, even when students could voluntarily opt out of these activities. In 1968, the *Epperson v. Arkansas* decision was unanimous that states could no longer prohibit the teaching of evolution because the prohibition was motivated by religious beliefs.[16]

The ripple effect of these decisions was to remove any reference to God and Christianity from the public school textbooks. No wonder that students are unaware that the motivations of the separatists on the *Mayflower* were heartfelt and pushed them into a dangerous crossing. They don't understand the passion of the antislavery crusade, or the national convictions of Franklin Roosevelt, who spoke to the nation in a fireside chat two days after the bombing of Pearl Harbor saying, "the rest of the world is praying for us . . . our hope and theirs for liberty under God."

The ACLU still whittles away at the freedom of religious expression in public schools in its arguments before the high Court. In *Wallace v. Jaffree* (1985) the court ordered the termination of moments of silence for voluntary prayer or meditation because this practice conveyed "a message of state approval of prayer activities in public schools." In 1987, the Supreme Court ruled that states cannot require public schools to balance evolution lessons by teaching creation. In 1992, the Supreme Court in *Lee v. Weisman* stopped the practice of allowing ministers and rabbis to offer nonsectarian prayers at public high school graduation ceremonies.[17]

With the culture cycle amplifying every court decision, federal courts soon expanded on the precedents established by the Supreme Court. In 1990, the Seventh Circuit Court of Appeals in *Webster v. New Lenox* ruled that school boards had the right to prohibit the teaching of creationism because such lessons would constitute religious advocacy and, hence, such restrictions did not constitute an infringement on a teacher's free speech rights (in other words, religious speech is not included in the First Amendment right of free speech). Although the decision only influenced children in the states of Wisconsin, Illinois, and Indiana, the ripple-effect was nationwide.

After more than two hundred years of supporting traditional American values and beliefs, the public school system had a complete makeover as they are now the principal advocate of the secular worldview. Only forty years ago, students learned a respect for religious traditions and standards. Today a teacher or student can be suspended for even wearing a crucifix necklace.[18] Free speech? Hardly! Free exercise of religion? Same answer! Some argue that students still have the right to pray and participate in after-school religious clubs, but the threats of SLAPP lawsuits and media intimidation are so great that schools rarely take the risk of allowing any appearance of religious activity, even if it is technically legal. Schools operate in the "Whisper Zone," staying a long way from the "invisible fence" that will shock them if they do anything that supports traditional Judeo-Christian values. Some schools and school administrators relish being on the forefront of this values revolution, and there is nothing silent or subdued about their effect on America's future. A curriculum that is not taught is just another form of censorship by the public schools.

HOW SLAPP LAWSUITS PARALYZE SCHOOLS

In September, 2004, the ACLU filed a lawsuit in federal court against a California school district for requiring pregnant students and students with children to attend alternative classrooms. The school district required that students receiving the benefits of child-care and parenting skills classes must participate in alternative classrooms. The suit was filed on behalf of two young women students, one fifteen and one seventeen years old, both of whom were parents.[19]

According to the ACLU, their attack on the school was justified by federal and state laws.

> The lawsuit references violations of Title IX, the landmark 1972 federal law that prohibits discrimination on the basis of sex in federally funded education, as well as the Fourteenth Amendment's equal protection and due process clauses, reports the Associated Press. Additionally, the California law that governs the program states specifically that school districts must "ensure that enrolled pupils retain their right to participate in any comprehensive school or education alternative programs in which they could otherwise enroll."[20]

This same press release quotes Nancy Solomon of the California Women's Law Center, who admits that out-of-wedlock births are destructive to both mother and child, yet she believes that there should be no consequences to the student that might discourage the same behavior from other teenagers. "[This] lawsuit should be a wake-up call to school districts that they cannot deny pregnant and parenting students their rights without consequences."[21]

The case demonstrates the dilemma we have as a nation: by protecting the rights of those who practice destructive behavior, and by insulating them from the consequences of their actions, we encourage and promote more destructive behavior. In business there is something known as "Gresham's

Law," which holds that "bad money drives good money out of circulation." It means that debased coinage gradually replaces good coins. We think the same law applies to culture: "bad behavior drives out good behavior." This has clearly happened with government support of teen pregnancies. While it is good to encourage compassion and support for needy students, lawmakers must realize that the basis of any education is the discrimination between constructive and destructive behavior. If schools cannot make these distinctions, then there will be no deterrent against behavior that is ruinous in the lives of millions of Americans. There are ways to protect the rights of individuals without making destructive behavior a legal right protected by the government.

What happens when schools teach that it is acceptable to have children outside of marriage? A huge number of young women simply lose the life script that would lead them to marriage. Simply stated, we are jeopardizing our children's future and the future of this country by teaching children to forego marriage. Children of single mothers have more emotional problems, drug abuse, suicide, sexual abuse, and problems with the law. Worse, these maladies are like waves rolling through the culture and afflicting subsequent generations with poverty and troubled relationships.

Lawsuits inhibit any residual responsibility educators feel to encourage students toward constructive behavior. Scott LaFee, a contributing writer for *California Schools* described the out-of-control litigation threat facing all schools.

> In New York, a father sues a school district after it suspends his son for firing a frozen egg at a passing school bus, which shattered a window and injured a child. The father says the district violated his son's civil rights because the act took place off school grounds.
>
> In Texas, parents sue the principal and all seven school district trustees after their daughter, a sixth-grader, is ordered to not wear a Hoover Dam T-shirt to school. The daughter did so six days in a row and each day was sent home. The shirt read: 'Somebody went to Hoover Dam, and all I got was this dam shirt.' The parents claim her First Amendment rights were violated and that the punishment—being sent home—was excessive and punitive.
>
> In Wisconsin, a student who claims his vacation plans were spoiled by summer homework sues his school's district to end the practice, citing an unfair workload and unnecessary stress.
>
> And in North Carolina, parents sue a school board after it decides to adopt uniforms for middle school students.[22]

Little by little, but at an accelerating pace, experienced teachers and administrators are beginning to abandon the public schools rather than face the battles of discipline, process, and political correctness in education. The list of extraclassroom responsibilities and liability is growing and controversial, so much so that many teachers find the pressure, coupled with the low pay, unfulfilling. One newspaper reports that, "a quarter of the teachers in New York's failing schools (an official designation) left each year [and] to fill the gap, the Board of Education had been forced to hire uncertified teachers."[23] Even extracurricular activities are subject to legal scrutiny, such as the cheerleader case in Texas, which showed that the SLAPP strategy worked outside the classroom.

The curriculum itself has become a beachhead for secularists to expand their reach into the schools. In 2007, in Montgomery County, Maryland, schools overhauled their sex education curriculum to go deeper into sexual and gender identity. By a unanimous vote the Board of Education mandated that a revived curriculum consist of "lessons on respect for differences in human sexuality and a lesson on condom use for tenth grade students that includes a demonstration video."[24] The new lessons were developed to introduce students to sexual orientation and transgenderism as early as eighth grade. "Everyone's watching Montgomery right now, in no uncertain terms, to see whether the new curriculum survives an expected legal challenge," said Jean-Marie Navetta, spokesperson for Parents, Families and Friends of Lesbians and Gays.[25]

In the case of the cheerleaders in Hempstead, Texas, the school board issued a statement declaring that it had "fought hard for values that are held by a majority of the citizens in the community, and would continue to fight if it had the financial wherewithal."[26] Scarce resources were apparently no problem for the Montgomery County Board of Education which vowed to support the new curriculum out of its concern for the "health and safety of students," especially their "mental health."[27]

The SLAPP strategy and effectiveness can be explained by this one simple press release. Rather than face an expensive and intimidating showdown over the policy, the school board decided to back down. It was a familiar outcome: the district could not afford to risk an expensive legal fight and the media intimidation that inevitably accompanies SLAPP lawsuits.

Lawsuits against schools for upholding moral standards or allowing the free expression of faith would sound almost comical if they weren't so detrimental to our culture. Notice the following headlines: "ACLU Seeks to Jail Teachers Who Pray," "ACLU Contends Abstinence Education Violates Church and State," "Coach Forced to Halt Prayer after ACLU Threatens," and "ACLU Bullies District into Banning Bible Distribution."[28] The list of lawsuits could fill several volumes.

The implication is clear. Public schools are no longer able to proclaim values in the public arena. They are no longer able to say that some things are "right" and others are "wrong" or "harmful." Government policy now protects the rights of those who practice destructive behavior. When schools cannot set standards and enforce discipline without the fear of being SLAPPed with a lawsuit, it should come as no surprise that safety and learning continue to deteriorate in education.

THERE'S HOPE FOR CHANGE

Just as easily as a few court rulings excluded common sense and traditional values from public schools, America's government "of the people" can reverse the current trends. The culture cycle will quickly respond to judicial or legislative decisions that restore the legal rights of those with traditional views. In fact, parents and students now have many legal rights that are not exercised because of the complexity and confusion of the law . . . and the threat of lawsuits.[29] Organizations such as the Alliance Defense Fund support parents all over the country in restoring their legal rights and their freedom of speech in public schools.

For example, the Alliance Defense Fund successfully intervened in a court case in Arizona to defend school choice programs, and helped restore a student who was suspended for distributing materials outside of class time during an event that allows students to present a Christian viewpoint on homosexual behavior. In a case that received national attention, ADF attorneys ended a seventeen-year lawsuit seeking the removal of the Mt. Soledad National War Memorial cross in California.

The wedding of secular values to the public schools is one reason traditional parents are embracing the idea of school choice. The system of school choice uses tax credits, vouchers, or other means of support to send children to private/religious or charter schools, in addition to the public schools. Parents also have the option of home schooling. The idea is gaining support because it allows traditional values to be linked back into the curriculum. Public choice is gaining ground as courts have supported the arguments for choice, and thirteen states have adopted some form of choice legislation. The policy has been backed by persuasive arguments that creating a competitive educational marketplace will improve the offering of local schools.

If parents and grandparents with traditional views needed any additional motivation, they should ask themselves these questions: "How could my children who graduate after twelve years in public schools possibly believe that God and traditional moral standards are highly valued by their community and country? How could America's religious heritage be relevant to them when the government and schools forbid it from even being considered in the classroom? How can children stand up and say that teachers, schools, judges, and the entire government are wrong?" As children learn, their whispers get quieter and quieter.

The fight is tough, but it's winnable. The battle, however, is much bigger than just public schools. The next step for children is college, the next battleground for the soul of our nation.

Chapter Seven

America's Secular Cathedrals: Higher Ed or a Lower Way?

Free speech, exercised both individually and through a free press, is a necessity in any country where people are themselves free.

—Theodore Roosevelt

The contemporary American middle class dream has many parts, one of which is the day young men and women head off to college. About two-thirds of high school graduates continue their education within one year of graduation, but roughly half of all freshmen enrolled in four-year institutions fail to earn a degree within six years.[1] For those who remain, the guiding role of parents steadily dwindles during these years, and is most often reduced to long-distance phone calls and holiday visits. New friends, professors, and myriad campus activities become the new sphere of influence to shape the beliefs and values of college students. If these young Americans arrive at today's colleges and universities with strongly held traditional beliefs, they will immediately be put to the test.

Typical of their experience is that of a recent class of incoming freshmen students at Clemson University. They were all required to read a book entitled, *Truth and Beauty: A Friendship*, before arriving for orientation. The book was an autobiographical account by Ann Patchett of her twenty-year relationship with author and poet Lucy Grealy. It "etches an unflinching portrait that includes depictions of Grealy's raw sexuality, drug addiction, and ultimately her death."[2] The reading assignment was immediately questioned by traditionalists, including parents and a professor, for the graphic depictions and amoral handling of the loss of virginity, abortion, pornography, masturbation, drug use, and a host of other difficult and potentially overwhelming issues for young college students. One parent of a student wrote in a letter to the president of the university that he was "angered and appalled at your

91

serious lapse of judgment in shoving this offensive material down the throats of Clemson students," complaining that "requiring the reading of this book puts Clemson's seal of approval on deviant behavior. All this was done at my expense as a taxpayer and parent!"[3]

University officials ignored the complaints. Jan Murdoch, Dean of Undergraduate Studies, told the Associated Press, "We assume that students are coming here with the ability to read and reflect and to discuss issues from their own perspective, using their own value system."[4] For the most part, the media treated the critics like unsophisticated fools, accusing them of censorship, naiveté, and violating the university's right to freedom of speech. Included in one popular blog was the comment:

> In the book, a woman makes bad choices in her life and pays the consequences. Sounds like a good book for college freshmen with a new burst of freedom to read. But Dr. Woodard doesn't think the book was appropriate because the author didn't spoon feed the freshmen readers a sermon with the proper moral lesson.[5]

The university's arguments were not without merit. College students are young adults who need to be aware of the harsh realities of life, but is it the responsibility of colleges to teach them this as freshmen? We want to be unequivocal here: books, particularly books with acclaim such as *Truth and Beauty,* should not be censored on university campuses. However, when a university funded by state and federal tax dollars *requires* students to read a book, that book has the official endorsement of the university and the government.[6] The university may not be endorsing the behavior of the characters in the book, but in the case of *Truth and Beauty*, it is requiring students to be exposed to graphic details of deviant and immoral behavior that would result in students being dismissed if they behaved that way on campus.

Clemson University thinks they are advancing freedom of speech, but they are wrong. The university is not fighting for the freedom of students to read and discuss books; instead it is *forcing* the progressive worldview on students under the guise of academic freedom. Should the university require students to read *Playboy* magazine and listen to Howard Stern as part of their college experience? The faculty committee that selected the required book for incoming freshmen would not even consider a book that presents a positive view of traditional religious values. If they did, the ACLU would immediately attack the university for "forcing" religious ideas on young, naive college students. Real freedom of speech would encourage the discussion of books like *Truth and Beauty* along with other books that provide a moral social contrast. Honest discussion and debate would include the personal and social costs of ignoring traditional values.

The university and its faculty deluded themselves when they claimed that they were encouraging students to think deeply and consider a wide range of diverse ideas. How can the deliberate exclusion of the values of the majority of Americans, along with centuries of historical fact and tradition, be considered open-minded? How can they pretend to be encouraging deep thinking and open dialogue if those who practice destructive behavior are held up as noble but tragic heroines, while those who hold traditional values are scorned and treated like fools? How can a student holding traditional views be expected to do anything but whisper in this environment?

The large majority of America's colleges and universities, as para-government institutions, have adopted the secular-progressive worldview and removed virtually all vestiges of traditional beliefs and values from their campuses. There is little freedom of speech for students with traditional beliefs in college classrooms. One conservative faculty member in North Carolina lampooned the liberal sacred cows of affirmative action, ethnocentrism, gay pride, cultural sensitivity training, and multiculturalism in his book, *Welcome to the Ivory Tower of Babel*. He presented modest proposals, like university affirmative action programs for underrepresented Republicans, and a Men's Resource Center where victims of false rape accusations can retreat for counseling.[7]

Americans do not complain, however, because there is a widely held belief that our colleges and universities are providing our children with the best education in the world. A cursory review of the rankings of the world's greatest institutions of learning might convince most students and parents to think otherwise.

A 2004 ranking of the world's best universities found that thirty of the top fifty were in the United States. Harvard was listed as the top university in the world, with the United States taking eight of the first ten places on the list.[8] While the United States has achieved much in higher education, the imperatives of time and growing competition require that the nation evaluate the direction of university education and raise the bar to better serve the nation and the world community. Charles Miller, who heads the federal Commission on the Future of Higher Education, says the attitude of administrators on campus is not up to the challenges of the next quarter century. "The message from higher education has been, 'we're the best in the world: now leave us alone and send us more money.'"[9]

The smugness of college administrators comes from decades of dominance and the prestige that universities enjoy in society at large. It is not an exaggeration to say that much of our society observes a form of worship and awe toward prestige universities. Despite what the First Amendment to the Constitution says about there being no state religion in America, the country now has regular worship services at secular churches on the campus of virtually every university: the humanities and social science departments are the collective guardians of a postmodern orthodoxy as powerful as any religious sect, with an enforced creed of multiculturalism (one culture is as good as another), diversity (all values and lifestyles are equal), and liberal politics, embedded in an ever-growing curriculum. These ideas lie at the very heart of what it means to be educated in America and imply an acceptance of secular multiculturalism and liberal diversity. These disciplines are the wellsprings of both learning and culture. All this education costs more each year and is protected by the sacred mantle of academic freedom, which is used to justify virtually any course or curriculum offering. The "priests" in this secular church are the tenured faculty, who make recruitment and promotion decisions for the faculty in each department and structure curricula offerings.

As para-government organizations, universities speak and influence the government. Public universities get part of their operating revenues from states, and all universities receive grants from the federal government for research. Universities have the implied endorsement of government because they are supported in part by taxes (even private universities receive tax supported scholarships, Pell grants, tuition assistance, and tax exemptions) and enjoy a type of government-protected monopoly status (the government recognizes the accreditation system that keeps innovative competitors out). Universities, with the tacit stamp of approval by the government, are aggressive advocates of the secular worldview. Most have campus cultures that are openly hostile toward religion and traditional values.

Ninety of the first one hundred colleges in the United States were begun by Christian denominations. Faith and learning were seen as essential to the formation of virtue in the new republic. No more. Beginning in the first half of the twentieth century, and accelerating in the post–World War II era, the American intellectual class chose to emulate the secularism of European thinkers. On college campuses, prominent thinkers simply ignored "the religion factor" in learning and American life. Instead, they focused on the political, economic, and social aspects of learning and education. The dogma, reinforced in classrooms and in the textbooks written by the same people, was that religion was important—*once upon a time*. But the "progress" being made within progressive America was comprehensively and irreversibly the development of a secular society.

The new curriculum is working. Nearly two-thirds of Americans believe that the Bible holds the answers to all or most of life's basic questions, yet only half can name even one of the four gospels.[10] The university classroom flourished as a secular cathedral when religion was banished from the public square.

"Worship" takes place in classes with a new aggressive teaching philosophy that values relevance and empowerment. This takeover of the classroom for political ends is relatively recent. "To educate," as defined by *Webster's New World Dictionary,* means "to train or develop the knowledge, skill, mind, or character." "To advocate," by contrast, means, "to speak or write in support of."[11] While advocacy and activism have their place in culture, such activity is usually rooted in the realm of politics. It has long been the consensus of higher educators that the university mission was to open minds and sharpen critical thinking skills, not to indoctrinate or tell students what to believe.

This mission was made clear in the founding statement of the American Association of University Professors (AAUP) in 1915. More recently in 2003, the American Council on Education (ACE) and fifty-three other academic associations (including AAUP), submitted an important brief to the Supreme Court for the affirmative action case of *Gratz v. Bollinger* that stressed that the purpose of education was to instill the capacity for independent thought.[12]

> Educators believe that developing the powers of analysis this way is not merely one among many skills to be taught; it is the chief skill, because on it rests understanding and freedom. Socrates thought knowledge and freedom so essential, and so dependent on close reasoning, that the unexamined life is not worth living. The purpose of education, held the Stoics who carried his idea forward, is to confront the student's passivity, challenging the student's mind to take charge of its own thought. To strengthen the ability to reason is to enable the student to determine what to believe, what to say, and what to do, rather than merely to parrot thoughts, words and actions of convention, friends or family.[13]

Partisanship has always been seen as antithetical to education, but it is par for the course in the secular church of the postmodern university. For example, the contemporary political science curriculum extols the "living constitution," while sociology offerings explain the benefits of single parenthood as a way of dismissing any concerns about out-of-wedlock births. The psychology department advocates the mental health benefits of "mutual loving relationships: in gay marriage." Across campus, the English department is busy "deconstructing" American history by showing the racism and sexism of earlier writers and political leaders. Of course, questioning the personal backgrounds of people like Martin Luther King, Jr., Hugo Chavez, and Fidel Castro are considered off-limits. The theatre faculty is preparing a public presentation of the "Vagina Monologues," a play where various women share their views about their vaginas, including homosexual experiences, with the audience. Isolated from one another, these teachings are negative, but considered exclusively—since the other side is not permitted a response—they result in indoctrination, not education.

These are the services of a typical week in the secular cathedral of the modern university, especially the state university. Political advocacy and liberal activism are fixed purposes in the core curriculum and extracurricular activities. The established position of the faculty and staff of the university in sympathy with these ideals guarantees their success. No dissident asking if such actions undermine educational purpose or fall outside the authorized mission of the academy is taken seriously.

For example, Professor Mike Adams chronicles the familiar experience of having a "debate" on campus, only to discover that the two participants both favored affirmative action. Rampant anti-Americanism is often the serious subject of faculty scholarship that results in yet another tenured dissident. Professors frequently take opportunities to charge those with whom they disagree with harassment and/or racism. Such is the daily fare of America's institutions of higher learning.[14]

It is not limited to the classroom. According to a 2004 survey by the American College Health Association, nearly half of all college students report having felt so depressed that they had trouble functioning.[15] Many of them end up in their college mental health center where they suffer from eating disorders, self-mutilation, binge drinking, and a broad spectrum of other maladies. Ironically, counselors teach young people to be very particular about what they eat and to be ridiculously frightened of the dangers of second-hand smoke. Still the culture on campus is so steeped in political correctness that the professionals cannot ask the students about last week's hook ups or tell them about the long-range consequences of abortion. "We must recognize," says a counselor on a university campus who wanted to remain anonymous, "that campus counseling has been hijacked by repressive, radical ideologies [where] open discussion is opposed."[16]

How is it that such practices displaced the ideals of scholarship and teaching as the university mission?

THE NEW UNIVERSITY

The Founders led a nation that believed in a natural law doctrine of human equality and self-evident truths. By that we mean the moral standards for society were traceable to the nature of human beings, a divine creator, and the cosmos itself. After the Revolutionary War they were concerned about the education of citizens in the new democracy. A monarchy might reflect the king's values, but a self-governing democracy required sober and sensible citizens who respected each others' rights. James Madison wrote, "As there is a degree of depravity in mankind which requires a certain degree of circumspection and distrust, so there are other qualities in human nature which justify a certain portion of esteem and confidence. . . . Republican government presupposes the existence of these qualities in a higher degree than any other form."[17] In other words, in popular government the character of the people was, and is, essential to the functioning of the state.

The founders knew that there was an innate human tendency toward self-indulgent human freedom. Their reading of past political texts, and their understanding of history, was that democracy in any form was prone to dissension, wars, slavery, xenophobia, and racism. In Plato's most memorable diatribe against democratic whims he said, "each of them thinks he should captain the ship, even though he has not yet learned the craft . . . [and] they go further and claim that it cannot be taught at all, and are even ready to cut to pieces anyone who says it can."[18] To counter this tendency in human nature and these intrinsic problems with democracy, the Founders emphasized an educational system with a moral vision. By recognizing and accepting man's natural rights, the divisions of class, race, religion, and national origin would disappear. "The immigrant," wrote Allan Bloom in *The Closing of the American Mind*, "had to put behind him the claims of the Old World in favor of a new and easily acquired education."[19]

This civic knowledge formed the core of American public education. George Washington said in his first inaugural address that the foundations of American national policies would "be laid in the pure and immutable principles of private morality."[20] Thomas Jefferson believed that the purpose of a university education was to prepare citizens for self-government. He wrote that, "If a nation expects to be ignorant and free, in a state of civilization, it expects what never was and never will be."[21] A university education was the place, as Jefferson said, for a citizen "to understand his duties to his neighbor and country, and to discharge with competence the functions confided to him by either." Jefferson founded the University of Virginia as an embodiment of this ideal. The university would "form the statesmen, legislators and judges on whom public prosperity and individual happiness depends."[22] Education emphasized self-restraint overindulgence, and moral and religious training as much as practical instruction.

This view of learning came in for revision in the late nineteenth century, when a new and more radical movement began to transform American education and culture. Academic leaders became enamored with the doctrines of historical progress advocated by European thinkers like Immanuel Kant, G. W. F. Hegel, Karl Marx, Charles Darwin, and Max Weber. The principal goal of this movement was to shake the culture from its Judeo-Christian foundations, and replace the ideas of the Founders with a new ethic based on evolutionary humanism and historical progress.

After World War I, a vast cynicism settled over Europe. It was rooted in the conviction that a pointless war had been waged for pointless principles. In a spasm of debunking and disenchantment, European thinkers rejected any vestige of Judeo-Christian values as a justification for allied intervention, or of America's postwar idealism. The debunkers of the 1920s soon leveled their disenchantment on American values and ideals, directing their disdain and hostility toward America's admiration of heroism and civic virtue. American intellectuals and academics promptly adopted Europe's contempt for traditional values and beliefs. A university education assumed the face of cynicism. The faculty became synonymous with propagators of a new secular faith in reason. The new academic philosophy upheld scientific reason, situational ethics, and human dignity without God as the new standard. Once the *"wall of separation"* was imposed by government on the education system, universities *"came out of the closet"* to become the leading advocates for secular ideals as necessary for human improvement and a more progressive America.

From the time of Franklin Roosevelt's administration, progressive intellectuals became a powerful political movement in the American university. Doctrines of moral relativism became implicit, denying any objective truth. The prevailing ideal of historicism argued that moral "values" had evolved over time and were the product of the age in which they were held. If it could be shown that morality changed over time, and the nature of humans was evolutionary, then there was little reason to be concerned with the moral underpinnings of the American Revolution, or the original premises of the Constitution.

The postmodern ethic of "deconstruction" accommodated this view when it argued that the Founders were racist, sexist, and homophobic, and their so-called antiquated ideas weren't worth emulating. Take, for example, Thomas Jefferson's words from the Declaration of Independence that: "We hold these truths to be self-evident, that all Men are created equal, that they are endowed by their Creator with certain unalienable Rights, that among these are Life, Liberty, and the Pursuit of Happiness." To the postmodern academic mind, this statement reeks of prejudice. First there is the sexist language (men only), and the author, the racist Jefferson, who not only owned slaves but allegedly fathered children by one, Sally Hemmings. The idea of a Creator-God is an outdated eighteenth-century concept in the contemporary Darwinian university, which accepts evolution without question. "Pursuit of happiness" was a thinly veiled reference to John Locke's idea of property. The conventional academic is closer to Marx's pronouncement that property was theft. The rejection of the Founders' understanding of "self-evident" truths opened the door for newer replacement ideas, with historical progress proving tolerance and diversity as superior values.

The academic understanding of human nature as one where individuals are only important as to their class status or minority position, justified the replacement of natural rights as a guiding sentiment for government and society. The academic aim was to interpret the Constitution as a "living" or "evolving" document. Woodrow Wilson, an early proponent of this notion, wrote: "We think of the future, not the past, as the more glamorous time in comparison with which the present is nothing."[23] The political principles of the founding fathers, Wilson continued, "do not fit the present problems; they read like documents taken out of a forgotten age." Political scientist Charles Merriam, who had a dramatic effect on contemporary research in the discipline, summarized the progressive ethic in 1903 when he wrote that the natural law and natural rights of the founders had been discarded by intellectuals "with practical unanimity."[24]

The ideal of natural rights was replaced by the new ethic of historical relativity. Rather than people delegating limited power to the government, as understood by the founders, the revisionist view was that government existed to empower people. Supreme Court Justices Stephen Breyer, Sandra Day O'Connor, William Brennan, Anthony Kennedy, Thurgood Marshall, and others, incorporated this relativist secular approach into legal decisions. The needs of people were now of concern to a large bureaucratic class of "experts," many of whom had ties to the academy. The exercise of political power by this new "knowledge class" was indispensable for defining and achieving standards of "social justice" in the emergent welfare state. So-called experts were interested in "the people" in only an abstract way. What they really sought was power, absolute and unchallenged.

The progressive theory of education created a new type of university for the modern welfare state. Universities were radically transformed: small, quiet, and dignified institutions of scholarly pursuit suddenly ballooned into sophisticated megabusinesses with a distinct political agenda. Hundreds of thousands of men and women became involved in "teaching" and "research." Collectively they offered "instruction" to millions of young adults—future leaders of America—who paid record high prices for degrees that were increasingly filled with "relevant" twenty-first century courses.

Partially as a result, colleges and universities collectively became big businesses, spending over $200 billion a year. Going to college is now easier than ever, but some classrooms are increasingly out of reach for many because of the higher costs. "In the past ten years, average spending on instruction per student at the wealthiest baccalaureate colleges—those in the top quartile, public and private—increased by thirty-seven percent; at the same time, spending by those in the bottom quartile grew by only six percent."[25] The product the university purportedly sells is education, and government is deeply involved in funding what it produces. This is one reason why the university embraces the secular ethic so tenaciously; it wants to avoid lawsuits that might inhibit federal funding. The ACLU would no doubt attack universities with lawsuits and calls to cut funding if they found evidence of the teaching of morality on their campuses, not to mention what they would do if religious instruction was offered. No wonder, then, that the most striking characteristics of higher education are its secular worldviews accompanied by the political ideology of the unaccountable, permanent professoriate.

A large-scale survey of American academics was conducted in 2003 using professional association membership lists from six fields: anthropology, economics, history, philosophy (political and legal), political science, and sociology. These are the historical heart of the social sciences in the university curriculum. The results were astonishing. University faculty heavily skewed toward the leftist politics of the Democratic Party. "The most heavily lopsided field surveyed was anthropology with a Democrat to Republican ratio of 30.2 to 1, and sociology with a partisan proportion of 28.0 to 1. . . . [T]he least lopsided was economics with a 3.0 to 1 relation."[26] In today's university the word "diversity" has almost sacred meaning, but it does not apply to the ideological and political affiliation of professors. This disparity has been around for some time. A study by Everett Carl Ladd Jr. and Seymour Martin Lipset in 1975 found that "only 12 percent of all professors thought of themselves as Republicans," compared to more than one-third in the general population.[27]

Not surprisingly, through an incestuous seniority system, now liberal professors supervise a curriculum replete with identity politics, radical feminism, multiculturalism, and postmodernism. Courses in "ethics" and "values clarification" are little more than opportunities to get students to talk about abortion, sexism, and the outlandish crimes of American foreign policy—subjects in which they have little expertise—in a way that meets the expectations of their teachers (i.e., their indoctrinators). These advocacy movements on American campuses, which are really moods with academic verbiage, have eviscerated the traditional learning in the humanities.

A typical deconstruction argument on campus is that Shakespeare was a prisoner of his time and place. The Bard "wrote in" those prejudices, and they now demand a postmodern reconstruction in light of twenty-first-century revelation. His plays must be read as instruments of the imperialist, racist, sexist, and mean-spirited English bourgeoisie culture. David Horowitz, himself a reformed 1960s leftist who now fights against this indoctrination, has written, "Conservatives don't get what the left gets, which is that the left has already colonized and converted whole university departments—women's studies, black studies, sociology—into political parties with an academic veneer."[28]

The progressive revisionist ethic is pervasive on campus. In 1996, the chairman of the theatre department at Arizona State University dismissed a popular untenured theatre professor from his teaching position because, "the feminists are offended by his selection of works from a sexist European canon that is approached traditionally." So much for academic freedom and the spirit of diversity in the university curriculum. The teacher had failed to adopt the postmodern ethic in his class instruction. The idea that Shakespeare could have any permanent insight into the behavior of human beings, and that this knowledge was worth learning, was lost in the controversy of the new ethic.

Today, identity politics, "victimology," radical feminism, multiculturalism, and "educating for a difference" all are presented under the innocent-sounding umbrella of "diversity." Veneration for this ideal fuels the university preference for gender and racial quotas in hiring and promotion. Administrative positions are similarly filled with preferences, and whispered acknowledgment is spread across the campus that the new associate dean position is reserved for a female, or even more exciting, a *black* female. The creation of women's studies programs, African American studies programs, ethnic studies programs, and gay-lesbian-bisexual-transgender studies programs, as well as the ubiquitous campus speech codes, are all hallmarks of today's postmodern universities.

The resources of the general academic budget are devoted to a bureaucracy of residence advisors, multicultural affairs officers, women's studies centers (for feminists only), ethnic dormitories, and special recognition for gay and lesbian students. The perpetuation of this bureaucracy depends upon the professors and staff uncovering campus "victims" and social inequities. The search is relentless. One campus advisor opened a session with students by saying: "I'm gay, and I've had sex with an animal. Do you have a problem with me?" As students come to realize that their racial, sexual, and ethnic attributes are all that matter in college, they escalate their demands accordingly. Group-based identities become academic causes, and the equivalent of learning becomes the asserting of an identity in the name of "diversity."

For example, African American students find that their in-class essay exams are strengthened if they interpret any question in terms of race. So a discussion of interest groups (political science), family life (sociology), mental health (psychology), or income disparities (economics) is taken as an opportunity to talk about how racial identity explains these issues. No white professor would dare deduct points from such exams, because they "don't understand" the issue. The same tactic is used by female students, Asians, Hispanics, and gays, as an assertion of their victim status resulting from their class, sexual, and racial disadvantages. All others failing to fall into sanctioned, designated identities are marginalized. "Transgressors" are admonished or ostracized and undermined if they already have tenure.

THE CARTE BLANCHE CURRICULUM

Consider this assigned story on the class reading list at a state university: The protagonist is a sixteen-year-old boy tortured by Guatemalan soldiers by having his fingernails removed. The death scene in the story is especially gruesome, as the protagonist is soaked in gasoline and set on fire. The description of these events was retold by the boy's twenty-three-year-old sister in the book, *I, Rigoberta Menchú*, published in 1983. The story itself was based on nearly nineteen hours of taped interviews given by the victim's sister to an anthropologist, Elizabeth Burgos, in Paris. The story reads like oral history.

The book propelled Menchú and Burgos to international fame and acclaim. Menchú received fourteen honorary doctorates, a welcoming reception from Pope John Paul II, and many visits with heads of state. Notable achievements were public awards like France's Legion of Honor and the Nobel Peace Prize in 1992. The book also served to revive student activism on campus, as it was welcomed into the nascent canon of multicultural literary writings and became a standard on most universities' required reading lists. While the collapse of Communism in 1989 discredited left-wing movements at the university, these activists boasted an overnight celebrity, saint, revolutionary, and icon. The burgeoning ethnic and women's studies departments raised Menchú to untold heights.

Only one problem emerged. Closer investigation by a Middlebury College anthropology professor, subsequently confirmed by the *New York Times*, found that Menchú's book was bogus.[29] It contained factual discrepancies and political distortions, including the eyewitness account of the murder. Admittedly, Menchú's brother and parents were killed by the army, but not in the way described by the book.

The exposure of *I, Rigoberta Menchú* created a firestorm of worldwide controversy. The author dismissed her critics as being racist. In press reports she gave a classically postmodern answer as to how she felt about the controversy: "I didn't find anything in these reports that changes the fact that my people are dead . . . and that is *my* truth."[30] One Spanish professor at Wellesley College said, "Whether her book is true or not, *I don't care*. We should teach our students about this brutality of the Guatemalan military and the U.S. financing of it."[31] The book continues as required reading, but this time for what it *symbolizes* more than what it *says*. The way the book arrived on the reading list is unimportant to college students who must read it, and why they read it speaks loudly about the mood of "political correctness" on campus.

The dogmatic and partisan nature of the academy's current diversity obsession obliterated any discussion of the truth or falsity of the book. A belief in fixed principles grounded in unchanging human nature was passé. In 2003 the Supreme Court ruled in two University of Michigan cases that the educational benefits of diversity in higher education—improved teaching and learning, better preparation for the workforce, and enhanced civic values— could justify a limited use of race in admissions decisions.[32] That decision has morphed into a new diversity, and the right to discriminate to achieve an advantage. In the name of "Diversity," American institutions of higher learning have deeply compromised their claims to educational integrity. On the postmodern campus, experimentation is valued more than truth. Everything is fluid and free; nothing is given and everything is up for grabs. The curriculum is "remade," "reinvented," "redefined," "reconstructed," or "revised" to accommodate change. The task for campus social engineers is to endlessly reinvent the world, en route to what postmodern philosopher Richard Rorty calls "achieving our country." Virtually any course is permitted, nothing is required or forbidden, and literally nothing is unthinkable.

Allan Bloom, author of the bestseller *The Closing of the American Mind,* wrote in 1987 that the goal of a university education was "the knowledge of the permanent concerns of man as man, not of the fragments of man that we find in this time and this place."[33] The old curriculum in theory, if not always in practice, at least affirmed that higher education should emphasize the origin and development of civilization, especially Western civilization. This was done by the study of enduring works in philosophy, science, sacred readings, literature, and the arts. These books were known as the classics, meaning they had proven their merit to generations of students. A college graduate was someone who had exposure to this body of knowledge, what E. D. Hirsch called "cultural literacy," or a national literacy, in order "to foster nationwide effective communication."[34]

That curriculum is now dead.

In 1996, the National Association of Scholars issued a seminal report entitled, "The Dissolution of General Education." It concluded that during the last thirty years, the commitment of American higher education to providing students with broad and vigorous exposure to major areas of knowledge had virtually vanished. "A quite plausible argument can be made that general education has become a residual category of American academic life. . . .

[H]aving fewer challenging requirements . . . is likely to improve the reten-
tion of students . . . [and] administrators can more easily avoid troubling the
academic waters by abdicating judgment on the merits of the [curriculum]."[35]
The university classroom resembles the shelves of a supermarket, bulging
with items of dubious nutritional value, but marketed with flash and pizzazz.

The new curriculum recognizes mainly race, class, gender, and sexual behavior as fit concerns for scholarly inquiry. The transformation of the university into a bastion of politicization was accomplished by expanding the number of courses and allowing students to choose the ones they liked. This
wasn't necessarily a negative thing, after students had mastered the classics.
The problem was that the new curriculum *replaced* the classical one. One
study concluded that "the prevalent smorgasbord approach to the curriculum,
allowing students to select almost any combination of courses, results in
patchwork education that reflects youthful interests, but at the expense of life-
long educational needs."[36] A study by the American Council of Trustees and
Alumni found that over two-thirds of the top seventy schools in the country
no longer required students majoring in English to take a course in Shakespeare.[37] At the same time, the English departments featured a multitude of
courses on popular culture, feminist literature, gay and lesbian writing, and
minority exploitation.

Georgetown University, for instance, dropped its "Great Authors" requirement for English majors in 1999. Previously, majors were required to take
one or more of the three writers regarded as preeminent representatives of
English literature—Geoffrey Chaucer, William Shakespeare, and John Milton. No more. English majors are now free from the strict academic burdens
of the past and can choose to study such topics as: "Hardboiled Detective Fiction," "AIDS and Representation," and "History and Theory of Sexuality." A
liberal education has come to be defined as a cafeteria self-selection approach
that leaves the choices up to the student. If students are as wise as the universities, the question is, why are they attending college? Cornell, which offers a minor in homosexual studies, boasts that "there is no course that students must take, and there are nearly 2,000 from which they may choose."[38]

The women's studies programs are often affiliated with English Departments on campus, and their speaker programs reflect the intellectual curricula prejudices. For example, Temple University Women's Studies Program
invited the following speakers between fall 2002 and spring 2004:

- Anne Sprinkle, former porn star and performance artist;
- Arlene Stein, author of *Sisters, Sexperts, Queers: Beyond the Lesbian Na-
  tion*;
- Octavia Butler, a feminist science fiction writer;

- Marina Walter of the United Nations Civil Service Leadership Development Project, speaking on "Gender and Peace-Keeping in Bosnia and other War-Torn Regions";
- Miriam Cooke of Duke University speaking on "Women's Jihad Before and After 9/11,"
- Gerda Lerner of the University of Wisconsin, author of *The Creation and Patriarchy* and *The Creation of Feminist Consciousness*; and
- Cynthia Enloe of Clark University, speaking on "Militarism and Empire: Some Feminist Clues."

No speakers were invited as part of the series that would defend a traditional perspective on gender.[39] The program has the effect of stifling speech on campus by only funding speakers from one side of the debate. Traditionalists are free to bring in speakers, it's just that the university will not pay to have them on campus.

Women's studies programs are results oriented—their goal being to turn feminist theory into political action and cultural change. The academic and the ideological are merged. The women's studies curriculum is not founded on nature, but on revolution—the purpose being (to use the Marxist word) "praxis" or action. The term *gender studies* has been proposed because it is less identifiable with the feminist movement. The announced effort of the curriculum is to attract funding from faculty and administrative committees without alerting the wider community to these designs.

The English major requirements, and the growth of "victim" studies curricula, are only part of a larger problem of declining literacy in a host of fields. In 2002, the National Association of Scholars commissioned a poll to compare the general knowledge of college seniors with high school graduates and college seniors at mid-century. The questions asked, with occasional modifications required to remove dated allusions, were identical with those asked of random samples of the American public at various times in the 1940s and 1950s by the Gallup organization. "When given the test covering four areas of general knowledge, American college seniors score at about the same overall level as did high school graduates of fifty years ago."[40] The study was constrained by small numbers for comparison, but was nonetheless suggestive of campus problems today. Today's college seniors did somewhat better on questions pertaining to literature, music, and science than their high school educated predecessors; about the same on questions about geography; and worse on questions dealing with history.

The findings about historical knowledge are especially troubling. College graduates today have suffered a collective amnesia when it comes to American history and government. The Roper organization surveyed college seniors at the top fifty-five liberal arts colleges and universities on their knowledge of history and government. At 78 percent of the institutions surveyed, students were not required to take any history at all, and no institution required American history. "In the country that gave birth to Jefferson's conception of an educated citizenry, colleges and universities are failing to provide the kind of general education that is needed for graduates to be involved as educated citizens."[41]

Administrators of colleges and universities are presiding over the dissolution of an academic core curriculum that made American universities the envy of the world. Despite widespread lip service to the importance of a general education, surveys repeatedly find that a solid core curriculum in higher education has evaporated. As a consequence, college students are graduating without the basic knowledge that was once considered the hallmark of a liberal education.

GRADES AND RESEARCH

The carte blanche curriculum has translated into a predictable effect on grade inflation. The fear of failing has all but disappeared. The changing ethic on campus is *not* to distinguish—the word now used is to "discriminate"—among students. Professors who have demanding standards in their class obviously believe that their course is important. Such a conviction is outdated in the egalitarian university where every course is equally valuable. Quite average students now leave college with the designation of "cum laude" on their diplomas. Grade point averages are easy to pad when hundreds of classes dot the registration lineup—minus a core of "challenging" coursework. Students soon learn which classes convert into grade point advantages, and which professors to avoid. University websites even allow students to grade professors, encouraging professors to "please" students rather than challenge them.

The data in table 7.1 suggests that grade inflation has kicked in over the past thirty years while at the same time learning has declined. Colleges have become the mythical Lake Wobegon of radio fame: "where all the women are strong, all the men are good looking, and all the children are above average."[42] The study in table 7.1 was of more than 9,000 students at every type of institution from two-year colleges to major research universities. While grade inflation was universal, it has been raised to an art form at the elite Ivy League schools. At Princeton the median GPA grew from 3.08 in 1973 to 3.42 in 1997. Grades of "A" were awarded to more than 30 percent of the students. At Dartmouth the "A" or "A–" grade went to 44 percent of the student body. At Harvard the figure for "excellent" was 46 percent. Admission to an Ivy League school is now synonymous with graduation with honors.

Table 7.1.   Cumulative Grade Point Averages Reported by Undergraduates: 1969, 1976, 1993

Cumulative GPA	1969	1976	1993
Disaggregated			
A+ or A	2	8	13
A–	5	11	13
B+	11	18	18
B	17	22	21
B–	19	15	13
C+	23	15	12
C	18	10	7
C– or below	7	3	2
Aggregated			
A– or higher	7	19	26
C or below	25	13	9

Source: Arthur Levine and Jeanette S. Cureton, *When Hope and Fear Collide: A Portrait of Today's College Student* (San Francisco: Jossey-Bass, 1998), p. 125.

Grade inflation is a reality across higher education, from the most prestigious research universities to the least selective colleges, and the reason is the egalitarian emphasis on "politically correct" courses. Schools increasingly cater to the temptation to keep students happy rather than uphold academic standards. Professors know they face student rancor and criticism if academic demand is heightened, so they expect less. The ascendancy of the loose curriculum has allowed students to avoid taking challenging and objectively graded courses. By compressing all grades near the top, grade inflation obscures student distinctions. "In short, grade inflation undermines the integrity of a college education just as monetary inflation undermines a nation's economy."[43]

Evaluating the quality of education, or the credentials of graduates, has oddly become a secondary priority of most universities. Research is now the main product of the university system. The quality of the research from universities varies and is primarily produced to assist aspiring professors in gaining tenure. In the social sciences, many of the publications are nuanced and obscure. The papers bristle with mathematical formulas and are studded with mysterious equations. To the outsider these publications appear as important contributions to knowledge, but they are not all that they seem. The unspoken secret in every academic hallway is that almost no one reads academic journal articles. They wield no influence beyond the campus. Instead they are a derivative of the "publish or perish" mania of higher education, especially prevalent at elite schools. Academic publications pile up on the shelves of university libraries, largely unread. Professional conferences offer a prelude to journal publication, presenting topics just as dense (but, by necessity, politically correct) as the subsequent articles.

Scholarly work is vital and is the authentic voice of any given discipline, but the quality of academic research remains questionable. As a presidential advisor in both the Nixon and Reagan administrations, Martin Anderson worked on both economic and domestic policy issues. Anderson's distinguished credentials for those positions (undergraduate and master's degrees from Dartmouth, and a PhD from MIT), provide a perspective that is indicative of this era's campus research climate. "Not once in all those years, in countless meetings on national economic policy, did anyone ever refer to any article from an academic journal . . . not once did anyone use a mathematical formula more complicated than adding, subtracting, multiplying or dividing."[44] The people who have the responsibility for advising and making economic policy have little or no use for the *American Economic Review*. Political decision makers and political campaign professionals rarely, if ever, read the *American Political Science Review*. They hold no animosity for the academic intellectuals, they just consider them irrelevant.

If academic research were innocuous that might be forgivable, but increasingly the subject matter is outrageous and so partisan as to make any pretense of academic credibility laughable. A social science conference recently presented a litany of research papers about alternative sexual orientations and the like: "A Life Course Analysis of Long-term Gay and Lesbian Couples," "Latina Bisexual Experiences and Identity," "The Mother Daughter Dynamics of Incest," "Applying Gaze Theory to the Playboy Centerfolds," and "Comic Books and the Communities of Memory."[45] Be forewarned: these papers typify academic research today.

Consider the task of a student entering a PhD program in anthropology, economics, history, philosophy, political science, or sociology fields. The student faces two years of coursework, preliminary exams, and a dissertation proposal, followed by a time of gathering data and writing. One student, who finished her first year in graduate school, shared with one of the coauthors, "I am so clearly seeing that getting a PhD is equivalent to joining a privileged club."[46] In this process of escorting the new initiate to graduation, that club tends to admit new members who agree with its ideological premises. Dissertation advisors, the ones who decide whether or not a student will receive a doctorate, are tenured academics, who not just subscribe to the secular drift of a discipline, but demand such views in the next generation.

Every PhD candidate faces a time of rewriting and gaining the confidence of his or her dissertation committee. Once this process is over, the candidate enters the job market. If the goal is an academic job, the competition is fierce, with dozens of applicants and several rounds of interviews. The task of gaining tenure is approximately a six-year process, and is based on publication in "highly regarded," (i.e., dust-collecting) journals. David Hamilton, a reporter for *Science* magazine, concluded at the end of his examination of academic research that most of it "resembles intellectual quicksand."[47] Regardless of the new candidates' publishing credentials, the only way he or she can win the regard of superiors is by imitating their ideological and political ideals. If they believe differently, they must whisper or abandon their higher education teaching goals. In this way, the tenure and promotion system works to reinforce the politically left views of the professoriate.

PROFICIENCY OF UNIVERSITY GRADUATES

These changes in our university system could, perhaps, be partially overlooked if the quality of graduates were to continue to lead the world. Unfortunately, academe's growing emphasis on faculty research, values clarification, and societal transformation results in graduates who yield neither the character nor capabilities to compete in the global economy. While many exceptions exist to these deficiencies in our university graduates, a growing body of evidence demands that university system decline must be addressed. As the American Association of State Colleges and Universities reports, "The evolving national conversation regarding higher education's academic outcomes, buttressed by data showing significant proficiency gaps for college graduates, make clear that the call for better measurement of learning outcomes cannot be evaded."[48]

Derek Bok, the former president of Harvard University, bemoans "the lack of attention that most faculties pay to the growing body of research about how much students are learning and how they could be taught to learn more. Hundreds of studies have accumulated on . . . improving critical thinking, moral reasoning, quantitative literacy, and other skills vital to undergraduate education . . . yet . . . fewer than 10 percent of college professors pay any attention to such work. . . . College faculties have long been able to ignore education research and avoid discussions of teaching methods because they risk no adverse consequences."[49]

President Bok, author of *Our Underachieving Colleges: A Candid Look at How Much Students Learn and Why They Should Be Learning More*, reports that "most undergraduates leave college still inclined to approach unstructured 'real life' problems with a form of primitive relativism, believing that there are no firm grounds for preferring one conclusion over another." Bok quotes other concerned authors focused on the state of American higher education. Little consensus of what constitutes educational ideals, purposes, or vision is to be found:

- "There is no vision, nor is there a set of competing visions, of what an educated human being is." (Allan Bloom)
- "The story of liberal education has lost its organizing center—has lost, that is, the idea of culture as both the origin and goal, of the human sciences." (Bill Readings)
- "Without a compelling, unifying purpose, universities are charged with allowing their curricula to degenerate into a vast smorgasbord of elective courses."[50] (Derek Bok)

Employers are the final judges of the quality of America's university graduates. The question for them is simple: Do they feel the need to whisper about the inability of recent graduates to read, write, analyze, and explain material? Here the news is not good. Increasingly, employers expend considerable resources to "remedy deficiencies in the writing and computational skills of the college graduates they hire."[51]

As one survey of Silicon Valley employers reported, "Business school deans return from meetings with corporate executives where complaints are lodged that the graduates cannot write well. Even deans and senior faculty members at top-rated business schools hear this complaint regularly from industry."[52] Employers complain that even those graduates from very selective and expensive institutions "lack the clarity of purpose, emotional maturity, and practical skills to cope efficiently with the demands and responsibilities of the workplace."[53] All this disruption occurs at a time when "American graduates will no longer be competing only with themselves but with hordes of ambitious, hard-working young people from countries such as India and China intent on claiming a piece of the world's most prosperous economy. In this new environment, American students can no longer afford to graduate without the best possible education."[54]

SUMMARY

American universities are the intellectual engines and the economic "seed corn" for this country and for much of the world. Campus environments train and shape future leaders, frame national policy, and provide societal standards for the next generation. Yet college campuses today function more under a paradigm of "secular-church" indoctrination, rather than offering true liberation—they choose to propagate rather than prepare. Political leftist views are so widespread that one rarely hears anything else in the classroom, faculty lounge, or professional journals. Students are invariably graded on politically correct hoop-jumping, and the antitraditionalist para-government groups have a readily available resource for their legal arguments. The purpose of a university education has become unclear. What is clear, however, is that America's higher education system is no longer serving the best interest of students or the common good of our nation.

When students leave the college classroom and gain voter status, they exercise a reinforcing effect on the cultural development cycle. They have been shaped by secular government; in turn, they seek to shape the future of governments. Graduates who go through "secular church" confirmation, upon having their group and "victim" status confirmed, are easy prey for politicians serving up victimization in order to manipulate their vote. If college students fail to understand the premises of democracy, free enterprise, and competition, they are unlikely to support marketplace values of freedom. If they are afraid to speak out against moral depravity, their whispers will be powerless to improve our culture.

As with public schools, universities and colleges are filled with administrators, faculty, and students who share at least some aspects of the traditional Judeo-Christian worldview. The assumption of a "wall of separation," however, stifles the freedom of speech of traditionalists and prevents them from bringing their ideas and opinions into the campus debates. Their voices are reduced to whispers. The campus advocacy of secular views has not only led to costly declines in social morality, it has fostered anticapitalistic and socialistic views of economics along with liberal political views among voters. This has contributed to bigger government, huge national debt, and less personal freedom. Americans must act quickly to force government to restore their freedom of speech at all levels of education. Whispers cannot overcome the secular education monopoly, but if traditional views are given equal standing in the public debate, Americans will choose to follow the principles that made our nation great.

Chapter Eight

War of the Worldviews: Attacks and Counterattacks

Everybody favors free speech in the slack moments when no axes are being ground.

—Heywood Broun

Since the 1960s, Americans have been indoctrinated with the secular worldview in government-controlled public schools and universities. In spite of this effect, many people still cling to, and endorse, traditional values. They understand and appreciate that an education without God, without an eternal backdrop, is a betrayal of American history. It is also a prelude to a corrupting spirit of materialism. In the face of secular indoctrination in schools, media intimidation, and opposition from fellow citizens, an increasing number of Americans are speaking out against government policies that are destroying our culture.

But the costs for such courage can be high. In March of 2007, the chairman of the Joint Chiefs of Staff touched the electric fence. On the record, General Pace declared: "I believe homosexual acts between two individuals are immoral and that we should not condone immoral acts."[1] Instead of apologizing, General Pace later said his mistake was focusing his comments on his view of morality instead of the official "don't ask, don't tell" military policy. The *New York Times* editorialized that the remarks were "offensive" and "bigoted."[2]

The war of the worldviews rages. Traditionalists who try to exercise their freedom of speech are often attacked by government-sanctioned para-government groups allied with the media. Though faced with the overwhelming interference of government, Americans are standing up and fighting back. Courageous groups all around the country are following the example of the

Boy Scouts. They are proving that traditionalists can prevail in the cultural battle if they stay in the fight. But more Americans must enter the fray to make a difference, and there must be a greater sense of urgency if we are to stop the decline of our culture.

When Americans demand equal treatment for traditional values and religious speech, they are surrounded by a cloud of confusing legal arguments that only serve to disorient the public and discourage their participation. Many conclude, "Maybe I can, maybe I can't, but I am not going to risk public humiliation to find out if I have the right to speak out." Secularism advances largely through the subtle tyranny of silence amid a cloud of legal doubt. The government stifles free speech and promotes injustice through judicial complexity and confusion.

ATTACKS AGAINST INDIVIDUALS

Recent attacks against religious speech at public high school graduations provide a vivid illustration of how legal confusion robs individuals of their freedom of speech. In 1992, a legal liaison for the Duval County School Board in Florida issued a memorandum to principals regarding high school graduations: "due to the recent Supreme Court ruling in *Lee v. Weisman*, there should be no prayer, benediction, or invocation at any graduation ceremonies."[3] After receiving a number of letters that suggested that student-initiated and student-led prayer *may* be allowed, the legal liaison issued a second memo that said prayer was allowable if schools carefully followed a complex legal formula: a brief graduation message of a religious nature is allowable if a majority of the graduating class approves and the message is prepared and delivered by a student volunteer, elected by the graduating class as a whole, without the assistance or direction of the school board or its employees.

Some school board members, spooked by the ambiguous guidelines, proposed instead a "moment of silence" at graduation. The motion was defeated four to three by the whole board, so the 1993 graduating seniors were allowed the freedom to choose. Ten of seventeen graduating classes in the district chose to recite various religious messages. The other classes opted for a secular message or no message at all.[4] Issue settled? Hardly!

A group of graduating seniors and one parent filed suit to stop the school district from allowing student-led prayer at graduation. They argued that prayer during graduation is per se unconstitutional, and that the school board could not avoid responsibility by delegating decision making to the graduating students. Representatives of the school board, as well as a majority of students and parents, responded by asserting *their* own First Amendment right of

Free Speech, arguing that student-initiated, student-written and student-delivered prayer at graduation is not subject to official monitoring by the school board or its employees. Therefore, such activities lack the government sanction condemned by the establishment clause of the First Amendment. The United States District Court for the Middle District of Florida ruled in favor of the school district and their new policy, which allowed student-initiated, student-written, and student-delivered prayers at graduation.[5] In this case the school won, but is there any wonder why most school officials choose not to protect the freedom of speech of students?

Reasonable people might suggest that the decision of the Florida District Court was a fair compromise between competing secular and traditional interests in society. The ACLU, however, has continued to threaten and badger schools and organizations throughout the United States whenever they find a hint of religious expression at public gatherings. School officials have responded by keeping their distance from the constantly moving "invisible fence" of legitimacy that marks the arbitrary "wall of separation" between what is allowed and what is not. Many school principals now screen the commencement speeches of students to censor any religious references. But some students, refusing to be cowed by the court ruling with attendant school policies, are not willing to whisper their strongly held beliefs.

One such brave American is Brittany McComb, the 2006 valedictorian of Foothill High School in Nevada. McComb had studied hard, earning a 4.7 GPA, the highest grade-point average in the graduating class. In her graduation address she wanted to thank God for her success. In Brittany's written speech, she made two references to the Lord, nine mentions of God, and one mention of Christ. School officials (i.e., government representatives) censored her speech, deleting the reference to Christ and several other references to God and two Bible references. But when Brittany McComb stood up to give her address, she also stood up for her right to freedom of speech. This was her speech, earned as a result of her academic record, and she believed she had the right to use her own words. Unfortunately, school officials were monitoring her speech and cut off her microphone before she could mention the word "Christ."[6]

Brittany's courage inspired the crowd, which jeered loudly in defiance of school officials. But the ACLU, whose representatives were advising the school, cited several court cases in defending the school's position. There are so many conflicting court cases that the ACLU can always find one that supports their antireligious position. An ACLU spokesman said that "a student was given a school-sponsored forum at a school and therefore, in essence, it was a school-sponsored speech."[7] McComb's response was succinct: "People aren't stupid and they know we have freedom of speech and the school district wasn't advocating my ideas. Those are my opinions . . . it's what I believe."[8] School officials went too far. If a student delivers a valedictory address, it is the student speaking, not the institution.

Just as attacks against freedom of speech and religious expression are amplified around the culture development cycle, so too are acts of courage like those of Brittany McComb. Her story made news all over the country, and the Rutherford Institute, a nonprofit civil rights group in Virginia, came to her defense. Rutherford filed a lawsuit on behalf of McComb asserting that school officials infringed on her freedoms of speech and equal protection. The lawsuit named the school principal, an assistant principal, and the school employee who pulled the plug on McComb's microphone.[9] Perhaps they were "stunned" to be called to account. This incident shows that Americans can SLAPP back, and this one counterattack against oppression reverberated around the culture development cycle. In candor, it must be admitted that the schools are at a loss to figure out what they can and cannot do. For so long they feared an ACLU lawsuit that they caved in at the very threat of litigation. After this victory, the shoe of intimidation is on the other foot: officials in other schools must think twice before censoring student speech, restricting freedom of religion, and cutting off the microphones of commencement speakers.

ATTACKS AGAINST PARENTS

The Supreme Court has recognized the traditional role of parents on several occasions. In 1944, the Court wrote: "It is cardinal with us that the custody, care and nurture of the child reside first in the parents, whose primary functions and freedom include preparation for obligations the state can neither supply nor hinder."[10] Again in 1972, in *Wisconsin v. Yoder*, the Court reaffirmed parental authority: "The primary role of the parents in the upbringing of their children is now established beyond debate as an enduring American tradition."[11] But the ACLU has no respect for "enduring American tradition" or the "primary role of the parents." As one of the best books on the ACLU declares: "[It] should be understood as not merely a liberal organization but a radical one, in the same sense that its early contemporary allies were radicals—pacifists, anarchists, socialists, and communists."[12] Representatives of the ACLU have stated, "The United States Constitution does not mention the right of parents to direct the upbringing of their children."[13] Secularists use court precedent like a sledge hammer when it agrees with their doctrine, but they conveniently ignore courts' decisions that support traditional values and beliefs.

Public schools are the venue secular-progressives use as a tool to circumvent parental values and authorities. When parents at an elementary school in Novato, California, filed a lawsuit to stop the school from subjecting children (some as young as seven years old) to blatant and explicit homosexual propaganda, they quickly found themselves facing the tremendous financial and manpower resources of the ACLU. The parents fought for two years, but were finally overwhelmed by the financial and emotional costs of seeking justice in courts where they were outspent and outnumbered. When the parents withdrew their lawsuit, the ACLU said: "The plaintiffs' decision to walk away at this stage of the case . . . sends a message throughout the state [of California] that schools have the authority to require mandatory attendance in tolerance-building and diversity education programs."[14] According to the ACLU, public schools have the authority to require mandatory attendance to any secular worldview indoctrination, but not to any activity that supports traditional American values such as saluting the American flag, reciting the Pledge of Allegiance, attending after-school Bible clubs, or even singing a Christmas carol.

In Chelmsford, Massachusetts, high school students were told they had to attend an assembly called "*Hot, Sexy, and Safer*" presented by AIDS activists. Parents were not notified about this assembly or warned of the graphic sexual nature of the information that was forced on their children. One witness told the *Washington Times* that the presenter, "asked a student to participate in a demonstration, and, holding a condom on one hand, she handed another condom to him. She slowly licked her condom and asked him to do the same. Then, saying, 'I don't want to waste this condom,' she invited a teen-age girl to come down. [The presenter] told the boy to kneel and instructed the girl to take the condom and place it over the boy's head."[15] Parents filed a lawsuit and the ACLU quickly came to the school's defense. Again, the cost of justice was too high. The parents lost.

In another school-sponsored event, a public school guidance counselor in Philadelphia arranged for a young female student to drive across state lines to have a second-trimester abortion to circumvent Pennsylvania's parental consent law. The counselor coordinated the trip with the girl's boyfriend, but did not notify her parents or seek their consent. The conservative Alliance Defense Fund filed a lawsuit against the school on behalf of the girl's parents. In this case, the parents won, and the school district was forced to establish a policy that forbids school employees from encouraging or assisting students in getting abortions.[16]

The attack on parents and parental rights extends well beyond public schools. The ACLU filed a lawsuit against a Virginia state law that made it illegal for teens to attend a nudist camp without parental accompaniment. In a shameless twist of their previous legal arguments, an ACLU legal director said, "By denying children the opportunity to go to this summer camp and by denying parents the right to choose where to send their children during the summer, *the state is trampling on their right to privacy and the rights of parents to direct the upbringing of their children.*"[17] Fortunately, a federal judge saw through the ACLU's duplicity, upholding the Virginia law and the rights of parents: a victory for common sense, parental responsibility, and traditional values.

The ACLU has led the fight to strip parents of their right to protect children from obscenity, even the worst forms of pornography—child pornography. "The ACLU has opposed federal legislation that allowed parents to notify the post office if they did not wish to receive sexually oriented advertisements in the mail. It also opposed legislation that would have labeled pornographic mail as such so the post office would know not to deliver it to families who did not wish to receive it."[18] The ACLU successfully fought the implementation of the Child Online Protection Act, which authorized fines and prison terms for posting material on the Internet that is harmful to minors. Paragovernment groups like the ACLU have used hapless judges and contradictory judicial precedence to diminish the traditional role of parents. While some counterattacks by parents have proved successful, reinforcements are needed to stop the erosion of our culture.

Americans have come to expect attacks against traditional values and religious expression at schools, football games, county council meetings, and other public forums. We have read about those who would take "In God We Trust" off of our money or take "God" out of our Pledge of Allegiance.[19] We have been numbed by countless lawsuits against Christmas manger scenes and the Ten Commandments on public property.[20] The excuse given by those sponsoring these attacks is that they are protecting "the wall of separation" between government and religion. But the presumed reach of what is "government" has now extended into all areas of our lives, far beyond the well-defined constitutional boundaries of government.

ATTACKS AGAINST CHURCHES

The last place you might expect the secularists to attack directly would be churches and private religious schools. But the ACLU and other paragovernment groups realize that by destroying the bastion of traditional belief in the country, they can destroy the orthodox-traditional worldview. The First Amendment protects religion from government intrusion, but the ACLU has been successful in redefining the meaning of the First Amendment. They conveniently ignore what the Amendment really says about religion: "Congress shall make no law respecting an establishment of religion, or prohibiting the free exercise thereof." In its place they hold that any expression of religious faith, especially Christianity and Orthodox Judaism, is illegal. Despite the obvious meaning that there should be no laws restricting religion, Congress passed laws and the courts made up laws that served to muzzle the free speech and the application of faith by churches and their members. These rulings by government have also severely restricted the freedom of churches to "petition the government for a redress of grievances."

Recent laws and regulations require that churches abide by the restrictions on political and legislative activities established in the Internal Revenue Code or lose their tax exempt status. The law includes two stipulations for churches: first, no substantial part of the churches' activities may consist of carrying on propaganda or otherwise attempting to influence legislation; and second, the church may not participate in political campaigning in opposition to, or on behalf of, any candidate for public office.[21]

The goal of these expanding regulations is to revoke the tax-exemption status of churches. The potential impact of this is apparent when one realizes that the average local government receives 64 percent of its general revenue from property taxes, and churches own a vast amount of untaxed property. One estimate is that in year 2000, church property was worth at least $300 billion.[22] State and local governments are strained to the financial breaking point, and courts have made it possible to remove the property tax exemptions enjoyed by the churches.

The Supreme Court's shift away from the time-honored position of tax exemption first became apparent in 1970 in the *Walz v. Tax Commission of the City of New York* case. In a close five to four decision, the court held that exempting church property was permissible, but not constitutionally required. In a case two years later, the court held that "tax exemption is a privilege, a matter of grace rather than a right." In 1983, the court held tax exemption was equivalent to a tax subsidy. An omen of impending change was sent in the *Bob Jones University v. United States* decision in which the court declared that tax-exempt religious schools had to comply with government policy or lose their tax-deductible status. The university had a religiously based practice that effectively discriminated against African Americans. The court upheld the Internal Revenue Service decision to withdraw the university's right to receive tax-deductible contributions because its practices were contrary to public policy.

The message of the *Bob Jones* decision was clear. If a university can be forced to comply with public policy mandates to retain its tax status, then all nonprofit institutions—with churches listed first—can be forced to do likewise.

Had these policies been in effect at the nation's founding, there would not have been an American Revolution. During the Revolutionary era, the pulpit played a key role in political activism. At the bottom of the original Declaration of Independence, the Continental Congress ordered copies of the document to be sent not to town clerks or newspapers, but to parish ministers. The Congress "required [them] to read the same to their respective congregations, as soon as divine service is ended, in the afternoon, on the first Lord's day after they have received it."[23] The political activism of ministers earned them the sobriquet, "the black regiment," for their robed resistance to England. In the 1770s, three out of four colonists were connected with Christian Reformed denominations and their theology. The beliefs held by these groups—along with fellow Calvinists in France and Scotland—made them suspicious of monarchies, and more willing to defy them when necessary.

For most American ministers, and many in their congregations, the religious dimension of the war was precisely the point of the revolution. Revolution would enable the nation to realize its destiny as a "redeemer nation," for the rest of the world. Much of the Revolution's ideological underpinnings were restatements of theological arguments advanced by Christians. Even when rationalists and deists spoke in favor of the independence movement, they usually employed if not the exact words, then the prevailing tone, of orthodox Christian discourse.

The ACLU has forgotten this history. The historic position is that the Constitution did not give the Congress, or the IRS, *any* authority to levy taxes on churches in the first place. In fact, the First Amendment appears to forbid "any law" about government regulation of churches and their activities. Yet today, if churches exercise their first amendment rights of free speech or petitioning the government with their grievances, the government will punish them with taxes. The ACLU, Planned Parenthood, and other organizations that work against traditional values and constructive behavior are free to actively pursue their agenda through the political process, but churches are restricted and silenced. A pastor cannot speak out against a candidate whose agenda diminishes the positive influence of religion and morals on our society, or endorse a candidate that stands for the things the church believes is in accordance with what the Bible teaches. A minister cannot declare that homosexuality is a "sin," if such statements conflict with local "sexual nondiscrimination" laws.

The exclusion of churches from the political process has contributed heavily to the discrediting of faith-based values in the society at large, and forced people of faith to stand alone against government attacks on values and morality. As The Rutherford Institute concludes, "In light of how the Internal Revenue Service (IRS) and some courts have interpreted [the relevant portion of the law] . . . churches and religious organizations may well consider this law as yet another example of the government's subordination of the rights of religious persons to 'matters of national public policy' or to other rights."[24] Get a Republican speaking on a political topic in a church, and the secularists are outraged by the perceived lowering of the so-called "wall of separation," but put a Democratic presidential candidate in the same situation, and leftists with their supporters are forgetful of these concerns.

In addition to muzzling the free speech and political activity of churches, the government, through the legal system, has begun the process of SLAPP-ing churches for disciplining their members. Critical to the viability of a Christian church is its responsibility to discipline members when they commit an immoral act. Until the past few decades, churches provided a national conscience, informing and educating Americans about what was right and wrong. The presence of a higher moral standard in society, even for non-members, helped to restrain destructive, immoral behavior in the wider culture. Churches were once a powerful positive influence in the culture development cycle. The government, however, has now crippled even this most sacred bastion of faith and constitutional privilege.

In the early 1980s, the case of *Guinn v. Church of Christ of Collinsville* became one of the first cases determining whether churches had the right to discipline members for violating moral standards and engaging in behavior inconsistent with church teaching. Marian Guinn was confronted with evidence that she was having an affair, and her church followed careful biblical principles to warn her and appeal to her to change her behavior. While she initially agreed, she did not end the affair and eventually terminated her membership. The church then excommunicated her in a public meeting. Guinn sued the elders and the church for invasion of privacy and outrage. The church was found guilty, and had to pay a fine of nearly $500,000.

Subsequent cases have both agreed and disagreed with the *Guinn* case, and the lack of predictability created by court inconsistencies has had a chilling effect on churches' willingness to stand for traditional moral principles. Professor Daryl L. Wiesen concludes:

> The unpredictability created by both the application of traditional, ad hoc free exercise analysis and the open-endedness of the intentional infliction of emotional distress tort may have a chilling effect on religious actions. Unable to predict the legal implications of their religiously motivated actions, risk averse religious actors may cease to engage not only in actionable conduct, but also in conduct that would be protected under the Free Exercise Clause.[25]

Many churches now stay away from the government's invisible fence, and the SLAPP Factor continues to move society in a secular direction. Like a dog inside an underground electric fence, churches now keep their distance from what were once clear moral rights. The loss of the moral influence of churches on society is immeasurable. For persons cheating on their spouse, the best thing that could happen to them, and the country, would be account-ability to a church body and subjection to public embarrassment. Public dis-cipline creates a deterrent for infidelity. It is the most compassionate thing to do for married couples and their children, and the most constructive thing for society. However, government has chosen to protect marital infidelity and en-courage the destruction of marriage. Churches, the conscience of our society for two hundred years, have been quieted, and another positive force in Amer-ica's culture development cycle has been reduced to whispers.

Protestant churches are not alone in receiving government scrutiny. Catholic schools are feeling the heat for upholding their standards as well. In 2005, the Catholic Diocese of Brooklyn was sued by Michelle McCuster, an unmarried kindergarten teacher who was fired after becoming pregnant. The attack on the church and school was led by the New York Civil Liberties Union. At the time of this writing, the matter remains unresolved, but the school has already been SLAPPed around by lawyers and the media. Jour-nalist John Leo, writing on his blog, provided an account of some of the me-dia attacks on the school:

> Much of the media seems convinced that dismissing a teacher over "Catholic morality" is an attempt to revive the Middle Ages. On CNN, Paula Zahn leveled a couple of sardonic putdowns at a defender of the school, William Donohue, of the Catholic League for Civil Rights. A jocular column by Adam Sommers in the *New York Daily News* said: "No harlots, no strumpets, no prostitutes. Next thing you know, con men, adulterers, drug addicts—all sorts of other sinners— will be coming to this church looking for compassion."[26]

Leo argued that the Catholic Church was well within its rights, and pointed out that taking these rights from a church destroyed its purpose.

Another Christian school in California, operated by the California Lutheran High School Association, was sued for expelling two girls for al-legedly being lesbian. While most courts have sided with Christian schools in similar cases on the basis of religious freedom, the plaintiffs are now saying that because the school charges tuition, it is a business. In California, *busi-nesses* cannot discriminate based on sexual orientation. The results of this case will be another SLAPP that will be heard throughout the culture.

Unfortunately, the SLAPP Factor has already impacted the willingness of other churches and religious schools to stand up for their rights. Unless the Catholic Diocese of Brooklyn gives in, and settles, they will probably win their court case. No one knows what will happen to the California Christian school. But what is known is that, in the process of defending themselves, both will spend thousands of dollars they don't have and endure many additional media attacks in the process. In the future, thousands of other churches and schools may find it easier just to lower their standards.

ATTACKS ON BUSINESSES

Another large part of the private sector that many assume has freedom of speech, freedom of conscience, and freedom of association is our nation's businesses. The secular tentacles of government, however, limit the ability of private businesses to establish traditional moral standards or to offer activities with religious content for their employees. New laws and court rulings increasingly force businesses to adopt a totally secular worldview.

The Employment Non-Discrimination Act, a bill that has been introduced in Congress, threatens to create a federal law that would require all businesses and organizations (such as the Boy Scouts) with more than fifteen employees to hire homosexuals and bisexuals. This law would create a new boom for lawyers, who could sue companies anytime a homosexual wasn't hired or promoted. The result could be chaos in the culture development cycle, with a host of traditional values abolished almost overnight.

Companies like Wal-Mart, that once had policies against adultery in the workplace, have been forced to drop standards that attract lawsuits for discrimination based on marital status. Wal-Mart, along with other retailers that have pharmacies, had refused on moral grounds to sell the Plan B morning after pill. But three women, backed by abortion rights advocates Planned Parenthood League of Massachusetts, National Abortion Rights Action League (NARAL), Pro-Choice Massachusetts, and other groups, filed a SLAPP-type lawsuit in 2006. When the state pharmacy board ruled in their favor, Wal-Mart agreed to change.[27]

New guidelines proposed by the Equal Employment Opportunity Commission, according to the Senate testimony of Chick-Fil-A executive Dan Cathy in June of 2005, will force their company "to eliminate all references to religion, which would significantly change the culture and morale at Chick-Fil-A."[28] The company has a history of supporting voluntary groups, including Christian groups, and closing on Sundays for religious reasons.

The safest policy for businesses has become a totally secular, religion-free workplace. As Michael K. Whitehead, general counselor to the Southern Baptist Convention's Christian Life Commission, notes, "Employers trying to avoid lawsuits want a clear-cut, simple rule which can be understood and obeyed by all employees, whether high school drop-outs or Harvard MBAs.

Their primary aim is not to be sensitive to EEOC's intentions or to maximize religious liberty. Their bottom line is to find a policy that will help them stay out of court."[29] Ambiguity in court decisions and regulatory guidelines leave businesses little choice but to adopt secular policies in order to reduce risks.

SLAPP has worked to remove religion and morality from the workplace, and the loss of these convictions with regard to honesty and truth telling have been obviated by government policy. Capitalism demands certain virtues, but the effect of these rulings has been to take away the virtues of hard work and replace them with whispers. The only strategy that can keep companies out of court is to avoid anything religious and to put no restrictions on the moral behavior of employees.

Whether individual, parent, church, or business, Americans holding traditional values are trapped in a "whisper zone" surrounded by invisible electric fences that threaten to "shock" them if they cross unmarked legal lines. It is not hard to understand why most Americans whisper when it comes to religious or moral issues. There is real danger in suggesting that almost any behavior is wrong. There is very real liability for businesses, churches, or other organizations that attempt to impose traditional standards of behavior. Americans, however, must stand up against the enemies of our culture, because the risk of losing our country is very real.

Chapter Nine

America's Secular Culture: The Cost in Dollars and Sense

If freedom of speech is taken away, then dumb and silent we may be led, like sheep to the slaughter.

—George Washington

Conspicuously absent from the political debate, as elected officials and judges continue to throw traditions overboard from the ship of state, is the mounting cost in dollars, debt, and human suffering.

Historically, societal standards have played an important role in restraining an inherently independent citizenry. Americans have always wanted to determine the course of their own lives and to live by their own moral values without government interference. This inclination toward independence only increased as societal standards declined. In his book, *Moral Freedom,* sociologist Alan Wolfe conducted in-depth interviews with people in eight distinct communities across the United States and found that most people still want to autonomously determine how to construct a virtuous life. Instead of deferring to traditional institutions like churches, Americans today want an individualized faith and personal self-discovery. "Listening to the way our respondents talked," wrote Wolfe "gives a certain amount of credibility to those who argue that contemporary Americans have too much freedom for their own good."[1]

It is quintessentially American to be antiauthoritarian and embrace individual autonomy. Because the United States is so advanced, so free, so diverse, and increasingly unconstrained by custom and tradition, the nation is especially prone to social experimentation. Some of this behavior has been sanctioned by government, and has come to the attention of social commentators. Economists are now interested in the mutual interaction of social forces and market behavior. For example, one text declares that "marital sortings have an enormous influence on the values, preferences, and skills of . . . children."[2] In short, social behaviors, like marriage, divorce, abortion, and same-sex marriage have consequences and costs. If government sanctions destructive behavior, the whole country suffers.

The costs and results of some government-sanctioned behaviors have not captured the attention of the mainstream media or policy makers. Politicians often make decisions that please major interest groups, while losing sight of what is best for the nation. To be sure, the job of government is not easy. For instance, cigarette smoking is a simple example of the type of dilemma confronting politicians. The issue of smoking also provides a vivid illustration of how government action can change behavior and at the same time work at cross-purposes. Following the 1966 report by the U.S. surgeon general that resulted in warning labels on cigarette packages, the government continued a long-standing policy of giving crop subsidies to tobacco farmers. The government provided both incentives and disincentives for smokers and tobacco farmers, and the number of smokers in America continued to increase.

Smoking is legal, and most Americans agree that individuals should have the right to smoke. A Gallup poll in 2005 found that 83 percent of those surveyed thought smoking should not be made illegal.[3] However, smoking is also known to create serious and costly health problems for individuals who smoke, and for those around them. The same survey found that 81 percent thought that smoking was "very harmful" for adults.[4] The consequences of smoking are estimated to be about $157 billion a year, and result in 440,000 premature deaths.[5] As a result of smoking, health insurance costs for everyone increase, and taxpayers must pay more for Medicaid and Medicare.

Recently, secondhand smoke was found to be a serious health problem for those who live and work in proximity to smokers.[6] As a result, new federal laws were passed to prohibit smoking on airlines, public transportation, and in most federal buildings, while states and municipal governments moved to restrict the areas where people can smoke. These actions by government established a precedent that removed the threat of discrimination-based lawsuits against private-sector restrictions on smoking, empowering many businesses to voluntarily restrict or prohibit smoking in the workplace. The government's mandates for health warnings on cigarette packs, and laws restricting smoking, subsequently empowered citizen groups to say that it is "wrong" for smokers to endanger public health and to force Americans to pay more taxes.

Is this growing opposition to smoking de facto discrimination against the rights of smokers? Selling cigarettes and smoking are still legal, but new mandates by government have resulted in citizens having the right to say that smoking is "wrong" when it affects others. This, in turn, has created a public stigma against smoking that has reduced the number of smokers and given nonsmokers freedom from secondhand smoke. While many Americans still choose to smoke, government action has saved countless lives, reduced costs to taxpayers, and improved the quality of life for everyone. We find a principle here: when the law discriminates on behalf of the common good, the culture development cycle promotes more constructive behavior.

Laws restricting smoking, and punitive taxes on cigarettes, are examples of constructive action by government in the culture development cycle. Though they came decades after research found a relationship between smoking and cancer, the new legislation did reduce the incidence of cigarette use and cancer. This does not mean that those who smoke are "bad" or those that don't smoke are "good." It simply means that government acted to discourage behavior that hurt the nation as a whole. The principle is that government can assist in the improvement of society by setting standards and providing incentives. The detrimental effects of smoking on individuals and society make it "right" for the government to discourage smoking . . . just as it does with so-called "sin taxes" on alcohol use, gasoline consumption, and other behaviors that have secondhand consequences on society. It is also "right" for the government to favor behaviors that promote the common good, such as home ownership, attending college, charitable giving, retirement investing, and job training. Citizens who own a home are not better than other citizens, but home ownership has a proven benefit for societal stability.

Unfortunately, government at all levels has been slow to respond to more politically charged behaviors that have proven much more destructive than smoking cigarettes. For example, the most costly policies by government are those that punish, demean, and weaken the institution of marriage. Previous chapters gave several examples of government attacks on traditional values and beliefs. This chapter gives an estimate of the staggering costs of government's policies on marriage, as well as the cost of other destructive behavior legitimized by government.

THE ECONOMIC BENEFITS OF MARRIAGE

Marriage and family are indispensable institutions of any civilized society. The family provides a responsible framework for stability—including sexual stability, a nurturing environment for children, an extended care network for older and younger generations, and a mechanism to transmit societal values to future generations. The security of marriage and a "home" that children can call their own contributes to the physical, emotional, and economic health of men and women as well as children. The byproduct of this stable family dynamic benefits the nation as a whole. All credible research shows that marriage leads to:

- greater health and longevity;
- greater mental health;
- more happiness;
- more education;
- more income;
- less abuse of adult women;
- less abuse, including less sexual abuse, of boys and girls;
- less poverty;
- less crime;
- less addiction;
- less depression and anxiety; and
- less violence and abuse.[7]

In the words of former senator Rick Santorum, "Strong families generate values and virtues. . . . [T]hey are moralistic, and so they are moralizing, [and] they teach right from wrong."[8] Marriage is a "wealth-enhancing institution." The longer a marriage lasts, the greater the family wealth. Despite this plethora of evidence, government has done more to discourage marriage than to support it.

Marriage is not a contract for cohabitation, but a vow of togetherness. Its purposes transcend what social scientists can measure because it is a sacramental act, a spiritual experience. "When the state usurped the rite of matrimony," write Robert P. George and Jean Bethe Elshtain, "it was inevitable that it should loosen the marital tie."[9] The state is not a representation of eternal values, and it often disregards them for the whims of the moment. But this spiritual, sacred aspect of marriage transcends government interference, and demands that the state leave traditional marriage as it is.

When government does intervene, the results can be disastrous. The arrival of the welfare state, and the accompanying government support payments for single women, show this clearly. Paternalistic federal laws and regulations diminish incentives to grant women economic liberty. Authors Kimberley Strassel, Celeste Colgan, and John Goodman argue in their book *Leaving Women Behind* that federal institutions overseeing employment, employee benefits, child care, taxation, health care, education, and retirement have twisted the definition of the traditional family beyond recognition.[10] While women's realities have changed dramatically, the government laws haven't kept pace, and they actually serve to ruin incentives for marriage and stability.

Premarital and Extramarital Sex

The fates of family and society are forever intertwined. Strong and loving families make for better citizens, while unstable, disruptive, and unhealthy families become a burden on relatives, neighbors, friends, and—ultimately— government and its taxpayers. In the past fifty years American society has become more accepting of sex before marriage, and the result has been a weakening of marriage. A 2001 poll found that 60 percent of adults said it was not wrong for a man and a woman to have sex before marriage.[11] A subsequent study found that 95 percent of those interviewed reported having had premarital sex.[12] Women aged eighteen to twenty-nine were much more likely to have had premarital sex than were their parents and grandparents.[13]

The elimination of sexual restraints, and the acceptance of an unconstrained sexual ethic by the culture at large, has destroyed past civilizations. One study of more than eighty early societies found "an unvarying correlation between the degree of sexual restraints and the rate of social progress. Cultures that were more sexually permissive displayed less cultural energy, creativity, intellectual development, and individualism, and a slower general cultural ascent"[14]

America's acceptance of unrestricted sexual behavior increased significantly after court decisions in the early 1960s removed the constraining principles of religion from education and public policy development. Traditional marriage did not collapse from its own weight, it was dismantled by those who believed its abolition was necessary to advance human freedom. "The legal, social, and economic supports that sustained marriage over centuries," writes columnist and social observer Maggie Gallagher, "have dispatched it with astonishing speed, and marriage has been reconceived as a purely private act."[15]

It is a private act with public consequences. Old certainties are gone, but no satisfying new answers have emerged to fill the vacuum. "In the early 1960s, roughly three-quarters of American adults thought that premarital sex was wrong. By the 1980s only a third of adults thought that premarital sex was 'always' or 'almost always' wrong.[16] Today, few are willing to say that any type of sexual behavior is wrong. The cost to the nation of this dramatic change in the culture development cycle has been enormous.

THE COST OF SEXUALLY TRANSMITTED DISEASES

One of the costs of sex outside of marriage is the increase of sexually transmitted diseases. "Sexually transmitted diseases (STDs) continue to be a major health threat in the United States. The Center for Disease Control (CDC) estimates that 19 million STD infections occur annually, almost half of them among youth ages fifteen to twenty-four. In addition to potentially severe health consequences, STDs pose a tremendous economic burden, with direct medical costs as high as $15.5 billion in a single year."[17] Other estimates have the direct annual medical cost of STDs at $17 billion, and these direct costs do not include the cost of other health problems such as cervical cancer that are caused by STDs.

The direct medical costs of STDs to the nation are approximately the same as the annual federal spending for the Department of Justice, the Department of Energy, or the NASA space program. As sexual activity increases at earlier and earlier ages, these costs will continue to rise at a dramatic rate.

By the twelfth grade, 65 percent of American high school students (both male and female) have had sexual intercourse, and 20 percent have had four or more partners.[18] Approximately two-thirds of people who acquire STDs in the United States are younger than twenty-five.[19] Each year 25 percent of America's teenagers will contract a sexually transmitted disease. More than half of all Americans will have an STD at some point in their life.[20] Many of these diseases are incurable and can lead to other serious health problems such as cervical cancer, infertility, birth defects, and brain damage.

These statistics, as frightening as they are, likely underestimate the degree of the health problems caused by promiscuous sex because not all STDs are required to be reported to state health departments and the Center for Disease Control. The most serious diseases, such as HIV and HPV, are among those that are often not reported. Privacy interests can understandably trump the public good, and as a result no one really knows how extensive this epidemic is.

The most serious and fastest growing STD cases are among men who have sex with men (MSM). This group carries two-thirds of HIV infections (even though less than 5 percent of males say they are homosexual), and of those who have the disease, about 25 percent don't know they have it.[21] When direct and indirect costs are considered, HIV/AIDS cases account for nearly half of the total costs associated with STDs.[22] Cases of rectal chlamydia, gonorrhea, and syphilis are also increasing at alarming rates among the MSM group. "The syphilis rate among U.S. men soared 81 percent between 2000 and 2004, primarily as a result of increases in reported cases among homosexual males."[23]

While HIV is considered deadly and expensive because it causes AIDS, the human papilloma virus (HPV) causes far more deaths among women in the United States each year. HPV is the name of a group of viruses that include more than 100 different strains that are sexually transmitted. Today it is the most prevalent and common sexually transmitted disease. "Thousands of

American women die from it. . . . In fact, it is estimated that 90 percent of cervical cancer cases are caused by HPV, and the virus itself cannot be eradicated once it is in the system."[24]

The problem has been growing for decades. It was diagnosed in 1992 at the University of California at Berkeley, which found that 47 percent of female students coming to the campus health center for routine gynecological exams carried HPV. "Every one of them will suffer painful symptoms for the rest of their lives, and some will die of cervical and uterine cancer. The most disturbing news is that the HPV can be transmitted while the male is wearing a condom."[25]

The majority of Americans are unaware of the link between certain types of HPV and cervical cancer. In one national survey, 70 percent of women were unable to name the cause of cervical cancer. Fewer than half of the clinicians responding to a Centers for Disease Control (CDC) survey in 2004 were familiar with various types of HPV. Lack of knowledge, misinformation, and confusion has left many patients puzzled or angry about the facts of the virus.[26]

Every American pays a high price for STDs as a result of a cultural preoccupation with sexual freedom. Taxes are higher and health insurance costs more for everyone. American productivity is lower, and our economic future is diminished. The lifetime medical cost for just one HIV patient is approximately $200,000. One study of patients receiving care for HIV found that 47 percent were paid for by the government programs Medicaid or Medicare, 33 percent had private insurance (which makes insurance more expensive for everyone) and 20 percent were uninsured (which shifts the cost of health care to those who pay).[27] STDs create secondhand consequences for all Americans.

The cost and misery of sexually transmitted diseases is only one consequence of the fascination the American culture has with sexual license. Yet government does little or nothing to encourage youth to delay sex until marriage. Calls for teaching abstinence in schools are met with accusations of religious bigotry, so teaching so-called "safe sex" has become the de facto policy of government. The result: today in America, it is unlikely that children will reach the altar without having an STD or marrying someone who already has contracted one. And for those who do marry, divorce rates will be higher for those who had sex before they married. Everyone will suffer, and everyone will pay. The CDC estimates that 65 million Americans have incurable sexually transmitted diseases.[28] Still, few are willing to even whisper that sex outside of marriage might be both harmful *and* wrong for individuals and the country. People may have the *right* to have sex outside of marriage, but is it right to ask others to pay for the consequences?

ECONOMIC COSTS OF COHABITATION

The growth and acceptance of sexual promiscuity, coupled with the devaluation and attempts at "redefinition" of marriage, have led to a corresponding increase in unmarried couples living together. Cohabitation can be defined as "two romantically involved individuals who share living space and related responsibilities—without a formal, legal commitment." Between 1960 and 2004, the number of unmarried cohabiting couples in America increased by over 1,200 percent.

Over 5 million couples now cohabitate in America, and over half of all first marriages are preceded by cohabitation.[29] Couples can legally live together and have the freedom to do so. However, the serious question for Americans to consider is, once we understand how costly and destructive cohabitation is to the country—and especially to both children, and the lack of long-term continuity of their parents' relationship—should others be forced to bear the cost? Should government enact policies to discourage behavior that hurts all aspects of our culture?

While most couples who move in together say they will eventually get married, only about 30 percent actually do. For those who ultimately get married, the divorce rate is 80 percent higher than for couples who chose marriage directly as an expression of commitment. A comparison of cohabitation and marriage found that couples who cohabit before marriage not only face a greater risk of divorce, they were also less emotionally healthy than married couples.[30] Cohabitation has not proved to be as safe as marriage, with nearly three times the alcohol problems, and couples are less faithful in their relationships than married couples.[31] Physical abuse is more than twice as likely among cohabitating couples as for those who are married, and the top three problems for unmarried couples who live together are drunkenness, adultery, and drug abuse.[32] Only about three out of a hundred couples that cohabitate ever end up in a successful marriage. The other ninety-seven are often left with heartache, misery, and despair.[33]

Since one-third of cohabiting couples include children, such households are prone to emotional, behavioral, and educational difficulties.[34] Despite mountains of social science evidence and thousands of years of history, government policy does not support marriage. Tax laws and other governmental policies actually discourage marriage and encourage cohabitation. Marriage reduces welfare eligibility for low-income Americans, and income taxes are often higher for many married couples than for singles living together. Many states now have antidiscrimination laws that prohibit landlords from favoring married couples. And older Americans often hesitate to remarry because of concerns about Social Security or the loss of other government benefits. State laws that once made cohabitation illegal have either been eliminated or not enforced because of the threats of lawsuits.

Schools and universities do little to support chastity, marriage, and fidelity. In fact, in many universities, cohabitation is being taught as an acceptable alternative lifestyle and as a good strategy as a test run or trial before marriage. A study by Norval D. Glenn of the University of Texas in Austin of twenty recently published undergraduate marriage and family textbooks found an extremely pessimistic view of marriage. "These textbooks highlighted the so-called 'dangers' of marriage, while ignoring its benefits and gave the exact opposite treatment to alternative relationships, extolling such alternatives as single parenthood and cohabitation."[35]

It is one thing for public schools and universities to promote alternative lifestyles, but it is another to promote a destructive marriage alternative under the guise of learning. Cohabitation is far more threatening to marriage as an institution than promiscuity. It blurs the line between marriage and unmarriage by coming with the external appearance of union without the internal, moral, legal, or emotional reality of such a union. Americans send their children to public schools to get an education—not for indoctrination about the alternatives to marriage.

Unwed Births

Children born to unwed mothers are by far the most costly and destructive result of premarital sex. A *Detroit News* editorial opined: "While single parenthood gains social acceptability, concerned officials say the decline in marriage in the United States since the 1960s has resulted in a rise in crime, poverty and other social problems. They point to research showing that children born to unwed mothers have more social and educational difficulties, costing taxpayers billions a year."[36] Women bearing children out of wedlock are likely to have a much lower income than married women; are six times more likely to be on welfare and 40 percent less likely to be working full time.[37]

Government action, amplified by the culture development cycle, has significantly changed American attitudes toward unwed births. In 1968, "Love Child" by the Supremes was a number one hit. The woman singer, portrayed by Diana Ross, pleaded with her boyfriend not to pressure her into sleeping with him for fear they would conceive a "love child." The woman in the song, herself from a fatherless home, did not want her child to endure the shame and the pain of growing up in an "old, cold, run-down tenement slum."

Today, the shame of unwed birth is gone. Illegitimacy is now fashionable. "Baby Mama," the 2005 hit record by American Idol's Fantasia Barrino,

extols the "virtues of being "a baby mama." The song even supports the belief that unwed mothers are entitled to more public support than they are getting: "I see you get that support check in the mail. Ya open it and you're like
'What the Hell' you say 'This ain't even half of daycare' saying to yourself
'this here ain't fair.'"

In 1964, 6.8 percent of children were born out of wedlock. In 2002, 34 percent were of this classification.[38] Among blacks, two out of every three births
are outside of marriage. The secondhand consequences of these fatherless
homes are devastating. Fathers who conceive a child outside of marriage are
less likely to marry and more likely to cohabit again, while unwed mothers
are much less likely to marry than are single women without children.

Children living in the home of their married biological parents are much
less likely to be abused and neglected than children living alone with an unmarried mother or in a nontraditional home environment. A child living alone
with a single mother is fourteen times more likely to suffer serious physical
abuse than a child living with both biological parents united in marriage. A
child whose mother cohabits with a man who is not the child's father is thirty-
three times more likely to suffer serious physical child abuse than is a child
living with both biological parents in an intact marriage.[39]

A Prevent Child Abuse America study, using data from the U.S. Department of Health and Human Services, the Department of Justice, the U.S. Census, and others, concluded the annual direct costs of child abuse and neglect
in the United States was over $24 billion.[40] This total included over $6 billion
for hospitalization, almost $3 billion for chronic health problems, over $14
billion for child welfare related costs, and over $340 million for the judicial
system.[41]

The same report estimated that the indirect annual U.S. cost was nearly $70
billion. This total included $8.8 billion for juvenile delinquency and over $55
billion in related adult criminality (13 percent of all violence can be linked to
earlier child maltreatment).[42] While not all abuse occurs in nontraditional
families, the overwhelming majority does. But while the cost of abuse is significant, it is small relative to the other government spending on children born
to unwed mothers.

"In fiscal year 2000, federal and state governments spent $199.6 billion in
means-tested welfare aid to families with children. This means-tested aid includes programs such as Temporary Assistance to Needy Families (TANF),
the Earned Income Tax Credit (EITC), public housing, food stamps, Medicaid, WIC food program, SSI, and dozens of other programs. Of the total
means-tested aid to children of $199.6 billion, *some $148 billion (or 74 percent) went to children in single-parent families.*"[43]

The direct government spending on children of unwed mothers was more
than four times the amount the federal government spent on education in

2001, more than three times the amount spent on the Department of Veterans Affairs, more than twice what was spent on the Department of Agriculture, and three times more than was spent on the Department of Transportation.

"On average, a mother who gives birth and raises a child outside of marriage is seven times more likely to live in poverty than is a mother who raises her children with a stable married family. Over 80 percent of long-term child poverty in the United States occurs in never-married or broken households."[44] More than 70 percent of all juveniles in state reform institutions come from fatherless homes.[45] The average annual cost to incarcerate a youth is $43,000.

The total long term cost to the nation of unwed births is difficult to estimate, but the cultural consensus confirms that it is astronomical. Without question, out-of-wedlock births are a primary cause of America's most serious and costly socioeconomic problems. Any society that protects this behavior under the guise of compassion, individual freedom, and political correctness is foolish and self-destructive. Unwed births are the cause of untold misery and hardship. *Now* is the time for our nation to establish a goal to reduce the long-term obstacles in children's lives, and the generational cycles it spawns.

President Bill Clinton spoke forcefully about this problem in his 1994 State of the Union Address: "The American people have got to want to change from within if we're going to bring back work and family and community. We cannot renew our country when, within a decade, more than half of the children will be born into families where there has been no marriage. We cannot renew this country when thirteen-year-old boys get semiautomatic weapons to shoot nine-year-olds for kicks. We can't renew our country when children are having children and the fathers walk away as if the kids don't amount to anything."[46]

THE COST OF DIVORCE

Until the 1960s, marriage was widely acknowledged and practiced as a lifetime commitment, and divorce carried a severe societal stigma. Divorces were almost as rare as unwed births. The number of divorces in America went from 16.4 percent of marriages in 1935 to 50 percent in 1995, an increase of more than 200 percent.[47] Between 1960 and 1980 the divorce rate more than doubled, and it has remained high ever since. Today, one-fifth of all adults have been divorced. Attitudes toward divorce changed dramatically between the early 1960s and the mid-1970s. In 1962, only half of all respondents disagreed with a statement suggesting that parents who don't get along should stay together for the children. By 1977, over 80 percent disagreed. Attitudes have changed little since the 1970s.[48]

Government action, primarily through court rulings and changes in divorce laws, served as the primary catalyst for America's change in attitude and behavior. A 1998 study found that no-fault divorce laws fostered a 17 percent increase in state-level divorce rates between 1968 and 1988, and its enactment led to more divorces in forty-four out of fifty states.[49] The importance of marriage, marital fidelity, and the stigma of divorce all relied heavily on historical, moral, and religious principles. Once court rulings removed religious discussions from public schools and public policy in the early 1960s, the value of marriage was diminished, and the culture development cycle worked to remove the stigma of divorce.

In the United States, "the average divorce costs nearly $50,000, and . . . $175 billion is spent annually on divorce, mostly on litigation."[50] In addition to direct legal costs, "marriages that end in divorce also are very costly to the public. One researcher determined that a single divorce costs state and federal governments about $30,000, based on such things as the higher use of food stamps and public housing, as well as increased bankruptcies and juvenile delinquency. The nation's 10.4 million divorces in 2002 are estimated to have cost the taxpayers over $30 billion."[51] Costs go beyond dollars. For many women, the stories of their lives after divorce read like a tragic novel replete with wanderings and poverty.

The lives of children are just as tragic. As Judith Wallerstein has written in her landmark study of twenty-five-year effects of divorce:

> It's feeling sad, lonely, and angry during childhood. It's traveling on airplanes alone when you're seven to visit your parent. It's having no choice about how you spend your time and feeling like a second-class citizen compared with your friends in intact families who have some say about how they spend their weekends and their vacations. It's wondering whether you will have any financial help for college. . . . It's worrying about your mom and dad for years—will her new boyfriend stick around, will his new wife welcome you into her home?[52]

Children of divorced parents suffer many of the same problems as children of never-married mothers. These children are more likely to lie, steal, get drunk, hurt others, skip school, use drugs, carry a weapon while on drugs, smoke cigarettes, suffer poor health. And they are more than twice as likely to favor having children out of wedlock than children of married parents.[53] While many resilient children of divorced parents avoid these problems, on average, divorce is a costly and crippling problem for America.

More than thirty years ago Americans created a "no-fault divorce" culture in an attempt to redefine marriage. The basis of that ethic was that marriage should only last as long as one person wanted it to last, and it was almost exclusively about adult happiness. Looking back, it is clear that many adults are worse off, and virtually all children suffered. As a culture, we made radical changes in the family without realizing how the next generation would be affected. It is time to restore marriage to a place of respect in society.

THE ECONOMIC EFFECTS OF ABORTION

Forty-four million unborn American children have been aborted since the U.S. Supreme Court made the procedure a right in 1973. Regardless of personal opinions about the morality of government-sponsored abortion, the social and economic consequences of this decision have been dramatic. The availability of abortion encouraged more sexual promiscuity, which, in turn, led to a rapid increase in sexually transmitted diseases. Before *Roe v. Wade*, unwed pregnancies usually resulted in marriage before birth. Today, because of abortion, pregnancy is now a woman's problem rather than a man's responsibility.

The average cost of a surgical abortion ranges from $350 to $800 depending on geography, gestational age of the baby, and other factors. If $500 is used as an average, total spending on abortion since *Roe v. Wade* in America would equal about $22 billion. This does not include the significant medical costs of postabortion psychological problems, infertility, and increased cancer risk. The direct costs of abortion, however, are small relative to the total economic cost of the loss of 44 million American workers, consumers, and taxpayers. Secularists would argue that the cost of abortion and postabortion services is less than that of childbirth and childrearing. This is the argument of economists Steven D. Levitt and Stephen J. Dubner, who declare that legalized abortion led to less crime.[54] Our response is that only a misguided economist could place a dollar figure on the value of one human life.

The estimated 44 million abortions since *Roe v. Wade* are equivalent to the population of our fifty-seven largest cities from New York, Chicago, and Los Angeles, all the way down to cities the size of Anaheim, California and Buffalo, New York. Each passing year adds five more cities to the toll. If the cost to the country for the war on terrorism will run $300 billion or more, the cost to our nation for abortion on demand is far higher. *The estimated loss in downstream tax revenue alone is $11.5 trillion, and the loss in personal income is three to four times that. The economic toll is unprecedented. 44 million abortions brought an end to America's famous "youth market"—reducing our under-thirty population by a dramatic twenty-eight percent. . . .* Famed management consultant Peter Drucker calls [the loss of younger workers and consumers] "the number one management problem of the twenty-first century." . . . The mistake the "population explosion" propagandists made is that they saw children

simply as a cost, when in fact every child is a future consumer, a future producer, and a future taxpayer.[55]

Despite what population-control advocates predicted in the 1960s and
1970s, the chief demographic problem facing most countries is not overpop-
ulation, but its opposite. All over the world, populations are aging. Especially
in the wealthier nations, a combination of declining birthrates and increased
longevity mean that their populations have a smaller proportion of young
workers and a higher proportion of disabled and elderly persons. The European Union, for example, had an estimated fertility rate of 1.47 in 2005, well
below the replacement figure of 2.1. The United States rate is 2.08, and if it
follows the European model, then the nation will face what demographers call
the approaching "demographic winter."
    Abortion on demand continues to contribute to this crisis, and to a funding
turning point for Social Security and Medicare, which dwarfs any financial
problem ever faced before by the nation. Since these programs depend on
younger workers to pay the benefits of retirees, they are now hopelessly underfunded. The shortage of American workers has also contributed to waves
of illegal immigrants, whose presence will fundamentally change national
values as well as our social and economic structure. Current estimates on the
cost of addressing the current illegal immigration problem now exceed $100
billion.
    Considering the cost and destructive impact of abortion on our economy,
our government's promotion and forced funding of this malignancy on our
culture is unimaginable. Planned Parenthood, the country's largest abortion-
for-profit enterprise, has received about $1.5 billion in taxpayer funds since
1997. Not only has Planned Parenthood committed millions of abortions, it
has become one of the most powerful lobbying groups in Washington, D.C.
For the seven years ending June 30, 2004, Planned Parenthood spent $193
million to influence public policy. This full-court spending to pressure politicians is more than the Federal Elections Commission allotted to either George
W. Bush or John Kerry during their 2004 presidential campaign.[56]
    Planned Parenthood also subverts parent-to-child values transmission via a
website that encourages premarital and perverse sex. This site "is so raunchy
that South Dakota governor Mike Rounds and the State Library Board rightly
insisted that a simple link to the website be removed from the state library
homepage." In addition, Planned Parenthood initiated hundreds of SLAPP-
style lawsuits to intimidate states that passed laws to protect the next generation—states that have also moved to protect parental rights from unwar-
ranted, invasive (and violent) actions upon minors. Planned Parenthood is a
para-government organization that uses laws, courts, and tax dollars to undermine the culture and diminish our future.

Abortion's legacy scars those living after the procedure. A psychological and philosophical toll is felt by those indoctrinated with secular beliefs that reduce ethical decisions to mere human reasoning. Millions of postabortive men and women reexperience the abortion in their memories and dreams. The result is often severe psychological distress and depression. To cope with these feelings, women adopt defense mechanisms of denial, hyperactivity, and low self-esteem. Such trauma can lead to depression and even suicide. An Italian study concluded in August of 2001 that elective abortions led to a higher than normal number of suicides by women.[57] In a tragic twist of fate for the feminist cause, emerging evidence also indicates a clear link between breast cancer and abortion.[58]

THE COST OF PORNOGRAPHY

Pornography glorifies nonmarital and perverse sex and leads to countless negative effects on the culture. In 1973, the U.S. Supreme Court set a test for determining whether speech or expression could be labeled obscene in the case of *Miller v. California*. Justice Potter Stewart, who did not mean to be funny, said he could not define obscenity, but "I know it when I see it." Nevertheless, contrary to established law and previous court precedents such as the *Miller* obscenity standard, American courts ruled that the First Amendment right of free speech protects most forms of pornography.[59] Even after Congress moved to limit child pornography with the Child Pornography Protection Act of 1996, the Supreme Court struck down some of the provisions, allowing computer-generated "virtual" child pornography. The government has perverted the First Amendment to make one of the most destructive of human behaviors a constitutional right.

Credible research confirms that even nonviolent pornography leads men (who are the primary users of pornography) to:

- increase callousness toward women;
- trivialize rape;
- develop distorted perceptions about sexuality;
- heighten appetites for more deviant, bizarre, or violent types of pornography;
- devalue the importance of monogamy and marriage; and
- believe that nonmonogamous relationships are normal and natural behavior.[60]

Repeated studies reinforce what most parents intuitively know: continued exposure to pornography desensitizes people to rape as a criminal offense and leads to an increase in sexual crimes. One psychologist concludes: "In my clinical practice, I have daily treated both children and adults who have been unequivocally and repeatedly injured by exposure to pornography, where the cumulated evidence over many years demonstrates a cause/effect relationship between such exposure and a variety of harms."[61]

In a nationwide study, University of New Hampshire researchers Larry Baron and Murray Strauss found a strong statistical correlation between circulation rates of pornographic magazines and rape rates.[62] These researchers are not sympathetic with traditional values, but they are responsible scholars who follow the evidence wherever it leads. Another study found that "half the rapists studied used pornography to arouse themselves immediately prior to seeking out a victim."[63] Defining the social effects of pornography is difficult, yet hundreds, if not thousands, of crimes and incidences of sexual harassment can be linked to exposure to pornographic images.

The saturation of Internet pornography led BBC (British Broadcasting Corporation) News to report that the U.S. is the "worst" for online child abuse. An Internet Watch Foundation investigation found nearly 2,500 U.S. sites containing illegal images. The same report found that 50 percent of online images of child abuse can be traced to the U.S.[64] Approximately 22,000 porn websites were operative in 1997. Today, over 300,000 exist. Seventy-three percent of the world's Internet pornography is produced in the U.S.[65] Internet pornography is the new crack cocaine, leading to addiction, misogyny, pedophilia, and erectile dysfunction, according to clinicians and researchers who have testified before a U.S. Senate committee.[66]

One witness before a subcommittee of the Senate Commerce Committee was Mary Anne Layden, codirector of the Sexual Trauma and Psychopathology Program at the University of Pennsylvania's Center for Cognitive Therapy. She called porn the

> most concerning thing to psychological health that I know of existing today. The internet is a perfect drug delivery system because you are anonymous, aroused and have role models for these behaviors. To have a drug pumped into your house 24/7, free, and children know how to use it better than grown-ups know how to use it—it's a perfect delivery system if we want to have a whole generation of young addicts who will never have the drug out of their mind. Layden added that pornography addicts have a more difficult time recovering from their addiction than cocaine addicts, since coke users can get the drug out of their system, but pornographic images stay in the brain forever.[67]

CBS's *60 Minutes* aired a special in September, 2004, entitled "Porn in the U.S.A." The program estimated that Americans now spend approximately $10 billion a year on adult entertainment, which is as much as Americans spent attending professional sporting events, buying music, or going out to the movies. "Consumer demand is so strong that it has seduced some of America's biggest brand names, and companies like General Motors (owner of DirecTV), Marriott and Time Warner who are now making millions selling erotica to America." Pornography is now a major source of profits for TV cable systems, in-house hotel systems, and satellite systems.[68]

The government, by lack of law enforcement, and the courts by judicial activism, have sanctioned the production and use of pornography as a constitutional right. Governmental protection of what is essentially a virtual prostitution industry now has some of America's largest and most respected companies selling smut to adults and children. Pornography is so profitable that these companies funnel profits to lobbyists who seek to influence public policy in their favor and to the detriment of the public. This aspect of the culture development cycle at work under the governmental umbrella serves as a catalyst for destructive moral decline. What chance do individual Americans have when they stand up against this government-supported industry behemoth to say that pornography is wrong, exploitive, and harmful?

THE COST OF SAME-SEX MARRIAGE

In the early 1990s, gay marriage came to the Nordic countries of Norway and Sweden. Ten years later, out-of-wedlock births spiraled to where 60 percent of first-born children had unmarried parents. Same-sex marriage has advanced the Scandinavian trend toward the separation of marriage and parenthood, with the state picking up the bill.[69] Legal marriage between homosexuals has done little to encourage fidelity or reduce the spread of HIV and other STDs. A study published by Dr. Maria Xiridou in a 2003 edition of *AIDS* reveals that homosexual couples in Amsterdam engage in what can be called consensual infidelity, and that HIV spread more rapidly among couples who considered themselves to be in a "steady" relationship.[70]

Radical homosexual activists in America are trying to convince politicians and judges that our government should redefine marriage to create legal sanction and official endorsement of homosexuality. The goal is to use society's most sacred institution to legitimize a behavior that has always been considered morally wrong and socially destructive. Same-sex marriage advocates are saying that parental gender does not matter for the family or for children.

Government policies have already caused untold damage to marriage, but if there is a "last straw" for the institution, it would be the approval of same-sex "marriage." Official government endorsement of homosexuality will result in further deterioration of marriage in America. Government-approved same-sex marriage has convinced Scandinavians that virtually any family form is as good as another. Traditional marriage will suffer the same fate in America if same-sex marriage receives government sanction.

The case for same-sex marriage and civil unions is being made in the courts. The energy behind the movement is fueled by the secular idea that all personal domestic relationships are of equal value to society and that the law should not favor any one relationship over another. However, we have already reviewed the benefits to society of successful marriage, and the high cost to society when traditional marriage is diminished. A compassionate society never intentionally creates fatherless and motherless children. Lynn D. Wardle, writing in the *University of Illinois Law Review*, concludes, "If we want to put children's needs first, we must preserve for them the basic social institution which has over the millennia been the most beneficial of all imperfect human institutions for children's welfare. . . . [W]e should think very carefully before accepting the invitation to legitimize the brave new world of homosexual parenting as a desirable environment in which to rear future generations."[71] Traditional marriage is clearly the best way to propagate our culture and values, and government has a responsibility to support and encourage it because of its unique benefits to the nation.

The arguments against legitimizing the homosexual lifestyle with the institution of marriage are irrefutable. Many are not willing to listen to the truth about homosexuality, but this lifestyle is notoriously unhealthy and destructive, with huge financial costs to society. Studies consistently find poor health and destructive lifestyles among homosexuals. Dr. John R. Diggs Jr., MD, in his report, *The Health Risks of Gay Sex*, compiles dozens of studies over several decades. He concludes that "the medical and social science evidence indicate that homosexual behavior is uniformly unhealthy."[72] Dr. Riggs writes:

> As a physician, it is my duty to assess behaviors for their impact on health and well-being. When something is beneficial, such as exercise, good nutrition, or adequate sleep, it is my duty to recommend it. Likewise, when something is harmful, such as smoking, overeating, alcohol or drug abuse, and homosexual sex, it is my duty to discourage it. . . . Sexual relationships between members of the same sex expose gays, lesbians and bisexuals to extreme risks of Sexually Transmitted Diseases (STDs), physical injuries, mental disorders, and even a shortened life span.[73]

Dr. Riggs details many of the health and societal problems caused by same-sex relationships:

- Homosexuals, though probably less than 2 percent of the population, account for the bulk of cases of syphilis, gonorrhea, Hepatitis B, the "gay bowel syndrome," tuberculosis, cytomegalovirus, and HIV.[74] Homosexuals also experience a high rate of anal cancer, incontinence, parasitic and other intestinal infections, Hepatitis A, and cervical cancer.

- High levels of promiscuity among homosexuals exacerbate the spread of STDs and other health problems. One study found 75 percent of white, gay males claimed to have had more than 100 lifetime male sex partners; 15 percent claimed 100–249 sex partners; seventeen claimed 250–499; fifteen claimed 500–999; and twenty-eight claimed more than 1,000 lifetime male sex partners.[75]
- It is well established that there are high rates of psychiatric illnesses, including depression, drug abuse, alcoholism, and suicide attempts among gays and lesbians. An extensive study in the Netherlands undermines the assumption that public stigma in America (homophobia) is the cause of increased psychiatric illness among gays and lesbians. Severe psychological problems persist among homosexuals even though the Dutch are accepting of the lifestyle and offer legal same-sex marriage.[76]
- Homosexuals, on average, lose twenty years of life expectancy. The probability of a twenty-year-old gay or bisexual man living to sixty-five years was only 32 percent, compared to 78 percent of men in general. The damaging effects of cigarette smoking pale in comparison—cigarette smokers lose on average about 13.5 years of life expectancy.[77]
- Long-term sexual fidelity is rare in gay, lesbian, and bisexual (GLB) relationships. One study reported that 66 percent of gay couples reported sex outside the relationship within the first year, and nearly 90 percent if the relationship lasted five years.[78]

Dr. Diggs summarizes by using an old African proverb: "Don't tear down a fence until you know why it was put up." He continues:

The societal implications of the unrestrained sexual activity described above are devastating. The ideal of sexual activity being limited to marriage, always defined as male-female, has been a fence erected in all civilizations around the globe. Throughout history, many people have climbed over the fence, engaging in premarital, extramarital, and homosexual sex. Still, the fence stands; the limits are visible to all. Climbing over the fence, metaphorically, has always been recognized as a breach of those limits, even by the breachers themselves. No civilization can retain its vitality for multiple generations after removing the fence.

But now social activists are saying that there should be no fence, and that to destroy the fence is an act of liberation. If the fence is torn down, there is no visible boundary to sexual expression. If gay sex is socially acceptable, what logical reason can there be to deny social acceptance of adultery, polygamy, or pedophilia? The polygamist movement already has support from some of the advocates of GLB rights. And some in the psychological profession are floating the idea that maybe pedophilia is not so damaging to children after all.[79]

Homosexuality is not a simple difference in sexual orientation. Studies over several decades consistently find that homosexuals have hundreds, even thousands, of sexual partners during their lifetime—with up to half of these encounters with total strangers.[80] The contention that the legalization of homosexual marriage or civil unions will create longer-lasting, healthier relationships is not supported by research. In *The Male Couple*, authors David P. McWhirter and Andrew M. Mattison reported that in a study of 156 males in homosexual relationships

> [o]nly seven couples have a totally exclusive sexual relationship, and these men all have been together for less than five years. Stated another way, all couples with a relationship lasting more than five years have incorporated some provision for outside sexual activity in their relationship.[81]

Similarly, in *Male and Female Homosexuality*, M. Saghir and E. Robins found that the average male homosexual live-in relationship lasts between two and three years.[82]

Americans may have a right to practice homosexuality and to believe that it is "right." We are not suggesting that government make homosexuality a crime, but like cigarette smoking, government should discourage behavior that has costly secondhand consequences to society. The argument that homosexuals are born genetically programmed to desire same-sex relationships is unproven. Thousands of homosexuals have stopped the behavior and escaped the lifestyle, proving that at least for many, homosexuality is a choice. Even if research could show a genetic predisposition toward homosexuality, government should never encourage behavior that is destructive to individuals and the common good.

Government has the responsibility to encourage behavior that builds up our culture and to discourage costly and destructive behavior. Government must also protect the right of citizens to say that this behavior is "wrong," and to shield citizens from the cost of the major health problems associated with homosexual behavior. As Dr. Diggs demurs:

> The impact of the health consequences of gay sex is not confined to homosexual practitioners. Even though nearly 11 million people in America are directly affected by cancer, compared to slightly more than 1 million with AIDS, AIDS spending per patient is more than seven times that for cancer. The inequity for diabetes and heart disease is even more striking. Consequently, the disproportionate amount of money spent on AIDS detracts from research into cures for diseases that affect more people.[83]

If government is intent on improving the quality of our culture, objective data demands that public policy should discourage promiscuous, out-of-wedlock sex, and set goals to reduce sexually transmitted diseases, unwed births, pornography, abortion, and homosexuality. Traditional marriage, while suffering from decades of neglect and poor government policy, is society's best hope of improving the quality of life for all Americans. If married parenthood is allowed to become a minority phenomenon, then the cultural pathologies we identify here will spiral completely out of control.

THE COST OF GAMBLING

Gambling is another costly and damaging behavior that is supported and promoted by government. In 1960, all states had prohibitions against state-run lotteries and most other forms of gambling. Nevada was the only state that allowed casinos. State-run lotteries had flourished in nineteenth-century America as a way to support government and social services without taxes, but every state had stopped the practice because of fraud, corruption, and the societal problems that inevitably accompanied the gambling industry. Thirty-five states passed constitutional prohibitions against state-run lotteries.

Churches and religious groups of all denominations had long pressured state and federal governments to prohibit gambling, but after major court decisions in the early 1960s separated religion from the public square, the temptation to raise new revenues through lotteries was too much for most states to resist. New Hampshire was the first to fall, reinstating a lottery in 1964. Other states quickly followed. Once a state introduced a lottery, neighboring states were almost forced to have their own or risk losing millions of "tax" dollars to other states. Forty-two states and the District of Columbia now have approved lotteries.

In fiscal year 2003, Americans spent $45 billion on lottery tickets. This is $155 for every man, woman, and child in the United States—money that didn't go to house payments, groceries, or other consumer products that grow our economy. Less than a third ($14 billion) actually made it to state treasuries.[84] The rest went to winnings, advertising, and administration. States spent $400 million in 1997 to advertise their lotteries, and this figure has likely more than doubled since then. Advertising now has made lotteries one of the most visible activities of state government, ironically encouraging participation in an activity that they prohibited only forty years ago. "Get-rich-quick" advertising for lotteries preys on America's poor and less educated, who spend a disproportionate amount of their income on lotteries and other forms of gambling, while the proceeds of lotteries often pay for a college education for middle- to upper-class Americans.

Like tobacco, governments benefit from gambling revenue. The irony is that many states purport to earmark gambling revenue for education, but in the process they have become as addicted to gambling as to nicotine.

In addition to the poor economics and regressive nature of state lotteries, this over-the-counter "drug" has also become a "gateway drug" to more destructive forms of gambling. Such risk-taking is addictive for a significant number of Americans, and that addiction afflicts an increasing number of victims as technology makes gambling more accessible and anonymous to more Americans. Following a study of Internet gambling, one author writes:

> A number of the studies have concluded that the proliferation of legalized gambling has had a detrimental impact on society. Aside from the moral issues involved, these studies point to the human cost of compulsive gambling, the spread of crime, particularly organized crime, cannibalization of other consumer spending, and increases in illegal gambling as costs of legalizing betting. As the industry moves online, many of these problems will be exacerbated due to the ease of accessing and the difficulties involved in regulating online betting. . . . [D]ata has shown that after gambling is legalized, communities experience a 100 to 550 percent increase in the number of addicted gamblers.[85]

When government legalizes a destructive behavior, it sanctions the behavior as "right," thus encouraging an increase in the behavior. Studies have shown that:

- more than 1 percent of Americans are compulsive gamblers;
- the percent of problem gamblers increases to 5 percent in mature gambling markets;
- every compulsive gambler impacts between seven and seventeen other people;
- compulsive gamblers average a debt between $52,000 and $92,000;
- 40 percent of white-collar crime can be traced to people with serious gambling problems; and
- gambling drains society in many other respects.[86]

Crime explodes when gambling is legalized. Within three years after gambling was introduced in Atlantic City, crime tripled and the city went from fiftieth to first in per capita crime rate. Comparing crime rates for murder, rape, robbery, aggravated assault, burglary, and motor vehicle theft reveals Nevada (the first state to allow casinos) is the most dangerous place to live in the United States.[87] When gambling is legal:

- child abuse and domestic violence increase;
- burglaries and the writing of bad checks increase;

- divorce and bankruptcies grow;
- the cost of law enforcement often doubles;
- alcohol problems grow; and
- suicide rates increase five to ten times among compulsive gamblers.

"The costs to society of rehabilitating compulsive gamblers, if it so chooses, would amount to $17,000 to $42,000 for each addict. . . . [T]he national price tag for compulsive gambling is currently estimated at $56 billion a year."[88] This is four times the amount ($14 billion) that states receive from lotteries! The cost of gambling to society far outweighs its benefits.

As states moved to promote legalized gambling, Congress passed the Indian Gaming Regulatory Act in 1988, opening up gambling even in states that prohibited it. Congress allowed Indian tribes to open casinos and promote gambling in states where gambling was illegal. By 1994, Congress realized that gambling was growing out of control and that federal and state governments had unleashed a plague on the American people. They authorized the National Gambling Impact Study Commission, which published its findings in 1999. The commission unanimously recommended that the nation "pause" the expansion of legalized gambling until the social and economic impacts could be better understood. The study included more than a dozen recommendations on how the industry could fight gambling addiction. The findings of this study were almost universally ignored.[89]

Today, legalized gambling opportunities exist in all but two states, with 443 commercial casinos operating in eleven states, plus racetrack casinos in six states. Indian casinos comprise the fastest growing segment with 354 casinos in twenty-eight states. Studies show that gambling addiction often doubles within fifty miles of casinos. "With government sanction and sponsorship of gambling, the vice has been gaining in prevalence and acceptability."[90] In other words, when the government makes something that was "wrong" "right," people embrace this new "right" and the restraints that discouraged the behavior are dissolved.

The next major political battle related to gambling is the legalization of Internet gambling. "A substantial part of the population has a latent susceptibility to compulsive gambling, and different individuals get hooked by different gambling opportunities. Making gambling widely available to everyone with a computer and modem, and making it available in people's living rooms, will clearly draw out much of this latent addiction. Moreover, video gambling, because of its instant feedback mechanism, is known to addict gamblers faster than other forms of gambling; hence, sociologists and psychiatrists widely refer to it as the 'crack-cocaine of gambling addiction.'"[91]

Most states have laws that make Internet gambling more or less illegal, and the U.S. Department of Justice has officially stated that Internet gambling is illegal, but unofficially it is not so sure. Even though Congress has attempted to address the issue, there is enough ambiguity in our laws to encourage the growth of the industry. The first online casino began in 1995. Now, at least 452 gambling-related websites have revenues exceeding $50 billion a year.

By 1993, Americans were spending more than $500 billion on legal and illegal gambling. With the expansion of state lotteries and the advent of online gambling, this figure now likely exceeds $1 trillion. Is there any wonder that Americans now have a negative savings rate and are heavily in debt. Congress needs to act, but because of the heavy influence of the gambling industry in political campaigns, it is unlikely that anything will be done without intense public pressure. History is beginning to repeat itself. Gambling is corrupting our political system just as it did in the nineteenth century before gambling was banned. The "Abramoff" scandal that rocked Congress in 2005 and 2006 was the result of gambling interests attempting to manipulate public policy. Gambling is destructive to our society, and it's time that Americans stop whispering, stand up, and say that it's wrong for our government to promote it.

SUMMARY

Sixty years after its founding, the editors of *Time* magazine wrote a celebratory piece entitled "What Really Mattered?" on the underlying values that had guided the nation through the twentieth century, "[t]he fundamental idea that [what] America represented corresponded to the values of the times. . . . [N]ot merely free, it was freed, unshackled . . . to take chances . . . of breaking away . . . from any constraints at all."[92] The quest for the unfettered "moral freedom" described by Alan Wolfe has come at a high price.

The direct and indirect costs of personal satisfaction at the expense of these cultural changes are astonishing. We estimate the direct costs of the issues we discussed to be $500 billion annually, with the indirect costs at $2 trillion! Add it up! The cost of diminishing marriage, including sexually transmitted diseases, divorce, cohabitation, unwed births, pornography, same-sex marriages, and abortion, along with the cost of government-sponsored gambling, likely exceeds our total annual federal budget. The consequences of these behaviors have been devastating to millions of individuals, families, and the nation as a whole.

Even small reductions in the destructive behaviors referenced in this chapter could eliminate untold suffering and save Americans tens of billions of dollars a year. At a time when our nation is facing the most severe financial crisis in our history, citizens should demand loudly that our elected officials act immediately. This is not a matter of subjective personal opinions about morality or religion. Our government has sacrificed the good of the nation to accommodate destructive behavior and appease interest groups. Politicians, judges, schools, and universities are ignoring the "general welfare" clause of our Constitution, and instead, promoting costly and destructive behavior that could destroy our nation. It is time to speak up and fight back!

Chapter Ten

Contrasting Worldviews:
Intolerance or Compassion?

The public interest is best served by the free exchange of ideas.

—Judge John Kane

Signs of a conflict over values are all around us. "In 1999, the Miss America Pageant changed its rules to allow contestants who had been previously married or had an abortion."[1] The secular worldview seized the public square by declaring that it was time to change the rules, but traditionalists responded that such changes were both illogical and self-destructive. The battle was joined, and the question became: whose agenda is better for America?

Secularist claims that their policies are compassionate, while traditional views are bigoted and intolerant, don't square with the facts. The documented outcomes of decades of secular policies reveal more cruelty than compassion. The real intolerance in twenty-first-century America is directed toward those with traditional beliefs. The freedom of speech of those with traditional views is quashed throughout the culture development cycle, from public schools and universities to businesses and even churches. Government control and involvement in all areas of our society has made it virtually impossible to say that any destructive behaviors are "wrong." Media advocates of the secular government ethic regularly "shock" citizens who speak out for traditional views and consistently work to purge our society of restraints that have protected individuals, families, and communities for generations.

The country is paying a high cost for the destructive behavior that is now encouraged by government.

There is nothing wrong, and much right, with letting religious faith serve as the wellspring of public action. Two hundred years of social progress under the traditional worldview is evidence enough that these values work. As a constructive guide to politics, religion and related moral principles should be very much in the public square. Nevertheless, critics feel justified in attacking any moral stand simply because government has ruled that religion must be separate from decision making and public policy development. This criticism deserves a response.

We have all seen enough of Iranian mullahs, the Taliban, and other theocratic governments to conclude that the United States government should not be run by religious zealots. There *should* be a formal separation between the two. But this separation should function more like different chemicals mixed in the same solution than chemicals kept in different jars.

To those who are not Christians—as well as to those of us who are—the prospect of theocratic rule is frightening. We readily agree with Soren Kierkegaard, who said that when Christianity becomes part of the state, it ceases to be Christianity. We emphatically want a faith unencumbered by state procedure. However, for most of our history, and even in the present day, the moral imperative of the American nation was self-consciously Judeo-Christian. Legal scholars of the nineteenth century, taking their cues from Blackstone's commentaries, proclaimed that Christianity was part of the common law of England. Christmas is a national holiday, and Thanksgiving has decidedly Christian, even Puritan, roots. Thousands of laws currently on the books were enacted in response to the efforts of Christian churches. The debates over slavery, and the more recent civil rights movement, were conflicts infused with theological overtones.

Before the 1960s, religion and government coexisted: separate and distinct, yet mutually supportive. Religion did not rule the government, but religious principles were integrated into all aspects of public and private life. When the courts created an adversarial relationship between religion and government, major shifts rapidly occurred in the culture cycle. Many long-held beliefs about "right" and "wrong" reflected in our laws were immediately discredited because of their religious connection. In fact, a number of state and federal laws have since been found unconstitutional because they violated the new antireligious position of our government.

How is it that these changes happened so dramatically and so completely? We have given several answers in this book, but we think one overlooked reason may lie in the postwar generation itself. In the 1950s, the faith and values that empowered the nation during the Depression and the Second World War were replaced by an unprecedented affluence. The old America, threatened by fascist dictators and economic collapse, began to disappear. In its place arose a more secure society, which seemed to worship materialism and readily accept a world of unending economic expansion. The evils of modernity became a target of campus radicals, but most of the generation accepted progress as the new ideal. In a world of newfound comfort and apparent security, a "felt" need for God and religion declined. The idea that the government should divorce itself completely from religion seemed an insignificant threat, and the self-appointed spokespersons for the postwar generation did not find a wall of separation between church and state as offensive.

The school prayer decision, and subsequent cases that removed religion from the public square, were explained as a way to protect religion from government intrusion. Only later did it become clear that the separation of church and state argument was being used to silence the voices of traditional America from active involvement in public debate and policy development. The recent court battles over the Ten Commandments provide a good illustration of the problems created by the "separation" decision by the courts.

Before the 1960s, the Ten Commandments were considered such an integral part of the legal system that they were permanently displayed on the walls of our Supreme Court, the U.S. Capitol, and state government buildings throughout the country. The government did not enforce the Ten Commandments, but the laws and cultural values reflected their religion-based requirements of honesty, faithfulness, respect for fellow citizens, and a respect for God. Like a mixture of separate and distinct chemicals, each performing different functions, the government and religion worked together to form a decent, productive, and cohesive society.

The shift began in the 1960s and accelerated later. The set of presuppositions largely derived from a Christian ethic faded with each succeeding year. The fact that government now views the influence of these religious principles on public policy as discriminating against nonreligious people demonstrates how far adrift we are as a nation. Americans have lost respect for laws because many of the principles supporting them have been discredited. Instead of supporting what is known to be "right," government now stands on the side of what many Americans know to be "wrong." Law has lost its moral authority, and has no transcendent point of reference. As Richard John Neuhaus has written, the strict prohibition provided by religiously grounded principals were the foundation of law. Take that away, and there is "the outlawing of the basis of law."[2]

CONTRASTING SECULAR AND TRADITIONAL
APPROACHES TO PUBLIC POLICY

Without a transcendent reference point, or a "north star" by which to judge social behavior, the culture was guided by the "rule of men" rather than the "rule of law." The new purveyors of values were secular elites who dominated the media, Hollywood, universities, and the courts. The public has come to believe that the law is only the current opinion of the collective ruling conscience. The practice of law is seen as moneymaking and legal manipulation of the first order. Lawyers are not seen as guardians of principle, but as professionals who can manage the rules to their own end.

From the perspective of some forty-five years, it appears that America lost both its innocence and its intactness in the 1960s. From a moral and legal point of view, the traditional impulse was quieted to private whispers. Supporters of the decade will argue that after the changes, government was acting with tolerance and compassion, and that it was protecting citizens against discrimination and intolerance. However, when the results of policy changes since 1960 are assessed, they can hardly be viewed as compassionate. Millions of Americans are now suffering from disease, poverty, poor education, incarceration, addictive disorders, high taxes, and heartbreak because of government endorsement of destructive behavior.

Government attempts to expand individual freedom, and to show compassion by insulating people from the consequences of their own actions, led to countless casualities of compassion. Many of these innocent victims are children, particularly the poor, who grew up in the post-1960s era without the positive support and restraints of family and faith. No group in America was harmed more by these policies than African Americans.

With the passage of new civil rights and antidiscrimination laws in the early sixties, black Americans appeared poised for a generation of growth and development. Arguments for equal rights for black Americans had been successful based on appeals to "equal under God" and "content of character" by Rev. Martin Luther King Jr. and others who assumed that religious arguments should be a part of public policy development. Religious values united the black community and a majority of Americans to change public policy. The enactment of civil rights for black Americans was one of America's pinnacle moments.

Faith and tradition were integral to the black community in 1960. The unwed birth rate among blacks was only slightly higher than whites, and divorce rates were actually lower. High school graduation rates were improving, and juvenile delinquency was about the same as whites. Though often poor, black families were strong and admirable given their commitment to church and community. Black youth grew up with a strong work ethic and a sense of personal responsibility.

At the very moment when equality was guaranteed by new civil rights laws, the powerful secular government of the 1960s moved to strip the black community of its greatest strength—family and faith. God and prayer were removed from schools just as blacks were allowed to attend better-funded, previously all-white schools. The teaching of evolution and the emphasis on personal freedom stood in distinct opposition to what was being taught at home and at church. New welfare programs subsidized unemployment and encouraged government dependency and unwed births. Legal abortion, now readily available at government expense, encouraged promiscuous sex and the spread of sexually transmitted diseases.

On May 17, 2004, Bill Cosby addressed the NAACP in Constitution Hall to mark the fiftieth anniversary of the famous *Brown* decision. In a surprise speech, he indicted the black community for its "culture of failure," including its twisted hip hop culture, high school dropout rates resulting in jail time for black males, and children having babies without bothering to marry.[3] Today, government attempts to show compassion without responsibility, and the results have effectively destroyed the African American community in America. More black children are aborted than are born, so much so that abortion is now the leading cause of death for black Americans—averaging 1,452 deaths per day.

> Unquestionably, the abortion industry targets the poorer African-American communities, and though blacks comprise only 12 percent of the U.S. population, black women account for 32 percent of abortions. . . . Without abortion, America's black community would now number 41 million persons. It would be 35 percent larger than it is. Abortion has swept through the black community like a scythe, cutting down every fourth member.[4]

Hispanics, with higher birth rates, and additional millions through immigration (both legal and illegal), have now replaced African Americans as the nation's largest minority.

African American children who escape the abortionist face a doubtful future, with more than two-thirds born to unmarried mothers. These children grow up in homes characterized by a greater exposure to abuse, violence, and drugs than any other group in America. Black youths are incarcerated at a higher rate than any group in the world: one in three black males born in 2001 is likely to spend some time in jail during their lives. Because of criminal records, one in seven African American males is legally prohibited from voting.[5]

In America today, while the government continues to spend hundreds of billions of dollars on poverty, more blacks live in it than ever before. Research shows that the poverty programs are anything but compassionate, yet government persists in the public provision of welfare subsidies.[6] "While poor African-American families were 3.8 times more likely than poor white families to live in high-poverty neighborhoods in metropolitan areas in 1960, they were 7.3 times more likely than poor whites to live in high-poverty neighborhoods in 2000."[7]

Many African Americans have escaped these conditions, demonstrating that they can compete and win in every sector of our economy. Blacks have achieved prominence in business, government, media, entertainment, and sports. These successes, while inspiring, were made in defiance of their circumstances. Surprisingly, media-designated black leaders continue to support secular-progressive solutions that have so miserably failed the African American community. Bill Cosby and Juan Williams are notable exceptions to this rule. They regularly appeal to traditional principles when challenging black students. In his book, *Enough*, Juan Williams raises a banner of proud black traditional values—self-help, strong families and a belief in God—that sustained the black community through generations of oppression.[8]

The traditional principles that guided the 1996 Welfare Reform Law stand in stark contrast to the failed secular policies that led to so much destruction among America's poor and minorities. The values of work, personal responsibility, and traditional marriage were integrated into public policies that effected a positive change in the culture development cycle. The results of this historic act, passed by the then new Republican majority in Congress and signed into law in 1996 by President Clinton, have been nothing short of dramatic. Millions of Americans moved from welfare to work, caseloads decreased by more than 50 percent, incomes improved, and child poverty fell further than any time since the 1960s. In sum, the law was one of the most successful social policies ever enacted.

Calls for welfare reform had been muted since President Lyndon Johnson made his Great Society a righteous pursuit in the early 1960s. An early critic of perverse welfare incentives in 1965, "the late Senator Daniel Patrick Moynihan, then an assistant secretary in the Department of Labor, published a government document arguing that black Americans were being held back economically and socially in large part because their family structure was deteriorating."[9] More specifically, at that time, one-quarter of black children were born outside marriage. The results of these nonmarital births and fatherless childrearing were predicted to be catastrophic. Although Moynihan's report caused an outpouring of rebuttal and even invective, the decades since the report have revealed with great clarity the perspicacity of Moynihan's vision.[10] Today one-third of all American children are born outside marriage, and the ratio for black children has reached the remarkable level of 69 percent.[11]

Charles Murray wrote a similar report in the *Wall Street Journal* in 1993 about the crisis in nonmarital births among whites. Unlike the 1965 Moynihan report, the Murray report was greeted by widespread acceptance and increased concern.[12]

It is worth remembering the melodrama from the secularists that accompanied the welfare reform package debate. Until 1996, welfare payments were distributed through a program known as Aid to Families with Dependent Children (AFDC). The federal plan was criticized because it bred a poor work ethic in recipients, encouraged out-of-wedlock births, and discouraged marriage and family values.

Attempts to change the status quo were met with cries from secular-progressive defenders that the proposed reforms were "anti-child," "mean-spirited," and would send "children begging for money." Senator Ted Kennedy called it "legislative child abuse," and Congressman John Lewis, a civil rights hero from Georgia, said the GOP was the grim reaper "coming for the poor, coming for the sick, the elderly, the disabled." Para-government groups, like the Children's Defense Fund, called the bill "national child abandonment."

Why the outcry? In retrospect it is clear that the new policy changed the underlying values of welfare from secular to traditional. The reformers declared that government programs should discourage illegitimacy and support incentives to get the unemployed working. The new policy chose to declare marriage and work "good," and out-of-wedlock births as "bad." The old welfare policies had become the "root cause" of many societal problems because they had created disincentives to work and to accept family responsibilities. However, as caseloads declined after the welfare program was reformed, states began to use part of their federal money that was no longer needed for welfare benefits to encourage work and marriage.

Most of the decline in America's culture can be traced to "root causes" related to out-of-wedlock sex, the devaluing and breakup of marriage, and government-sponsored programs such as pornography and gambling. For decades, government policies contributed to America's cultural decline while the government continued to spend billions fighting the problems caused by these very policies. Politicians decried poverty, crime, and social ills as they subsidized and supported the real policies at the root of cultural problems. As Patrick Fagan of the Heritage Foundation, one of the nation's foremost researchers and authors about marriage and its effects on our society, writes:

Although America has invested $8.4 trillion in social programs since the War on Poverty began in the 1960s, welfare dependency, juvenile crime, child abuse, school underachievement, drug abuse, suicide among children, and many other problems have increased. At the same time, federal and state governments still spend about $150 billion each year subsidizing single-parent families. This stands in stark contrast to the approximately $150 million they spend each year in an effort to reduce out-of-wedlock births and divorce—the two principal causes of single-parent families America. In other words, for every $1,000 that government spends providing services to broken families, it spends $1 trying to stop family breakdown.[13]

Welfare reform has not been a cure for all problems associated with poverty, but it was a necessary step in the right direction. Fagan continues, "Increasingly, liberal and conservative policy analysts agree that divorce and out-of-wedlock births have long-lasting detrimental effects on women, children and society; but evidence is growing in the private sector that government can help to reduce this pattern. . . . [I]t should be possible to reduce the divorce rate by as much as one-third to one-half in a few short years."[14]

While reform only partially addressed many of the problems cause by the welfare program, it did reduce dependency on government by encouraging employment, and allowed states to use some of their welfare funds to create programs that strengthen marriage and reduce divorce among the poor. Welfare reform demonstrated how one new law could effect change throughout the culture. The major change wrought by the 1996 Welfare Reform Law was not just in the thinking of politicians and administrators, new policies encouraged greater public participation in activities that improved our culture.

Ending welfare dependency has not turned poor mothers and fathers into child-centered soccer parents. But reform did send a clear message: children should be born to married parents who take responsibility for them. It also had a clear hope that changing the rules of welfare would lead to a revival of wedlock. Neither of these ideals has yet to be realized in practice. The picture seems to be that low-income single mothers now work jobs instead of receive welfare, but fathers are still absent, and children still underachieve. Welfare is only one part of the cultural puzzle, but it has given a decided edge toward marriage.

The welfare example is a good demonstration of how the culture development cycle works, and how it can be changed. Government welfare initially became the catalyst for dramatic increases in unwed births with considerable costs and consequences to society. Some early welfare policies began in the 1940s under President Francis Delano Roosevelt's New Deal. In the early 1960s, President Lyndon Johnson formalized and expanded government incentives for unwed births. Government effectively made illegitimacy a right, and critics like Senator Moynihan found themselves standing against strong currents in the liberal media and university culture. As the voices of reason were silenced, the problem magnified:

During the period 1950–1960, the (illegitimacy) ratio increased 36 percent; from 1960–1970, it increased 102 percent; from 1970–1980, it increased 72 percent; from 1980–1990, it increased 52 percent; and from 1990–2002, it increased 21 percent. Thus, the time of greatest increase in the illegitimacy ratio was the period 1960–80.[15]

As welfare programs expanded and costs grew exponentially, so did public concern. When the secondhand consequences became undeniable, the explicit voices of reason from taxpayers soon began to overpower the inertia of government endorsement of illegitimacy. The slowing of the rate of increase of illegitimacy in the decade before welfare reform is indicative of how the consensus opinion of the American people could reduce destructive behavior and force political change.

Public consensus eventually changed how people voted, and subsequently changed government policies. Republicans overthrew decades of Democratic control of the Congress in 1994 in part by riding the growing wave of public backlash against secular welfare policies and societal decline. By 1996, after overcoming two vetoes from President Clinton, "we the people" finally began to change the direction of our culture.

The policies included in the welfare reform package were important, but not as important as the messages that the reform sent through the nation. After years of government endorsement for out-of-wedlock sex, illegitimacy, and divorce: the expressed goals of the 1996 welfare reform legislation provided explicit government support for marriage and the formation of two-parent families, while officially disapproving of out-of-wedlock pregnancies.[16] As documented by the U.S. Department of Health and Human Services:

> Prior to TANF (welfare reform), disincentives to marriage were inherent to existing welfare rules. . . . When Congress enacted PRWORA (Personal Responsibility and Work Opportunity Reconciliation Act) and established the TANF (Temporary Assistance for Needy Families) program, States were given the authority to provide marriage support services as an acknowledgement that two-parent households are the most effective environment for raising children.

The new program provided funding, and more importantly, "permission" (freedom of speech) to use the media and schools to promote these goals.[17]

The specific goals and program recommendations in the law made it difficult for the ACLU, Planned Parenthood, NARL, NOW, and other para-government organizations to threaten, intimidate, and sue schools and governments when they promoted marriage and discouraged unwed births. Before these goals were explicitly spelled out in the law, critics would have charged that they violated the separation of church and state. In addition, welfare reform funding for media campaigns created opportunities to send positive messages through a media that had been historically hostile toward marriage and traditional values. While most states were initially slow to respond (in part because of fear of lawsuits and bureaucratic inertia), a number of states and communities have subsequently initiated programs to meet the goals of welfare reform.

For example, since its enactment in 1996, the Welfare Reform law led to $10 million being allocated to the Oklahoma Marriage Initiative for marriage and relationship training. In this program, participants can access training in high schools, universities, military bases, churches, and many other places.[18] Oklahoma's goal is to reduce divorce by one-third by 2010. In the same way, Louisiana authorized the State Health Marriage and Strengthening Families Initiative. The curriculum is designed to be administered by faith-based, community, or other organizations located within low-income communities. The state of Virginia has taken another innovative approach, incorporating a healthy marriage component into an already existing program that provides services for at-risk youth. Virginia's Right Choices for Youth, Mentoring and Fatherhood Program focuses on strengthening parent-child communications, promoting responsible fatherhood, and developing parenting skills.

In Colorado, the Strengthening Families Initiative helps communities throughout the State connect with resources, information, and services to strengthen and empower families. The initiative includes Colorado's Healthy Marriage Program which is supported by over forty agencies statewide, including local and faith-based organizations. In January 2004, eleven California counties in the San Francisco area joined the national movement by convening a Healthy Marriage Forum. The forum began the planning to integrate healthy marriage efforts into local services.

Florida became the first state to make learning marriage skills a part of the high school curriculum. Students who take the course get a 50 percent reduction in the cost of their marriage license fee. In one county, 32 percent of couples were now taking premarriage courses, mainly within their churches. However, Florida's high school initiative has not had widespread adoption because of the difficulty in changing public school curriculum.

Governor Mike Huckabee of Arkansas hopes to reduce the divorce rate by 50 percent by 2010. His strategy is to offer a $100 tax credit for couples who take premarriage courses that will be offered primarily through churches since pastors officiate 75 percent of weddings. Governor Jane Dee Hull of Arizona has authorized $1 million of TANF funds to develop community-based marriage skills courses, and Arizona is also one of several states to create Covenant Marriages (voluntary lifetime legal commitments with tough rules for divorce). Other states with marriage initiatives include Utah and Wisconsin, with additional states adding programs each year.

These programs are examples of American federalism at its best. The policies limit the national government by allowing states to experiment with real-world solutions. These state programs serve as laboratories of democracy, where experiments are tried and proven in real-world tests. If successful, the local programs are copied by others states, and eventually they influence the policies and procedures of the national government.

The spirit of the federal welfare law is beginning to work its way down to new state laws, which are fostering private sector activity that supports federal and state goals—another example of how federal law guides the culture cycle. "Communities that have established Marriage Savers congregations and Community Marriage Covenants are demonstrating the most success in decreasing divorce. The strategy: Help churches train mentors for engaged couples who can help them prepare for a life-long marriage commitment and help counsel marriages in trouble. Congregations with such mentors have helped up to 90 percent of troubled married couples who have come forward."[19]

This approach to public policy is rooted in something classically American: local religious values as a wellspring of culture. "As religion was rooted in human nature . . . so the church was in human society . . . [it] was one of the institutions that reflected 'the rational and natural ties that connect the human understanding and affections to the divine' helping to sustain 'that wonderful structure, Man.'"[20] In colonial America, faith was the wellspring of democracy and law.

Marriage Savers was started a decade before welfare reform in 1986. It is a full-service program for churches that includes activities like lessons in finances and child-rearing, as well as mentoring for stepfamilies and a program to strengthen existing marriages. In some cases, the results were dramatic, with 70 percent of separated couples reconciling and troubled marriages being restored.[21] Only a few pastors and congregations have implemented all of the activities in the program, but informal data indicates that even small efforts can significantly improve the success of marriages. Such faith-based efforts are far better than secular programs.

Over 135 cities have signed Community Marriage Covenants to motivate Marriage Saver congregations and civic leaders to rally communities behind efforts to strengthen marriage. This is a good example of how individual citizens and communities can stand up and shape the cultural values. Many cities with Community Marriage Covenants report reductions of up to 47 percent in their divorce rates. "For example, a covenant was signed by ninety-five pastors in Modesto, California, in 1986. Since then, the divorce rate has plunged 47.6 percent, while marriages have climbed 9.8 percent. In some cities, the divorce rates have declined twenty times faster than the national rate of 1.3 percent rate."[22]

One of the clearest examples of the effectiveness of community-based programs can be seen in the contrast between Kansas City, Kansas, which had a Marriage Saver program, and Kansas City, Missouri, across the river, which did not. While the Kansas side of the city only had forty pastors participating, it did have considerable media support from *The Kansas Star*, which published a number of stories about the initiative.

The number of divorces on the Kansas side plunged 32.5 percent in just two years, while the number of divorces actually increased during the same period on the Missouri side of the city. "The difference: . . . one state developed a visibly pro-marriage climate; the other plodded along without changing attitudes or expectations."[23] Kansas City, Kansas, used new laws as a catalyst to enlist the support of churches, the media, and the community as a whole. Their efforts made small changes in their communities, which changed attitudes and behaviors.

The key to the successes listed above: a change in law (1996 Welfare Reform Law) that restored and legitimized some aspects of traditional values in the public policy debate. This in turn restored the freedom of speech of traditionalists in schools, communities, and in the media, who were given some legitimacy to say that traditional marriage was "right" and unwed births were "wrong." Secularists have continued to fight the principles of welfare reform. Unfortunately, subsequent court rulings in some states favoring same-sex marriage have again made people reticent to promote traditional marriage, but some cultural progress has been made because the government through welfare reform reduced its support for a failed secular policy.

America can solve many of its most serious problems if it is willing to acknowledge commonsense, cause-and-effect relationships that drive human behavior. Government can assist those whose problems are out of their control without creating one-size-fits-all blanket protections for destructive behaviors. Unfortunately, the resistance to this commonsense approach of restoring cultural values will be intense. Many will be unwilling to admit that destructive, politically protected behaviors are the primary causes of America's problems. Few will be willing to publicly consider that some behaviors might actually be "wrong" because they hurt individuals and society. A recent article in the *Washington Post* provides an example of this resistance, as well as another contrast between secular and traditional approaches to solving problems.

The *Post* article reported a controversy over a government-sponsored conference on the prevention of sexually transmitted diseases. The conference was titled, "2006 National STD Prevention Conference, Beyond the Hidden Epidemic: Evolution or Revolution?" One of the sessions was called "Are Abstinence-Only-Until-Marriage Programs a Threat to Public Health?" When one member of Congress noticed that none of the panelists were supporters of abstinence-until-marriage education programs, he complained to the main organizer (Centers for Disease Control), and one of the panelists was changed. The title of the "abstinence" session was also changed to, "Public Health Strategies of Abstinence Programs for Youth." Not surprisingly, the government-funded participants on the conference panel were incensed.

"Bruce Trigg of the New Mexico Department of Public Health, the original organizer, condemned the decision as political meddling in the scientific process. . . . 'It is unprecedented that this type of interference takes place at a scientific meeting. . . . [Their] claim is this is about a public health program when it's really about ideology and religion.'"[24] The scientific community has learned to play the "religion" card whenever they want to discredit their critics, and there are plenty of government agencies willing to support the old welfare-subsidized-pregnancy ethic.

"William Smith of the Sexuality Information and Education Council of the United States, who was bumped from the panel for his abstinence until marriage views, said 'It was shocking to me. What does this say about the ability of politicians to influence what is going on in public health.'"[25] Smith's statement reveals much about the health profession elites; he does not believe that elected representatives of the people have any right to be involved in public health! He publicly expresses disdain for duly elected representatives of the people having a say in government-sponsored programs that they fund. Jonathan Zenilman, president of the American Sexually Transmitted Diseases Association, said he was "surprised and astounded. . . . This is the first time I've seen the process of peer review subverted by pure politics."[26]

An objective assessment of the views of these self-described "experts" reveals serious flaws in their thinking, and consequently, their ability to help solve the problem they claim to be addressing. First, there is an obvious unwillingness of these conference participants to recognize the "root cause" of sexually transmitted diseases: sex outside of marriage. If sexually transmitted diseases are a real problem, and previous chapters have documented that STDs are a serious and costly problem nationally, we must first address the "root cause" of the problem. It is patently absurd to claim that you want to reduce STDs without having as your primary goal the reduction of sex outside of marriage. It is also poor science to attempt to solve a social problem without attempting to understand how to minimize the behavior that is known to cause the problem.

Digging even deeper for "root causes," the question must be asked: "Why has sex outside marriage increased dramatically over the past four decades?" This book has suggested that the answer—and the real cause behind the dramatic increase in STDs and many other social maladies—is the government welfare program that encouraged premarital sex and unwed births, court decisions that separated religion-based moral restraints from our culture, and para-government intimidation that represses the voices of reason. The obvious conclusion is simple: the primary causes of the increase in STDs are government rulings and policies. Therefore, if we want to reduce STDs we must begin by correcting the government policies that caused the problem.

Apparently, the scientists being paid by taxpayers to solve this problem are more interested in continuing the funding of present programs than turning up any solutions. Their answer is to encourage people to have more sex outside of marriage by making them believe they can eliminate the risks of pregnancy, disease, and heartbreak. It should be noted that this national conference about STD prevention intentionally excluded any participation by those holding traditional views until one congressman challenged the sponsors. There was no free speech for those holding traditional views. The inclusion of *one* panelist with traditional views elicited outrage among "scientists" and the media, even though the secular policies advocated by the conference participants have consistently failed to accomplish their stated goals.

The safe-sex advocates are part of the problem, not the solution. It is time to change our thinking about these social issues. The secular presuppositions of these so-called scientists and educators are fatally flawed, and it is a mistake to believe that the same kind of thinking that caused our problems can now solve them. We must refute attempts to intimidate those who know better, and restore some balanced thinking to the culture cycle. An improved quality of life for future generations in America demands that we adopt some of the quality improvement methods of businesses that were outlined earlier.

Traditionalists approach the problem of sexual promiscuity, STDs, and unwed births differently. Supporting abstinence before marriage is a proven way to stress the importance of marriage while reducing unwed births and sexually transmitted diseases. Robert Rector of the Heritage Foundation provided a comprehensive analysis of the success of abstinence programs in his 2002 article entitled, "The Effectiveness of Abstinence Education Programs in Reducing Sexual Activity among Youth."[27] Rector answers critics with overwhelming scientific evidence that abstinence programs work. He writes, "Critics of abstinence education often assert that while abstinence education that exclusively promotes abstaining from premarital sex is a good idea in theory, there is no evidence that such education can actually reduce sexual activity among young people. Such criticism is erroneous. There are currently ten scientific evaluations that demonstrate the effectiveness of abstinence programs in altering sexual behavior."

Abstinence programs reported by Rector included Virginity Pledge Programs, which found that "sexual activity among students who had taken a formal pledge of virginity was one-fourth the level of that of their counterparts who had not taken a pledge." Another program named "Not Me, Not Now" reduced sexual activity among fifteen-year-olds across one county in New York from 46.6 percent to 31.6 percent during the intervention period. The pregnancy rate for girls aged fifteen through seventeen also dropped from 63.4 pregnancies per 1,000 girls to 49.5, significantly better than the state as a whole. Operation "Keepsake" in Cleveland, Ohio, reduced the rate of onset of sexual activity (loss of virginity) for twelve- and thirteen-year-old minorities by roughly two-thirds relative to comparable students in schools that did not participate in the program.

"A 2001 evaluation of the effectiveness of the virginity pledge movement using data from the National Longitudinal Study of Adolescent Health finds that virginity pledge programs are highly effective in helping adolescents to delay sexual activity." This study of more than 5,000 students concludes that taking a virginity pledge "reduces by one-third the probability that an adolescent will begin sexual activity compared with other adolescents. . . . When the virginity pledge is combined with strong parental disapproval of sexual activity, the probability of initiation of sexual activity is reduced by 75 percent or more."[28] A larger study of 7,000 students in Utah showed similar results, while a nonabstinence program that offered nondirective or value-free instruction in sex education and decision making, was found to have no impact on sexual behavior.

The evidence is substantial that abstinence programs can improve lives and, at the same time, save taxpayers billions. Although these limited programs are still operating in a hostile environment, even small efforts and expenditures have shown positive results. But the secularists are unwavering. In 2005, the Hollywood comedy *The 40-Year-Old Virgin* poked fun at a man who repeatedly had to explain why he had not had premarital sex. Our culture demeans virginity. The media is hostile to abstinence. The government continues to fund organizations like Planned Parenthood that work tirelessly to promote promiscuous sex, homosexuality, and abortion. The following statement about abstinence-only sex education is taken from the Planned Parenthood website:

> Abstinence-only education is one of the religious right's greatest challenges to the nation's sexual health. But it is only one tactic in a broader, longer-term strategy. Since the early 1980s, the "family values" movement has won the collaboration of governments and public institutions, from Congress to local school boards, in abridging students' constitutional rights. Schools now block student access to sexual health information in class, at the school library, and through the public library's Internet portals. They violate students' free speech rights by censoring student publications of articles referring to sexuality. Abstinence-only programs often promote alarmist misinformation about sexual health and force-feed students' religious ideology that condemns homosexuality, masturbation, abortion, and contraception. In doing so, they endanger students' sexual health.[29]

As a para-government organization, Planned Parenthood is essentially the official voice of government. It should be known that when this organization refers to libraries blocking sexual health information, they are complaining about Internet filters for pornography. When they refer to promoting "alarmist misinformation about sexual health," they are complaining about telling students the truth about the dangers of STDs. When they refer to "free speech" they mean the privilege to stop any view but their own. They also consider abstinence a religious philosophy, and therefore believe it has no place in public health. They use taxpayer money to oppose and mock virginity and chastity. Taxpayer funding of Planned Parenthood should be withdrawn because they actively promote antireligious, destructive secular policies.

This conflict is intense, and the outcome crucial. It is possible to forecast a coming American Dark Age if court rulings and bureaucratic mandates continue to make the government the primary instigator of costly and destructive societal values. Thankfully, there is an alternative: restore the freedom of speech of those holding traditional values. Give Americans the right to say that destructive behavior is "wrong." Let them say it in schools, community centers, churches, and universities without having to face the intimidation of school officials and ACLU lawyers. The critics are wrong: this is not a call for a theocracy. It is an objective and outcome-based pragmatism that can have the effect of regenerating the American culture at its roots. This movement can reverse the damage that poor governmental policies and misguided court rulings have foisted on the culture.

Opponents try to frighten Americans by declaring that this commonsense government encouragement of constructive behavior is simply a cover for religiously inspired conservatives who "want to impose their morality on others." However, it should be remembered that all actors in the political arena want to "impose" some view of the world on others, and as we have shown, government has been co-opted by antireligious zealots to impose destructive and costly secular policies on our culture. Our goal is not to use government to promote religion, but to encourage government to stop trying to shape the beliefs of Americans and start using policies that promote the "general welfare" of all citizens.

Edmund Burke was a British philosopher who contended that society was organic and flourished in times when government was restrained. "The nature of man is intricate; the objects of society are of the greatest possible complexity; and therefore no simple disposition or direction of power can be suitable either to man's nature, or to the quality of his affairs."[30] In other words, government does the most good when it allows community organizations like churches, schools, volunteer groups, and neighborhood associations to flourish. Americans will solve their problems as long as they don't have to whisper.

We have shown that even small increases in the number of young people waiting until marriage to have sex, as well as support for keeping marriages together, would cause significant reductions in unwed births, poverty, crime, child abuse, sexually transmitted diseases, pornography, and other costly social ills. We have also shown that these and other changes could save our nation hundreds of billions of dollars. The evidence is clear that we can achieve these changes more effectively and less expensively if we attack the causes, rather than continuing to spend billions on the symptoms. We now know that government is the major culprit in many of these problems.

GOVERNMENT'S CONTINUING ROLE
IN SHAPING AMERICA'S CULTURE

Today, the practice of religion and faith in politics is treated more like a private belief than a public worldview. There is some rhetoric of religion in the public square, in what is known as "civil religion," a label given to the practice by Robert Bellah.[31] It means that Americans expect leaders to utter vague platitudes that affirm the religious base of the nation and reinforce its preeminent position in the world. "God Bless America," has become the last line in many politicians' speeches. The platitudes of America's civil religion are accepted, but they are devoid of theology and do not affirm a distinction between right and wrong.

Two major initiatives by government in the 1960s and 1970s began seismic shifts in the culture by changing how decisions about right and wrong were made. First, the government (primarily through the courts) shifted its focus from promoting the general welfare to protecting individual rights—specifically an individual's rights to destructive behavior. For example, the *Roe v. Wade* decision affirmed the right of privacy and awarded a license to a host of activities once unthinkable. Courts also redefined the First Amendment to make pornography a right. What was right for the individual now trumped what was good for society. Second, the government (again, primarily through the courts) changed the historical coexistence of government and religion by formally declaring that religion must be separate from any government-sponsored activity. This meant that many "wrongs" that were prohibited by both religion and law, became "rights" trumpeted by para-government groups and the courts.

These fundamental changes are seen in the 1963 Supreme Court decision of *Murray v. Curlett*. The court ignored centuries of positive societal outcomes from the nominal integration of religious training in the public schools, and ruled in favor of the rights of one atheist who was offended by the practice. Prayers and religious activity were effectively banned from America's public schools. All of the positive and well-known benefits associated with a societal respect for religious principles, including respect for teachers and others, were thrown out in favor of one person holding antireligious beliefs.

At the time, the ruling seemed innocuous, with defenders offering reassurances that children could still pray whenever they wished and read the Bible on their own free time. Who could foresee that years later, teachers would be forbidden to wear crosses in front of their classes, chorus teachers could not have sacred music at school, and children would be threatened with expulsion for praying at mealtime. Today, students must abandon their religious beliefs as a prerequisite to receive an education, and no connection is made between the tasks of faith and learning.

The pattern of government intervention has continued. What began as a few precedents regarding prayer at public events grew into endless court cases ordering the removal of the Ten Commandments from public buildings and the expulsion of groups saying "Merry Christmas" during town Christmas parades. The nation founded as a bastion of religious liberty, where people of diverse faiths could worship without worry or persecution, has now evolved into a place where religious practitioners must act like they have no convictions.

The awkward truth is that millions of Americans rely on their religious traditions for moral knowledge that guides their lives, including their political lives. They do not like being told to be quiet, and they fear the consequences of a secular state. In one of the best studies on the rise of the Nazi ideology in Germany, author Fritz Stern found that, "Protestantism has been turned into a respectable shell for secularism," and that "people belonged to churches for the same reason they buy insurance before boarding an excursion train: through orthodoxy they try to buy themselves protection."[32] Americans fear politics divorced from religious principle, and they want churches to be a moral force in the political world.

The attacks against positive behavior such as marriage, traditional values, and religious standards have angered millions of Americans. They are astonished that many values they took for granted are now the target of the secular culture. The media, as documented in Bill O'Reilly's 2006 book *Culture Warrior*, increasingly attack almost anyone who does not espouse secular and progressive thought.[33]

> U.S. journalism is essentially in the grip of a pack mentality . . . when one in five media warriors does not believe in the existence of a supreme being, its not hard to figure out why many press people support secular causes like unrestricted abortion, gay marriage, and restraints on public displays of faith.[34]

The present day reluctance to acknowledge the religious, and specifically the Christian, basis of politics is puzzling given the past events of American history. The civil rights movement, to again take a familiar example, was replete with Christian preaching and deep theological arguments. Today, black Americans have a high confidence in organized religion and are more likely to treat the Bible as literal truth.[35] The only member of the clergy whose life is celebrated as a national holiday is Martin Luther King Jr., and his religious calling was central to his political crusade. Political dialogue, which once welcomed explicit religious witness, now views with suspicion people who talk about God in public.

Occasionally there are lapses in the political rules. Always there is the chance when dealing with religion that someone will not get the word and say something inappropriate. A prominent example was when Nobel Laureate Mother Teresa appeared at the 1994 National Prayer Breakfast. At the time, the Catholic nun had achieved worldwide recognition for her work among the destitute and dying in India. Here is an excerpt from her address:

> I feel that the greatest destroyer of peace today is abortion. . . . Please don't kill the child. . . . I want the child. Please give me the child. I am willing to accept any child who would be aborted, and to give that child to a married couple who will love the child and be loved by the child.[36]

The speech was made before Bill Clinton, a pro-choice president who vetoed a bill to end partial-birth abortion. These were strong words from a person who embodied all that was best in any public avowal of religious purpose. Yet they were quickly forgotten, and their implications were ignored by the secular press who found them embarrassing and inconvenient.

Today in America, similar suggestions that any behavior or public policy may be wrong are met with accusations of hate, intolerance, and discrimination. Few people are willing to stand up against the government, the media, and the entirety of the culture to say that something is wrong. With fewer willing to speak out against what they believe is wrong, most societal restraints against destructive behavior have disappeared. Americans no longer have the opportunity to grow up and live in a positive environment that is supportive of traditional moral values. Instead, they remain quiet. Parents who try to protect their children from destructive and negative influences have little chance of success.

"The legal culture that guards the public square," writes Stephen L. Carter in his book, *The Culture of Unbelief*, "still seems most comfortable thinking of religion as a hobby, something done in privacy, something that mature, public-spirited adults do not use as a basis for politics."[37] It is becoming abundantly clear that a public square without moral underpinnings only hastens cultural disintegration. Officials seem unwilling to accept the obvious fact that all behaviors and relationships do not have the same value to society.

Some activities, including personal and commercial relationships, create positive benefits to our nation, while others have costly negative effects. This is not a moral or religious judgment; it is simply a statement of objective fact.

Instead of genuine tolerance and civility, the changes in public life have only served to drive people into mutually hostile camps. Go to a public debate on a contentious political issue and you will see pseudo-civility and an intolerant tolerance at work. In the 2004 presidential election, there were both "Bush-haters" and "Kerrry-haters." Both were intense, and neither had any interest in listening to the views of the other. What is paraded today as tolerance and marches under the banner of pluralism is a new intolerance. This corruption of social civility is a result of three factors:

1. relativism in regard to truth, which results in a constantly shifting foundation for law;
2. a libertarianism "anything goes" ethic in regard to lifestyle; and
3. secularism in regard to social consensus.

"The result is a form of easygoing tolerance that starts out with inadequate respect for truth and people, and ends with no room for challenges of any kind."[38]

In its deepest sense, civility means respect for, and listening to, others. "Listening" to others is what makes freedom of speech so important in a democracy. In the traditional American experience, civility came from a belief that all people were equal in the sense of being made in the image of God. The genius of the American religious culture, and its relationship to the political culture, was that it lacked arrogance and self-righteousness while infusing common values into the cultural mix. Dogmas that divided the church shrank in the public arena. Commonly held beliefs gave substance to the cultural whole. The dismissal of Judeo-Christian thought meant an end to cultural solidarity, and an end of political civility. A 2003 Pew Research Center poll showed a nation "profoundly polarized between two political camps that are virtually identical in size but inimical in their beliefs on virtually all major questions."[39]

Truth is what frees. An open society is one where personal responsibility trumps societal obligation. The progressive weakening of liberty in the United States is a result of false philosophies that have weakened public discourse. Here's a recent quote from *Time* magazine columnist Joe Klein on the condition of civil discourse in America.

> But the smart stuff is being drowned out by a fierce, bullying, often witless tone of intolerance that has overtaken the left-wing sector of the blogosphere. Any-

one who doesn't move in lockstep with the most extreme voices is savaged and ridiculed—especially people like me who often agree with the liberal position but sometimes disagree and are therefore traitorously unreliable![39]

The present crisis and division portends a loss of civility based on a loss of commonly held values. The question then becomes: "should government encourage or restrain some behaviors that have been shown to be harmful to individuals in society?" The mere fact that people exhibit strong desires to behave in certain ways does not make that behavior right. A primary role of a civilized culture is to restrain harmful behavior and encourage behavior that strengthens the culture. For what is "natural" about a man and woman committing their lives to each other, sacrificing personal pleasures to raise children, and being faithful to one sexual partner for their entire lives? Society must create a strong support system for marriage to work. Conversely, society must also create a strong system to restrain natural desires that bring harm to our culture. This is not discrimination, it is good public policy.

American civility requires that tolerance and compassion be extended to people who believe that destructive behaviors are wrong. We should set the record straight: allowing the natural desires and weaknesses of our fellow citizens to shape the predominant values of our culture is not compassionate; encouraging unencumbered people to ruin their own lives, and destroy the lives of many others in the name of personal expression is not compassionate; and whispering when we know what is right and wrong is not tolerance—it's cowardice!

The question remains for the nation, "what role should government play in encouraging constructive behavior or discouraging destructive behavior that diminishes our culture and creates costly secondhand consequences for others?" A rational perspective would include Juran's and Deming's management ideals mentioned in earlier chapters, that assume the primary goal of leadership in every organization is to continuously improve the quality of outcomes by continuously improving the processes and inputs used to produce the final product. Rationality, however, has proven more of a slogan than a philosophy for the secularists who seek to guide America's public policy; as have their claims of compassion and tolerance. With secularists exposed, traditionalists should be emboldened to stand up and speak out against behaviors and policies that are destroying our culture.

Overcoming our Self-Imposed Silence, Regaining Our Voices, and Winning the Culture War

The jaws of power are always open to devour, and her arm is always stretched out, if possible, to destroy the freedom of thinking, speaking and writing.

—John Adams

"These are America's best days," writes David Frum, "and yet . . . [we] *aren't* satisfied."[1] In all but five of the past thirty-five years since 1965, a majority—often an overwhelming majority—of the American public has told pollsters that the country is on the "wrong track." With great success comes great responsibility. America has achieved unprecedented success, and as a result its citizens are heirs of a burdensome duty to leave the country and the world better than we found them. This responsibility rests squarely on the shoulders of the American people, not on the government. To solve the serious problems that threaten, Americans must first be reminded that the success of our social, economic, military, and political systems have always been dependent on traditional values and beliefs. Many of today's problems can be traced directly to the separation of these values from public life. The result has been a measurable and growing trend of cultural deterioration.

The good news is that what government has helped to break, it can also help to fix. The word "democracy," comes from the Greeks, and is a combination of two words: "demos," for people; and "cracy" for rule. In the end, America is ruled by the people, and when they speak in unison, there is no problem that cannot be fixed. Our conviction is that the most important task confronting Americans is a moral task. The job is to reclaim politics as a profession of ethical ideals. The notion that government can be neutral in this cultural dispute about social values is preposterous. Government, by its very nature, is a moral enterprise. "The aim of government is justice," writes George Will, "which is more apt to come about if government is more aware of, and forthright about, the fact that statecraft is soulcraft."[2]

Reversing government rulings that restrict and intimidate the voices of principled Americans will require that traditionalists proactively speak out with conviction, courage, and clarity. It was Plato who declared that "the price of apathy in public affairs is to be ruled by evil men." Constructive societal restraints and incentives are dependent on the unified voices of traditional values and beliefs. Given the critical importance of speaking out; why do we whisper? We whisper because:

- When government makes a destructive behavior "legal" (such as premarital sex and unwed births, homosexuality and same-sex marriage, pornography, and gambling) it implicitly makes that behavior "right."
- When government makes a behavior "right" and enforces that "right" across all areas of the public and private sectors, it becomes extremely difficult for individuals to say that the behavior is "wrong."
- When government makes a behavior "right," para-government groups and the media amplify the government edict, drowning out the voices of those who believe the behavior is "wrong."
- When government says that a behavior is "right," Americans no longer have the right to say it is "wrong."
- Those who believe that government-endorsed behavior is "wrong" must stand against the government (including courts, federal agencies, and public schools); para-government groups (including the ACLU and universities); and the media.
- When those who believe that destructive behaviors are "wrong" stop speaking out against those behaviors, societal opposition against destructive behavior is eliminated.
- When government says that constructive behaviors are "illegal" or "optional" (such as prayer, Bible study, personal responsibility, and traditional marriage), it removes societal endorsement of the behavior and implicitly says that the behavior is "wrong."
- When government says that constructive behaviors are "wrong," traditional values are excluded from public policy debates.
- When government adopts a secular ethic and then enforces a secular "right" and "wrong" throughout the culture development cycle, traditional views are stigmatized and traditionalists lose their freedom of speech.
- Principled Americans are now forced to whisper or else feel the heat of a government-imposed secular worldview.

Some may argue that government does not muzzle the freedom of speech of traditionalists, but there is too much evidence to the contrary. The Massachusetts public school example from chapter 6 provides just one of many recent examples. After a Massachusetts court declared same-sex marriages legal, public schools surmised that if it was legal, they should teach it; even to kindergarteners. When parents complained, they found that they did not have the right to say that teaching homosexuality and same-sex marriage was wrong. The government determined that this behavior was "right" and government agencies, including public schools, were going to enforce that it was "right." Traditional beliefs and arguments about homosexuality were silenced and treated as if they were "wrong."

Reversing the deterioration of America's culture is possible because the culture development cycle can work for good just as easily as it can work for bad. We think of it much like the circulatory system in the human body. A healthy culture, like a healthy body, constantly cycles in the "good" blood and cycles out the "bad" blood. Traditional values in the culture development cycle work like natural antibodies in the blood system. When traditional values are allowed to operate freely in society, they provide immunity against destructive agents that can infect the entire system. Unfortunately, government-endorsed secular values have weakened America's immune system, leaving our culture less resistant to destructive behaviors. America is sick, but not incurable.

Like an intravenous drip in a patient's arm, the government can "drip" decisions into society's bloodstream that strengthen or weaken our culture. Since the 1960s, governments at all levels in America have systematically killed off the traditional "antibodies" in the culture that had stabilized it for generations. Voluntary private-sector checks and balances have been weakened or overwhelmed by government-sponsored secular influences in the culture. But "we the people" can change what the government puts in the IV "drip."

At some point, and we believe *this* is the moment, Americans have to decide whether the desire to be coddled by government is greater than the desire to be free. It has now been nearly half a century since the explosion of government power and the accompanying shift in cultural values have placed the nation on a slippery slope. The consequences are everywhere apparent and devastating to view. The nation must know that only by finding their feet, mustering their courage, and raising their voices can they turn back the inroads the moral relativists have made in the culture.

The reconstituted American IV "drip" is freedom of speech. Restoring free speech for those who hold traditional values will do more to improve

America's culture than any other action. If government stops imposing secular beliefs on society, and restores the rights of traditionalists to freely advocate and live out traditional views in public and private settings, the culture development cycle will begin working to establish higher, healthier standards. The high standard of America's culture is dependent primarily on one key element of free speech: *the right to say that some things are "wrong."*

RECLAIMING OUR RIGHT TO SAY IT'S WRONG

Secularists like to say that they avoid making value judgments. But their "values-free" social science is often really only a justification for selfish passion tied to secular self-interest. At its founding, America was led by men concerned about the education of the individual through control of his passions. No more. Now secular intellectuals work to stifle any discussion of the noblest ends of life, replacing them with a credit card for indulgence.

As a result, government's exclusion of traditional values has virtually ended any public debate about what is "right" and "wrong." Finding a public school or university that teaches some behaviors are morally wrong will prove impossible unless the curriculum is rooted in some moral tradition. Yet the ability to discriminate between what is "good" and "bad" or "right" and "wrong" is foundational to any culture. People need behavioral boundaries established in what society values, including the consensus societal opinions about what is "right" and "wrong."

Despite government-imposed secular domination of our culture for several decades, Americans continue to hold strong moral beliefs. A 2006 Pew Research study found that:

- 88 percent of Americans believe it is morally wrong for married people to have an affair;
- 79 percent believe it is morally wrong not to report all income on tax returns;
- 61 percent believe it is morally wrong to drink alcohol excessively;
- 50 percent of all Americans believe homosexuality is morally wrong, with only 12 percent saying that it is morally acceptable (others don't believe it is a moral issue);
- 35 percent believe that sex between unmarried adults is morally wrong, with 22 percent saying that it is morally acceptable; and
- 35 percent believe gambling is morally wrong.[3]

Though often afraid to express them publicly, many Americans continue to value moral boundaries despite government and media efforts to purge traditional beliefs from the culture. The holding of traditional values would likely increase if the voices of traditionalists were not muted.

Moral boundaries are important, but morality is only one part of the cultural concept of "values." Behaviors must also be judged by the "value" they bring to society. This book has documented how traditional values not just preserve, but actually advance, the culture and save taxpayers billions along the way. Conversely, we have shown how secular values result in human suffering and astronomical costs to taxpayers. For these reasons, government must make value judgments about individual behavior and relationships. Government cannot act on behalf of the common good unless it is willing to make determinations about what is good and bad for the country as a whole. All legislation is moral legislation because it conditions the actions and thoughts of the nation at large. Government policies that proscribe, mandate, regulate, and subsidize guide behavior that will ultimately bolster or alter habits and values. Americans do not want their government to interfere with private behavior, but government must make value judgments about behavior that is either helpful or detrimental to society as a whole.

While government must make these value judgments, it should not make policy decisions based on particular moral or religious opinions. The more general question is: what decisions support our social, economic, and political systems, and which ones are detrimental. Government can only promote the "general welfare" by having a notion of human excellence and "the good." Constructive values and behaviors should be integral to court rulings and policy decisions. Government violates free speech and the establishment clause of the First Amendment when constructive values are excluded from public policy because of a religious heritage or a faith content. Government exclusion of traditional views means government is stifling the free speech of the majority of Americans and "establishing" secular views and beliefs.

The private sector has a different role from government in the cultural cycle. Responsible individuals and private organizations must make moral *and* value judgments. People must be free to say that some behaviors are wrong; either for moral and religious reasons, or because they are harmful to society. Americans must rediscover the power of the words "right" and "wrong." Telling a child that a behavior "may not be safe" will have a different result than saying that "it is wrong and you shouldn't do it." If traditional "speech" is allowed to operate freely in the culture, positive "antibodies" will restore the health of the culture. No government force is needed; only the restoration of freedom of speech.

Secularists will not easily relinquish their hard-won monopoly position as directors of public policy, or their role as cultural policemen. Secular paragovernment groups now control much of the culture cycle through government-sponsored antipathy toward traditional views in schools, businesses, and communities. Moral absolutes and value judgments are anathema to the secular worldview. While secularists join the chorus for character education, they also fight to disallow any inclusion of values or moral judgments; there can be no discrimination based on immoral behavior. Translation: Americans do not have the right to say that many destructive behaviors are morally wrong in schools, businesses, or any public setting.

Winning the war of worldviews requires a rational, businesslike, and non-specific, but nonetheless, moral approach.

PRACTICAL STEPS TO IMPROVING
AMERICA'S CULTURE DEVELOPMENT CYCLE

A mythical story is told about Max Weber, the famous German sociologist, who was visiting with friends near the end of his life. As he explained some of the chilling conclusions from his assessment of the modern world, someone asked, "If you're so sobered, why do you keep working?" Weber's famous reply was, "I go on to see how much I can stand." The bad news, which was recounted in previous chapters, is much like Weber's quip. Our own government has been the principal agent in the dismantling of our culture. But the good news is that what government has broken, it can also help to fix. Here are some practical steps to help improve the culture cycle once freedom of speech is again a daily option.

- Cultivate a willingness within society to say that some behaviors and activities are wrong—bad for individuals and the country. History provides ample evidence that parental, corporate, or societal *disapproval* will reduce undesirable behaviors. Positive and constructive behaviors must also be identified as "good" and "right" for our society. If America is unwilling to distinguish between constructive and destructive behavior, it is senseless to spend hundreds of billions of dollars trying to address social problems that will be ultimately insoluble.
- Federal and state governments, along with the private sector, must establish goals and make public commitments to solve cultural problems and improve outcomes—for example, tax incentives to encourage marriage and similar rewards if couples stay married. Currently, governments are spending billions to deal with the symptoms of problems, but there are few public goals to reduce the behaviors that cause the problems.
- Identify and address "root causes" first. It is senseless to continue to spend hundreds of billions of dollars as a nation on symptomatic problems (poverty, child abuse, drug use, juvenile delinquency, etc.) that are caused

by behaviors and activities that are actually encouraged by the government (out-of-wedlock births, the destruction of marriage, gambling, etc.).

- Federal and state governments, working closely with the private sector, must develop plans, strategies, and public/private partnerships to reduce destructive behavior, address causes, encourage constructive behavior, and improve outcomes.
- Results must be measurable, and quantitative measurements must be used to continuously improve policies and outcomes.

These steps should be guided by principles that reflect objective, moral philosophies, and criteria. The following principles are not necessarily inclusive, but are certainly worthy of consideration as Americans seek to reverse the decline in our culture.

Principle 1: Programs and policies must be based on readily identifiable standards that promote the common good, and not based on subjective opinions of some powerful interest group or legal wrangling. For example, traditionalists had argued for years that human dignity is tied to work and that government programs should encourage employment and family stability. While these arguments were supported by research, the position of traditionalists was criticized for years as lacking compassion until statistical data proved beyond any doubt that the welfare program was destructive to foundational social values. It was objective data, not opinion, that eventually led to reform.

Government can use social science responsibly to derive standards to promote the common good, but these objective standards should not be disqualified simply because they are consistent with traditional or religious principles. Beware: we will probably discover that monogamy is healthy, honoring parents wise, and lying wrong. All of these findings are consistent with the Ten Commandments, whether they are publicly displayed or not.

Principle 2: Programs and policies should be compassionate and not publicly judgmental toward individuals. The 1996 Welfare Reform Law did not demean single-parent households; it simply provided incentives for marriage and two-parent households. The intent of all cultural reforms must be to promote the public good, not to embarrass and demean individuals. Admittedly, it will be difficult to discourage destructive behavior without offending some individuals who practice the harmful behavior. However, if the government simply removes the incentives for destructive behavior, and allows the natural consequences of the behavior to accrue to the individual, there will be little need for individuals to be singled out.

Principle 3: Individual behavior must be connected with the consequences of that behavior, and the government should not act to insulate people from the natural consequences of their actions. For example, it is clear that out-of-wedlock sex has public, as well as private, consequences. This does not mean that society should abandon unwed mothers or those with STDs, but the government must remove the incentives for these and other destructive behaviors, and assure that individuals bear some of the costs of the results of their behavior.

Principle 4: The public must be protected from secondhand consequences of individual behavior. The government has a compelling interest in restricting private behavior that imposes costs and consequences on the public. In fact, public consequences should be one of the criteria that determine whether a behavior is private or public. It is convenient to say, "what people do in their bedrooms is their own business," but funding for unwed births and treatment for AIDS and STDs shows that we all bear the consequences and expense of these and other "private" behaviors.

Principle 5: Government-operated public schools and state-supported universities must teach and model behaviors that are consistent with federal and state policy goals. The public life of a person is officially endorsed by government (and implicitly by society) when an individual becomes a public school teacher or a public university professor. This means that teachers, like police officers and judges, are rightfully held to higher standards than people who work in other areas. We cannot have teachers—male or female—preying on children. America cannot develop constructive behavior patterns among citizens if public schools and universities do not support these behaviors. It is unreasonable to ask taxpayers to fund schools that teach and model behaviors that are destructive to society. America cannot continue teaching destructive values and behavior under the guise of academic freedom, especially when taxpayers are paying the teachers.

Principle 6: Churches and faith-based groups must have an equal right to participate in public activities and to compete for the opportunity to participate in government programs that serve the public. Many of the successes in improving the culture involve partnerships between government and churches or faith-based organizations. It is time to put an end to government-sponsored discrimination against religion and faith, and enlist the support of the faith community to improve the culture.

Principle 7: Citizens, as well as private businesses and organizations, must be guaranteed the freedom to set their own standards and to associate with individuals whose behavior is consistent with these standards. Discrimination against race, gender, religion, disability, or any intrinsic personal characteristic should not be tolerated, but Americans and private organizations must be permitted to discriminate—yes, discriminate—against behavior that is destructive. *All people are equal, but all behavior is not.* The elevation of destructive behavior to a civil right is a travesty that has been imposed on the American psyche for several decades. Americans must have the freedom *not* to accept or promote behavior they consider immoral or destructive, which is nothing more than "freedom of speech" and "freedom of association."

RECOMMENDATIONS FOR FUTURE ACTION

The American political system presupposes very little consensus among its citizens as to the common good, but it does presuppose a consensus on some core values. Majority rule requires an element of truth telling and honesty in public office. Once elected, officials take oaths and vows to guide their public behavior. The definition of a polity demands a comprehensive understanding of some things, and central to these beliefs is an ability to debate issues in the public square.

The most important action that principled Americans can take is to become more informed and engaged in the war of worldviews. The nation's transition to a secular society took place with most Americans being unaware that events were orchestrated by government and a select group of para-government groups who were changing the culture and diminishing our freedoms. Once Americans are fully engaged, there are several recommendations that will begin to reverse the decline of the culture and our nation. The following is not an inclusive list of possible action, but these recommendations should be considered as top priorities.

1. Major Reforms of America's Judicial System

As we have documented in this book, SLAPP lawsuits, used to intimidate and silence American citizens and organizations, must be brought to an end. The ACLU and other para-government organizations are using courts as a sledgehammer to self-fund lawsuits and forge a secular society that ignores the traditional wellsprings of religious faith as the source of character and values. The courts have become the most powerful factor influencing the culture cycle. No significant improvements in the culture will be forthcoming until major changes are made in America's judicial system.

Disparate court decisions at all levels of state and federal courts have created a complex and confusing array of judicial precedents. When people are unsure of their rights, there is no justice. Americans with traditional values and beliefs live in a "whisper zone" where they are surrounded by invisible legal fences. They are not sure of the legal boundaries and are afraid they will be "shocked" if they exercise their freedom of speech. This practice of intimidation is stopping any chance of societal reform. America's judicial system has become the playpen for lawyers and para-government groups who know how to use the courts to threaten and intimidate others. Justice is out of reach for most people because it is for sale at a price that risks too much time, money, and likely public embarrassment.

The Supreme Court must stop federal and state courts from continuing to pile one confusing precedent on top of another, and bring some clarity to the culture war. Consider these questions:

- Can schools teach that unwed sex is wrong and that traditional marriage is the most desirable environment in which to raise children?
- Can these schools be protected from expensive lawsuits that challenge their right to say some behaviors are wrong?
- Can schools teach "intelligent design" as one of the theories of creation or sponsor a Boy Scout troop?
- Can parents with traditional values demand the right to send their children to schools where they can learn in an environment that is consistent with their worldview?
- Can universities enforce moral standards for professors without fear of lawsuits?
- Can businesses require employees to uphold behavioral standards, and can organizations establish membership criteria that discriminate against inappropriate behavior?
- Can people believe in the Ten Commandments, and not have them publicly displayed?
- Can teachers intimidate students by telling them not to express their convictions because they have a religious base without accountability?
- Can professors attack grade inflation without fear of reprisals from administrators?

These are just some of the many questions people have, and the Supreme Court owes the American people some clear answers and reasonable approaches!

Where there is legal doubt, there is no freedom. Ask judges and lawyers about this problem, and they will hedge or provide you with a technical explanation of how there is no problem. Unfortunately, their explanations belie the reality of how legal complexity and confusion force traditional Americans into the shadows of "The Whisper Zone." The Supreme Court must act to eliminate the legal confusion that provides lawyers and judges control of our culture. Limiting the ability of lawyers to use SLAPP-style lawsuits would be an important step by the high court.

Lawsuits against public schools or public school teachers should be severely restricted. Judges and members of Congress have made themselves immune from lawsuits because they know that every decision they make would be challenged if they were not protected. Public schools face similar threats and should demand the same protections. There is plenty of accountability built into the public school system without allowing lawsuits to disrupt and distract schools from their educational mission. Public schools have elected school boards that are directly accountable to the people, and it is senseless to continue to allow the ACLU and others to threaten and intimidate teachers and principals with lawsuits. If a student is harmed, criminal charges can be filed. If someone doesn't like a school's policy, they can complain to the school board. If people don't like the actions of a school board, they can vote the members out of office. Public schools should no longer be paralyzed by the threat of costly lawsuits.

Likewise, lawsuits should not be allowed against churches. If "government can make no law" affecting religion, then certainly lawyers shouldn't be able to drag churches into court when someone doesn't like their policies. If a church violates the law, criminal penalties apply. Otherwise, churches should be protected from the intimidation of predatory personal injury lawyers.

The entire lawsuit system in America needs reform. SLAPP lawsuits are used not only to intimidate people and organizations of faith and values, they are also used to extort billions from business, industry, doctors, and hospitals, thus hurting the economy, sending more jobs overseas, and increasing the cost of health care. Without legal reform, organizations and businesses will continue to face frivolous, costly lawsuits or be sued when they "discriminate" against behavior that is destructive to their business or its values.

America is one of the few developed nations without some form of "loser pays" legal system that requires plaintiffs to pay the court costs of defendants when the plaintiff loses the case. This would deter lawsuits and encourage people and organizations to defend themselves against bogus lawsuits. The Supreme Court could improve the legal system, as could Congress. Americans need to elect congressmen and senators who will vote to reform our legal system (often called tort reform). Only then will the cultural cycle begin to reflect the views of the majority of the American people.

Several major Supreme Court rulings since 1960 have sent our cultural values spiraling downward. Federal district and circuit court judges have responded to these rulings by continuing to amplify and pervert the intent of the Constitution. Para-government groups have used these precedents to intimidate and silence the voices of reason. The following are just a few of the major rulings that must be addressed before Americans can regain their voices:

The Separation of Church and State

The establishment clause found in the First Amendment was intended to keep the federal government from establishing a national religion. It served this purpose for more than 150 years after the adoption of the U.S. Constitution. During this time, the federal government allowed states to regulate the interaction of church and state. Many states had laws that prohibited the use of public funds for religious purposes, but there was generally a constructive coexistence between religious principles and the operation of government.

Judicial precedent and confusion related to the 1962 "separation" court decision are likely too entrenched to be completely reversed. Ironically, in attempting to keep the government out of religion, the courts have actually created a new federal religion; secularism. The best appeal for traditionalists may be to demand the right to be separate from America's national secular religion.

Expanding school choice would be the most achievable short-term strategy to allow Americans to separate from government's secular religion. Despite the commitment of many dedicated teachers and administrators, America's government-run schools are consistently failing to prepare the majority of students to compete in a dynamic and fast-changing global economy. Countless studies document their shortcomings. Multilevel government regulations and bureaucracies, the reigning secular elite, along with the negative influences of the powerful teachers union, make it virtually impossible for schools to help students achieve their potential. Academic deficiencies, combined with the rejection of the teaching of discipline and character, make it imperative that Americans demand the freedom to separate from government schools and government secular religion.

A wide majority of Americans support school choice, and there is ample judicial precedent supporting the equal treatment of students who choose to attend nongovernment, independent schools.[4] Beginning with *Everson v. Board of Education*, and continuing with dozens of subsequent federal court rulings, the courts have upheld (with some consistency) allowing education dollars to follow students to the school of their choice. The 2002 *Zelman v. Simmons-Harris* Supreme Court decision confirmed that states had the right to provide vouchers for students to attend nongovernment schools. Secretary of Education Dr. Ron Paige hailed the decision in saying, "This decision lifts the constitutional cloud that has been hanging over school-choice programs for years and will open the doors of opportunity to thousands of children who need and deserve the best possible education."[5]

School choice has the potential to reverse decades of government-sponsored purging of values from our culture, and citizens must become more vocal about demanding that their states and local school districts provide this freedom. American parents should not be forced to send their children to secular, government-controlled schools.

In addition to school choice, Americans must search for other opportunities that could challenge the "separation" theology that has been imposed by the courts. Cities and states should not be threatened with constant lawsuits for allowing a Christmas display or even using the word "Christmas." These extreme (and seemingly laughable) cases create a powerful SLAPP effect among the public that warns and reminds people that faith and religion are, in effect, against the law.

Freedom of Association

Americans must also use court precedent to demand the freedom to associate with people and organizations of their choice. Like school choice, we must appeal to our right to separate from the government-sponsored religion that promotes destructive and costly behavior. The freedom to attend nongovernment schools and join associations that share traditional values would encourage positive activities and behaviors in the culture cycle. Currently, however, confusing laws and the impending threat of lawsuits have restricted the rights of private citizens to adopt and enforce standards in their organizations and workplace. For example, private clubs, volunteer organizations, and sport associations are often the target of para-government groups. However, the Supreme Court has established the needed precedent to reestablish our freedoms of association.

In the previously cited case *Boy Scouts of America v. Dale* in 2000, the Supreme Court overturned a lower court ruling that prohibited the Scouts from expelling a member who would not agree to their standards. The decision concludes that the lower court had interpreted too broadly the term "public accommodation" and writes:

> We are not, as we must not be, guided by our views of whether the Boy Scouts' teachings with respect to homosexual conduct are right or wrong. Public or judicial disapproval of a tenet of an organization's expression does not justify the State's effort to compel the organization to accept members where such acceptance would derogate from the organization's expressive message. While the law is

free to promote all sorts of conduct in place of harmful behavior, it is not free to interfere with speech for no better reason than promoting an approved message or discouraging a disfavored one, however enlightened either purpose may strike the government.[6]

These words are in harmony with the premise of this book. The ruling recognizes that the government should not be deciding what is right and wrong for individuals and organizations, except for promoting freedom of speech for positive, instead of harmful, behavior. The ruling also acknowledges that if the court does impose its view of right or wrong onto a private organization, it would be unlawfully restricting the freedom of speech and the freedom of association of a private organization. This ruling—this judicial precedent—should be equally applied to all private organizations, schools, and businesses. Chief Justice William Rehnquist, who wrote the majority opinion in the Boy Scout case, relied heavily on an earlier case, *Roberts v. United States Jaycees*, in which the court wrote that: "the Court has recognized a right to associate for the purpose of engaging in those activities protected by the First Amendment—speech, assembly, petition for the redress of grievances, and the exercise of religion."[7] The Court found a freedom of association because

choices to enter into and maintain certain intimate human relationships must be secured against undue intrusion by the State because of the role of such relationships in safeguarding the individual freedom that is central to our constitutional scheme. In this respect, freedom of association receives protection as a fundamental element of personal liberty.[8]

This right, the *Roberts* decision continues, is crucial in preventing the majority from imposing its views on groups that would rather express other, perhaps less popular, ideas. Government actions that unconstitutionally burden this freedom may take many forms, one of which is "intrusion into the internal structure or affairs of an association" like a "regulation that forces the group to accept members it does not desire." Forcing a group to accept certain members may impair the ability of the group to express those minority views, and compel obedience to those views, that it intends to express. Thus, "freedom of association . . . plainly presupposes a freedom not to associate."[9]

Americans must demand that these court precedents be applied equally throughout the private sector. If civic groups, churches, and businesses are free to establish and enforce behavioral standards of their choosing without the fear of government intimidation and expensive lawsuits, the private sector would begin to offset the negative influences of government policies that promote destructive behavior.

Critics will charge that this freedom of association would allow businesses and organizations to arbitrarily discriminate against behaviors of all kinds. While it may be true that some could impose unwise standards, any organization that must compete for members, employees, or customers will be forced to have reasonable and balanced standards if it is to succeed. A business that establishes a policy of "no smoking, drinking, or cussing on the premises" might eliminate some good workers, but it should have the right to associate with employees that are willing to comply with these standards.

More controversial, but just as necessary, would be similar standards for schools, especially those that require teachers to model positive behaviors. This could include rules prohibiting unwed pregnant teachers or those that publicly advocate nontraditional sexual behavior from being in the classroom. If courts will not allow government schools to establish constructive standards for teachers and students, then school choice initiatives would insure a rebirth of values as a foundation for education. Parents should have the freedom to "associate" their children with a school that teaches positive behavior.

Freedom of Speech

The courts' distorted interpretation of the First Amendment "freedom of speech" clause must also be changed before America can effectively fight the growing plague of sexually transmitted diseases, sex trafficking, pornography, and indecency. Currently, the courts limit constructive First Amendment speech while using a perverted view of "free speech" to support destructive and costly behavior. A *Washington Post* article in May of 2006 highlighted how the courts will continue to be the enemies of our culture, even after the legislative and executive branches of government take positive action.[10] The article, entitled "Prostitution Clause in AIDS Policy Ruled Illegal," reported that two federal judges ruled unconstitutional the government's policy of forcing U.S. health groups to denounce prostitution as a condition for receiving funds for international AIDS work. Both judges said that the requirement violated the First Amendment right to free speech. These rulings overturned standards in the Congress and the Justice Department, which mandated that USAID (the federal agency that distributes AIDS funding) require organizations to state that they oppose prostitution and sex trafficking, and sign a form before receiving funds designated to fight the spread of AIDS.[11]

Prostitution and sex trafficking are illegal in the United States, yet these judges ruled that government cannot say that these behaviors are wrong. Prostitution and sex trafficking are major causes of the spread of AIDS, yet the courts ruled that these behaviors are expressions of free speech. The stated position of those who brought the suits was that being against prostitution would inhibit the ability to help prostitutes by distributing condoms. In other words, judges want to use American taxpayer money to show people around the world how to practice prostitution safely. These court rulings force a ludicrous logic flow through the culture and legal community, both at home and abroad. This same message has been forced on Americans for decades: destructive behavior and destructive speech are constitutional rights, but constructive behavior and discrimination against destructive behavior are "prejudices," declared to be either illegal or subject to lawsuits.

Perverse interpretations of "free speech" have also been used by the courts to protect pornography — an industry that is promoting perverse sex, violence, rape, disrespect for women and marriage, and many other societal maladies. Courts have used "free speech" protections to discard library attempts to block Internet pornography in spite of Congress's attempt to stop government-sponsored dissemination of smut.[12] The Americans who wrote the Constitution and the Bill of Rights would be horrified if they knew that their efforts to protect the freedom of speech of citizens had been corrupted into the protection of many forms of prostitution, pornography, and perversion. The simple conclusion, reached by anyone familiar with recent court procedure, is that present justices have a better and more "enlightened" view of right and wrong than the Founding Fathers and most of the American people. Americans must force the courts to return to the original intent of the First Amendment and the American founding.

The Right to Privacy

As the United States approaches 50 million abortions since the infamous *Roe v. Wade* Supreme Court decision in 1973, Americans must renew their efforts to seek constitutional protections for unborn children. The *Roe* decision was the result of a newly invented constitutional "right to privacy" — a right that is not mentioned anywhere in the Constitution, but invented by justices. The court then extended this new right to include a woman's right to end the life of her unborn child. This decision made abortion a constitutional right and made it unconstitutional for any state to restrict abortion in most circumstances. Today when Americans try to speak out for those who cannot yet speak for themselves, they must stand against the federal government, the Supreme Court, and all the para-government groups who are "protecting" the constitution.

The "right to privacy" was used again by the Supreme Court in *Texas v. Lawrence* in 2003 to strike down state laws against homosexual sodomy. This decision overturned a 1986 court decision, *Bowers v. Hardwick*, which recognized a state's right to restrict homosexuality based on "longstanding moral antipathy toward homosexual sodomy." Justice Scalia, who was joined by the late Chief Justice Rehnquist and Justice Clarence Thomas in his dissent, lamented that "state laws against bigamy, same-sex marriage, adult incest, prostitution, masturbation, adultery, fornication, bestiality, and obscenity are likewise sustainable only in light of *Bowers'* validation of laws based on moral choices."[13]

The Supreme Court has effectively legalized homosexuality and set the stage for para-government groups to contest any law that restricts or discriminates against destructive behavior. Americans must challenge the direction of the Court and force it to define "privacy" in ways that protect individuals and benefit society.

2. Continue to Strengthen Marriage

Patrick Fagan has written: "Though cultural attitudes, social science findings, and social policies have begun to recognize the importance of supporting marriage and decreasing the incidence of divorce, the policies and activities of state government are still biased against marriage. This bias amplifies the damage caused by decades of misguided federal welfare policy that has virtually eliminated marriage among the poor and federal tax policy that is penalizing marriage."[14]

While welfare reform and community-based efforts are a start in the recovery process of America's culture, we have only begun to realize that federal and state governments are the primary cause of damage. The changes that must be made in laws and court rulings are a necessary first step in cultural regeneration and will ultimately reduce the pain and suffering of millions, while saving taxpayers billions of dollars a year. The following recommendations are intended to encourage discussion and debate, and to help Americans regain their voices.

One of the most important actions that could be taken by the federal government would be to pass the Federal Marriage Protection Amendment to the Constitution. Without constitutional protection, para-government groups will continue to "judge shop" in federal and state courts to chip away at the definition of marriage. "Forcing marriage to mean all things will ultimately force marriage to mean nothing at all."[15] The most important step Congress can take is to send a constitutional amendment that protects the institution of marriage. Courts currently ignore a federal law that defines marriage as the union between a man and a woman. Judges have also overturned state referendums that overwhelmingly supported the traditional definition of marriage. The federal government must make a definitive statement in support of marriage, and there is no stronger and more permanent way to do it than a constitutional amendment. On the most recent votes in Congress on the proposed amendment, the House and Senate fell well short of the two thirds super-majority that is required for a constitutional amendment. Americans will need to elect new members of Congress if they want to protect marriage.

States must resist the establishment of same-sex marriages and civil unions that officially recognize and endorse homosexual relationships. People can be free to have whatever relationship they desire, but governments should not legitimize behavior known to be destructive and in violation of the social traditions and morals of the culture. Laws that establish same-sex marriage or civil unions represent government endorsements of behavior that is a blatant repudiation of proven American values. The culture has translated appetitive nature into a political right. The ethic of contemporary homosexual activism is that sex is strictly for pleasure. "At the bottom of the contemporary debate over marriage, is the possibility that defenders of traditional marriage affirm, and its critics deny, namely, the very possibility of marriage as a one-flesh communion of persons."[16] Sexual behavior that undermines faithful, lifelong marriage between a husband and a wife is harmful to the culture at large.

Marriage is a public institution that unites men and women for the purpose of reproducing the human race and keeping a mother and father together to cooperate in raising to maturity the children they produce. Any law that supports gay unions, whether civil laws or marriage, will violate the freedom of conscience of Americans who believe that homosexuality is wrong. It will also lead to the dismemberment of marriage as we know it. This is not a question of what people are allowed to do, it is a question of what behaviors our government endorses and promotes.

The goal of the gay marriage movement in both Norway and Denmark, and in the United States as well, is not marriage, but social approval of homosexuality. Advocates of same-sex marriage seek to remove procreation from the definition of marriage and to redefine it as "a loving and committed relationship." Such a meaning places the definition of marriage on a "slippery slope" that could ultimately remove restrictions against marrying multiple partners at once, incest, relations with minors of either sex, a close blood relative, or a person who is already married.

As of late 2006, more than half the states have approved constitutional amendments protecting marriage as solely between a man and a woman.[17] Most other states have statutes designed to protect traditional marriage by defining marriage only as the union of a man and woman. Only five states have no statutory or constitutional protection for traditional marriage.

A federal constitutional amendment is still needed because nine states are now facing lawsuits that are challenging their traditional marriage laws. In four of these states, trial courts have found a right to same-sex marriage in state constitutional provisions relating to equal protection and due process—

in each case relying in part on a Massachusetts court decision that forced the state to accept same-sex marriage. This is another example of how one bad court decision can be multiplied through the culture.

Continuing to support the expansion of abstinence-until-marriage programs will also strengthen marriages, reduce the spread of STDs, and decrease the number of unwed births, saving the nation billions of dollars every year. Public schools, funded with taxpayer dollars, which speak for the government, must stop endorsing sex before marriage by teaching safe sex with no moral criteria. Teaching human sexuality in a biology class makes good sense, as does being honest with students about the risks and dangers of having sex before marriage, but most current sex education curriculums in the public schools are a de facto endorsement of unwed sex and a diminishment of the importance of marriage.

Patrick Fagan offers a number of specific recommendations for states to encourage abstinence and reduce divorce and out-of-wedlock births while strengthening marriages. The following are excerpts from his recommendations:

- Set a goal of reducing out-of-wedlock births and divorce by 33 percent in each state by 2010.
- Make a concerted effort to redirect the unused welfare revenues for Temporary Assistance for Needy Families (TANF) to programs that increase marriage and decrease divorce. States should consider creating an Office of Marriage Initiatives to encourage marriage and discourage divorce. States should also use the charitable choice provision of TANF and encourage faith-based organizations to compete for funding to provide services.
- Allocate state welfare funds to reward counties that reduce out-of-wedlock births and divorce.
- Make state laws more marriage friendly. Many states have a marriage penalty in their tax code. This penalty should be replaced with incentives for marriage and penalties for unwed births and divorce.
- Eliminate perverse incentives in state laws that reward unmarried parents for having more children. States should consider new or expanded benefits for married couples on welfare. At the time their child is born, 82 percent of unmarried mothers and fathers are romantically involved, 44 percent are living together, and over 70 percent of the mothers say their chances of marrying the father are "50-50." The long-term costs to society are immense for not making clear the reasons these couples should marry.
- Support initiatives to help troubled marriages get back on track. Divorce is the primary reason ("root cause") women and children fall into poverty. There are a growing number of programs that help to strengthen troubled

marriages and a state Office of Marriage Initiatives could make these programs more available to low- and middle-income citizens.

- Encourage the work of churches and faith-based organizations in poor areas. Few Americans realize the extent to which marriage has disappeared among the poor, in large part as a result of such government programs as welfare, marriage penalties, and family planning programs that promote sexual activity and childbearing outside of marriage. Because of the effectiveness of churches in strengthening marriages, churches in poor areas are probably government's most effective allies in efforts to decrease divorce and increase marriage in communities beleaguered by the effects of family breakdown.

- Ensure that government personnel support a marriage initiative. Encouraging marriage represents a paradigm shift by government, and it will be difficult to change the regnant ethic. Governors and state legislators should utilize county clerks, who process marriage licenses, as well as welfare workers, school counselors, teachers, public health, and school nurses who interact with young mothers, to encourage participation in marriage preparation and skills classes. Personnel who ignore or block good policy should be educated about the problem or replaced.

- Create incentives for couples to participate in premarriage preparation classes before receiving a marriage license. Something as simple as a discount on marriage licenses or a small tax credit will make a significant difference because it tells couples that their government believes marriage is important and right.[18]

The federal Department of Health and Human Services (HHS) has developed a marriage calculator that provides every state with a reliable method of calculating marriage penalties in their welfare and Medicaid programs. Since distribution formulas differ for every state, this will be an important tool for states to reduce the disincentives for the poor to get married. Congress has also funded a five-year, $100 million a year program through HHS to encourage healthy marriage. State and local governments, private nonprofit organizations, and faith-based organizations will compete for these funds to develop innovative programs to promote marriage.[19]

Critics abound on efforts by government to support marriage through the use of public personnel and welfare funds. Don Block, past president of the American Family Therapy Academy, said: "It is really taking money away from those at the thin edge, people who have a whole range of needs, health, nutrition, housing." Like many secular experts in the public policy realm, Mr. Block does not understand "cause and effect." America's poor often live on the thin edge because of the effects of the breakdown of marriage and family.

"The duty of government is to protect and foster the common good. For the past thirty-five years, government has played a major role in the destruction of marriage among the poor by subsidizing out-of-wedlock birth. . . . Preventing divorces in low-and-middle-income families is preventing poverty, and that is good public policy."[20]

Fagan offers a number of additional recommendations and programs that states could use to improve the lives of millions and save taxpayers billions. Evidence supports his contention that divorce can be reduced by 30 percent through community programs to strengthen marriage. A concerted effort by governments will eventually enlist the help of media, which will lead to significant shifts and societal attitudes and behavior.

3. Free Churches to Participate in the Political Process

Congressman Walter Jones from North Carolina has for years tried to pass a bill in the U.S. House of Representatives that would reestablish free political speech for churches. This bill would eliminate the IRS "gag rule" that threatens churches with the loss of tax exempt status if they endorse a candidate or get involved with political campaigns. The constitution protects churches from government interference, and it is time to encourage churches to participate in the political process. This would give the faith community equal standing with secular groups that work to influence the culture development cycle.

The record of faith-based ministries is impressive, but the struggle to participate often discourages individuals and groups from attempting to enter the culture wars. Consider what happened when a faith-based service organization entered America's prisons. The InnerChange Freedom Institute was begun by the Christian organization, Prison Fellowship, in 1997. The program utilizes a transformational model of change based on Bible teaching and personal responsibility. All participants volunteer for the program and are required to make a two-year commitment. The program is administered by contracts between states and IFI and operates in Texas, Kansas, Minnesota, Iowa, and Arkansas. The Texas Department of Criminal Justice and the University of Pennsylvania have both issued studies showing the IFI graduates are far less likely to return to prison than are other prisoners. The University of Pennsylvania study found that only 8 percent of InnerChange graduates returned to prison within two years of their release, compared to 20 percent of similar Texas prisoners.

In February of 2003, Barry Lynn and the Americans United for Separation of Church and State filed a lawsuit against the state of Iowa claiming that the faith-based programs violated separation of church and state doctrines. In a subsequent ruling, a federal judge held that this was the case and that IFI was "pervasively sectarian" and therefore could not receive federal funds. Despite the fact that the program was purely voluntary, the court ordered it closed and the more than $1.5 million received by IFI refunded to the state. Prison Fellowship has promised to appeal the ruling to the U.S. Supreme Court.

The InnerChange program worked with local church communities to provide volunteers to assist inmates and their families during incarceration and after their release. The judge's decision has had a chilling effect on the participation by churches in the political process. If faith communities are not allowed to participate, the culture cycle has only secular explanations for reality, and an integral constructive influence on cultural life will be lost. The assumption that a social good can be achieved by clever institutional relationships instead of an appeal to the soul in pursuit of excellence is bogus. The new politics has shifted from a question about the ends of life to a preoccupation with human passions.

4. Continue to Improve Welfare

Much has changed since the 1996 Welfare Reform Act was enacted. Millions have moved from government dependency to employment and independence. Unwed births among teenagers have declined, but there is still much more that can be accomplished. We must continue to improve welfare in ways that will broaden the incentives for education, work, and marriage, and create more disincentives for unwed births. The current welfare system continues to penalize married couples. Welfare benefits should be improved for married couples. Benefit levels should be upgraded for unwed mothers who identify fathers whose income could then be garnished to pay child support. Unemployed fathers should be required to participate in work programs. Unwed mothers who do not have the financial means or a willing father to care for a child should be encouraged to consider the benefits of adoption. All welfare participants should be required to take a course that explains that welfare benefits are temporary and that no one is entitled to receive subsidies from taxpayers.

5. Connecting Actions with Consequences

Congress should require that states have tough child support laws for fathers of illegitimate children. Expectant mothers who plan to use Medicaid or other public assistance should be required to identify fathers who would, in turn, be required to pay the medical expenses of childbirth. Fathers who could not pay medical expenses would be required to participate in community service or work programs. A co-pay should be required for all Medicaid and other health care services (e.g., health department or hospital emergency room).

Tougher child support laws in some states have already demonstrated that connecting the consequences of unwed births to fathers will significantly reduce unwed births. Researchers at the University of Washington and Columbia University in a study of over 5,000 women found that "states with the most stringent laws and strict enforcement have as much as 20 percent fewer out-of-wedlock births."[21] At a time when Medicaid is the fastest-growing expense for most states, tough nationwide child support laws could save states and the federal government billions of dollars.

Similar rules should apply to people using public assistance health care programs for sexually transmitted diseases. Significant co-pays should be required, and patients must reveal the names of their partners. These names should not be made available to the public, but the partners of those with STDs should be contacted to notify them of their potential infection.

6. Addressing the Growing Problems Associated with Gambling

The exponential growth in Internet gambling will soon complete America's transition from an antigambling to a government-sponsored pro-gambling culture. Individuals, churches, and communities have little chance to reduce the corrosive societal impact of gambling because state governments are now gambling's most ardent supporters. It will be very difficult for Americans to reverse gambling's grip on our culture. The gambling industry has become one of the most powerful political lobbying groups and among the largest campaign contributors to state and federal candidates. Both the Republican and Democratic parties receive considerable financial support from the gambling industry, so it is unlikely that either party will lead the effort to reduce the corrosive societal impact of gambling.

Dr. James Dobson, who was a member of the National Gambling Impact Study, writes, "Some religious leaders want new ethics rules for Congress, but that's only a band-aid fix. Politicians need to root out this infection. Gambling—all types of gambling—is driven by greed and subsists on greed. That makes it morally bankrupt from its very foundation. Gambling creates addicts, breeds crime and destroys families."[22] We need courageous office holders who will begin the process of shutting down lotteries, casinos and other gambling outlets." Unfortunately, millions of voters are now addicted to lotteries and other forms of gambling.

State governments are among those most passionately hooked on lottery proceeds and are moving to rapidly increase the variety of games and advertising to compete with the growth in Internet gambling opportunities. Many states were forced to adopt lotteries after neighboring states offered a lottery. Millions of dollars flowed across state lines as people in one state crossed over to another state to buy lottery tickets. Now it would be very difficult for states to wean themselves from these new revenues.

Government corruption and the destructive second-hand consequences of gambling will likely have to become more apparent before a majority of voters demand change. To help Americans understand the dangers, we need bold political leaders and citizens to stand up and say that gambling is wrong. Already we are seeing that gambling revenues come from the poorest black neighborhoods and are used in turn to fund the education of white, middle-class students. Short of outlawing gambling at the federal level, the best we can hope for at this stage may be for national leaders to demand that the federal government constantly study and issue regular reports on the impact of gambling on America. Hopefully, leaders will emerge that have the courage to stand against the current societal support for gambling.

THE NEXT ELECTION: POLITICAL IMPLICATIONS OF WORLDVIEWS

Voices and votes are the weapons that traditionalists must employ to win the war of worldviews. Every election represents an opportunity to support candidates who understand the importance of restoring freedom of speech and will fight to include traditional views in public policy debates. Few elected officials are aware of the full scope of the culture war. Like many citizens, politicians have been lulled into accepting the growing secularization of America's culture as a natural consequence of modernity. They assume that the government has little control over the decline in our culture.

As political "experts" report the increasing polarization of America, there is little awareness that this polarization has resulted from government promotion of a secular culture. The political divide in America is no longer conservative versus liberal, right versus left, or even Republican versus Democrat. Political affiliation in the future will be best defined by secular versus traditional values and beliefs. The implications of this new political dynamic are astounding. Historically, political parties have debated which ideas were best for America. Secularists have little use for national identity, arguing for the unbridled freedom of individuals irrespective of the impact on the nation.

The Democratic Party in America has largely adopted the secular-progressive worldview. Major financial and grassroots supporters of the Democratic Party include supporters of a secular, "central management" approach to government: the ACLU and personal injury lawyers, unions (including the teachers unions), homosexual groups, welfare and income-redistribution advocates, academics, Hollywood, and members of the media. A 2004 Zogby International poll confirmed that cultural and religious differences between the Democratic and Republican Parties were enough to swing the electoral votes in Red (Republican) and Blue (Democratic) states:[23]

- A solid majority (56 percent) of Red State voters reject the political, economic, and social values espoused by Bill and Hillary Clinton, while less than half (47 percent) of Blue State voters disagree with Clinton values.
- Seventy percent of Red State voters support marriage only between a man and a woman, while 55 percent of Blue State voters agree with the traditional definition of marriage.
- Over half (51 percent) of Red State voters attend church, synagogue, or mosque either once a week or more often. Conversely, a near majority (46 percent) of Blue State voters said they only attend religious services on holidays, rarely, or never;
- Only 5 percent of voters in Red States label themselves "progressive" (a new political term), but 11 percent of voters in Blue States claim that label.
- Nearly two-thirds (64 percent) of those living in Red States are married as opposed to 56 percent in Blue States.

It should be noted that many Democrats are deeply religious, highly moral people. However, many of them have fallen victim to the secular "separation" worldview that opposes the incorporation of meaningful values into public policy. It is not unusual to hear a Democrat say that they are personally opposed to abortion but believe that abortion should be legal. They fail to realize that by making abortion legal the government makes it "right," and actually promotes it with government force. Few Democrats would be willing to say that behaviors such as abortion, premarital sex, unwed births, homosexuality, or gambling are "*wrong*."

Republicans are not much better. Many in the GOP have also adopted the "separation" worldview and are afraid to publicly join the war of worldviews. Republicans whisper because they know they will feel the heat of media intimidation if they make public value judgments. In 1994 Republicans were swept into power and a Congressional majority because Americans were distressed about the corruption in Congress, wasteful spending, and the general decline of our culture. In 2006, Republicans were swept out of power for many of the same reasons. Republicans accomplished welfare reform and a balanced budget, but failed to keep their word about wasteful spending, corruption, and support of traditional values. Ironically, it was the preelection revelation that a homosexual Republican congressman sent perverse e-mails to underage male pages that provided the "straw that broke the camel's back" of the Republican majority.

Secularists will pursue significantly different domestic and foreign policies than traditionalists:

- Secularists will advocate "choice" from traditional values (such as marriage and abortion), but oppose "choices" that free people from dependency on a secular, controlling government (such as vouchers for schools).
- Secularists will oppose school choice, individual ownership of health plans, choices of health plans with Medicare and Medicaid, personal savings accounts for Social Security, and welfare-to-work programs that force able-bodied Americans to work; but they steadfastly continue to advocate abortion and homosexual marriage.
- Secularists will support government-sponsored health care for all Americans, continued government ownership and control of Social Security, more federal control of public schools, and more regulations on businesses and organizations.
- Secularists will support income redistribution through an increasingly progressive tax code, while opposing all attempts to create a simple flat tax that will expand America's economy and increase our global competitiveness.
- Secularists will support same-sex marriages, special rights for homosexuals, and antidiscrimination laws that prohibit the military, schools, businesses, and organizations from excluding individuals who are openly homosexual.
- Secularists will seek to solve societal programs with government programs rather than incentives for the private sector to meet the need.
- Secularists will substitute diplomatic hope for military power in foreign policy, believing that there is no "evil" in the world, only misunderstandings.
- Secularists will seek international consensus rather than national objectives.
- Secularists will continue to remove any vestige of religious symbols from the public square. Existing displays will increasingly come in for attack from groups like the ACLU and other liberal para-government group interests.
- No new displays of religious symbols or wordings will be presented for public display because government officials will fear litigation from secular groups.
- The president will not visit the National Jamboree for the Boy Scouts because he/she will be subject to criticism.
- Fewer elected officials will attend the National Prayer Breakfast because they will be criticized for doing so.

- Secularists will continue to "push the edge" in family television entertainment, suggesting that homosexual marriage is normal, abortion acceptable, infidelity inevitable, and divorce appropriate to one's happiness.
- Gay and lesbian studies majors will become a part of the curriculum of every major college and university.
- Federal judges will increasingly overturn legislative proposals that protect traditional values.

Because of a worldview that fails to understand both the evil and excellence of human nature, the secularist will advocate government policies that are advertised to show compassion to individuals but actually cause individual and societal deterioration. The secularist will then advocate government programs to reduce the suffering caused by their own policies. Because of secular domination of government for several decades, America is spending billions fighting poverty, crime, child abuse, disease, exploding health care costs, unemployment, and many other problems that are really just symptoms of deeper "root causes." Secular compassion (or, as we see it, "narcotic") provides free education and citizenship for children of illegals, along with free health care and legal protections from employment discrimination. These policies have contributed significantly to a massive influx of illegal immigrants and an expanding budget deficit. The consequences will be paid for by the American people for generations.

The pattern of secular government subsidies and protections extends to a host of other destructive behaviors. For example, America is now experiencing an epidemic of obesity that is leading to dramatic increases in diabetes, heart disease, cancer, and many other health problems. As the costs for health insurance, Medicaid, and Medicare expand in large part because of the health effects of obesity, the nation faces devastating financial consequences. A major cause of these problems is a consistent government policy that protects the behaviors that lead to obesity. Most public schools have eliminated or significantly reduced physical activities while at the same time funding a school lunch of pizza, burgers, and burritos. The government forbids employers from discriminating against obese applicants, prohibits insurance companies from charging more for obese policyholders, and has given obese Americans special privileges under the Americans with Disabilities Act. On their face, these policies sound compassionate, until we realize that millions of Americans are suffering with disabilities, illnesses, and costs related to obesity because of government protection of this unhealthy behavior. The government should provide incentives for healthy behavior as it now subsidizes obesity. Medical savings accounts would be a solid first step in improving the health of every American. If the private sector was allowed to make decisions about obesity, most Americans would have ample incentives to stay fit.

When it comes to foreign policy, few are aware of how cultural deterioration in America has diminished our moral authority abroad. The problem has weakened America's global war on terror and its well-intended attempts to establish democracies in the Middle East. The United States is universally disliked by people in other countries, and the reason is not envy. China, despite its Communist government, trade violations, and widely known human rights abuses, has a better image than the United States in most of the European nations.[24] Of course, if the army of the People's Republic of China suddenly marched across Russia into Western Europe, the United States would overnight become the best friend of the most outspoken anti-American European legion led by France and Germany. While Americans have come to believe that other countries are simply jealous of the United States for our wealth and freedoms, surveys regularly show that people throughout the world have a strong disdain for the nation's culture and character.

People around the world know America primarily through the media, movies, and the Internet. A large number of foreign college students also learn about America through universities where they visit and enroll. With these "spokesmen" for America, it should come as no surprise that most Western and Asian countries surveyed see Americans as "greedy" and "violent." Muslims around the world view Americans as immoral and in need of more religion.[25] Americans often assume that people in other countries want to be like us, but this is far from being true.

America no longer has the moral authority to spread its ideals and philosophy around the world. We are resented when we intervene, because we are not respected as a nation or as a people. Our cultural decline must be a part of any new foreign policy that reflects the fact that the rest of the world does not want to become what we have become. They do not want our brand of freedom or culture.

THE IMPORTANCE OF SPEAKING OUT

For freedom-loving Americans, the greatest weapons for changing the culture development cycle are our voices and votes. We cannot allow the enemies of freedom to silence our voices and discourage our votes. Hopefully, this book has helped to confirm what traditional Americans already know in their hearts. We must all stand up together and speak out together with confidence, because the facts support our case.

The majority of Americans are whispering for several reasons, the main one being that they are afraid. The postwar generation has presided over a rapid cultural decline, especially in the realm of personal ethics and family stability. In the past forty years a revolution has severed the roots of our culture. We have watched as the revolution of the 1960s has led to the victory of:

- the sexually active over virgins,
- cohabitation over marriage,
- divorce over monogamy,
- abortion over the right of an unborn child to life,
- a collapsing birthrate over the baby boom,
- gays over straights,
- moral chaos over moral consensus,
- situational opinions over historically tested truth,
- lust over modesty,
- lying over truth telling,
- atheism over religion,
- statism over freedom,
- dependency over responsibility,
- silence over speech,
- multiculturalism over America,
- the living Constitution over the written Constitution, and
- darkness over light.

Every reader should close this book realizing that our values and national character are not just matters for family and church; they are matters of the utmost importance for the survival of the nation. Understanding how to use the cultural cycle to reverse these trends is how we can reduce the suffering of millions and improve the quality of life for every American. It is how we can cut billions of dollars of unnecessary spending, reduce taxes, and improve our economy. It is how we can improve student performance and regain our competitiveness as a nation. And it is how we can restore respect for America around the world. To continue to "separate" character and values from public policy will only guarantee that we continue to decline as a nation.

There is a very real opportunity to shift the direction of the culture development cycle. The public is increasingly alarmed about the cost and second-hand consequences of government-sponsored destructive behavior. There have been some recent additions to the Supreme Court who appear to have traditional leanings. *And* there is the opportunity to elect a new president and Congress in 2008. This is not the time for whispers. Americans must join their voices in supporting partnerships for change at the local level and demanding change from their state and federal governments. As we raise the volume of our voices, we will increase our chances of saving America.

Notes

PREFACE

1. Alliance Defense Fund, "ADF Attorneys Help Secure Equal Access for Church Evicted from Local Community Room," December 13, 2006, available from: www.alliancedefensefund.org/news/story.aspx?cid=3949.

2. Ronald Reagan, "Inaugural Address," January 21, 1985, Ronald Reagan Presidential Library.

3. John Stuart Mill, "On Liberty," in *Classics of Moral and Political Theory*, 4th ed., ed. Michael L. Morgan (Indianapolis, IN: Hackett Publishing, 2005), 938.

4. Robert H. Bork, *Slouching Toward Gomorrah* (New York: Regan Books, 1996), 12.

5. William J. Bennett, *The Index of Leading Cultural Indicators* (New York: Simon and Schuster, 1994), 8.

6. William J. Bennett, *The Index of Leading Cultural Indicators: American Society at the End of the Twentieth Century*, rev. and exp. ed. (New York: Broadway, 1999).

7. George H. Sabine, *A History of Political Theory*, 4th ed. (Hinsdale, IL: Dryden Press, 1973), 163.

CHAPTER 1   FEELING THE HEAT

1. Valerie Bauerlein, "A Contest of Contrasting Styles," *State*, June 17, 2004, sec. A.

2. Aaron Gould Sheinin, "DeMint Says Gays Can't Teach in Schools," *State*, October 4, 2004, sec. A.

3. Jack Bass, *Charleston Post & Courier*, October 13, 2004. sec. B.

4. Barbara Miner, "Antigay Stance Fits Party Platform," *Myrtle Beach Sun*, October 21, 2004. sec. A.

5. Albert Eisele, "Taxplan, Gay Gaffes Cost DeMint Lead in SC Race," *Hill*, October 27, 2004.

6. Lauren Markoe, Aaron Gould Sheinin, and Jennifer Talhelm, "DeMint Apologizes for Remark." *State*, October 7, 2004, sec. A.

7. Dan Hoover, "DeMint Offers an Apology," *Greenville (SC) News*, October 7, 2004, sec. B.

8. Sandra Martin, *Myrtle Beach Sun News*, October 7, 2004, sec. A.

9. Lee Bandy, "DeMint's Missteps Give Boost to Tennebaum," *State*, October 10, 2004, sec. D.

10. Schuyler Kropf, "Neck & Neck," *Charleston Post & Courier*, October 24, 2004, sec. A.

CHAPTER 2   WHO IS RIGHT?

1. James Davidson Hunter, *Culture Wars: The Struggle to Define America* (New York: Basic Books, 1991), 42.

2. Robert N. Bellah et al., *Habits of the Heart: Individualism and Commitment in American Life* (Berkeley: University of California Press, 1985), 65, 77.

3. Geoffrey Layman, *The Great Divide: Religious and Cultural Conflict in American Party Politics* (New York: Columbia University Press, 2001), 11.

4. Brendan Sweetman, *Why Politics Needs Religion* (Downers Grove, IL: InterVarsity Press, 2006), 35–36.

5. Sweetman, 29.

6. George Marsden, *Understanding Fundamentalism and Evangelicalism* (Grand Rapids, MI: Eerdmans, 1991), 2.

7. Sweetman, 30.

8. From Thomas Aquinas, *Summa Theologica*, quoted in Michael Morgan, *Classics of Moral and Political Theory*, 4th ed. (Indianapolis, IN: Hackett Publishing, 2005), 464.

9. Sweetman, 17–18.

10. See George Marsden, *The Soul of the American University* (New York: Oxford University Press, 1994).

11. Sweetman, 67–68, with excerpts from: Christian Smith, ed., *The Secular Revolution: Power, Interests and Conflict in the Secularization of American Public Life* (Berkeley: University of California Press, 2003).

12. Chris Hedges, *American Fascists: The Christian Right and the War on America* (New York: The Free Press, 2007).

13. Richard John Neuhaus, *The Naked Public Square* (Grand Rapids, MI: Eerdmans, 1984), vii.

14. Sam Harris, *Letter to a Christian Nation* (New York: Alfred A. Knopf, 2006), viii, ix.

15. Harris, x–xi.

16. Neuhaus, 86.

17. Sweetman, 115.

18. Sweetman, 129.

19. Michael J. Behe, *Darwin's Black Box*, 2nd ed. (New York: The Free Press, 2006), 5.

20. Irving Kristol, *Reflections of a Neoconservative: Looking Back, Looking Ahead* (New York: Basic Books, 1983), 41.

21. Bill O'Reilly, *Culture Warrior* (New York: Broadway Books, 2006), 173–74.

22. Charles Pickering, *Supreme Chaos* (Macon, GA: Stroud & Hall Publishers, 2005), 52.

23. O'Reilly, 197–98.

24. Dana Blanton, "More Believe in God Than Heaven," FOX News.com. June 18, 2004.

25. Sweetman, 14.

26. Sweetman, 74–75, also see the overview of recent surveys of people's religious beliefs in George Gallup Jr. and D. Michael Lindsey, *The Gallup Guide: Reality Check for 21st Century Churches* (Loveland, CO: Group Publishing, 2002).

CHAPTER 3 WHO DECIDES WHAT IS RIGHT AND WRONG?

1. David McCullough, *John Adams* (New York: Simon and Schuster, 2001), 282.

2. Charles Pickering, *Supreme Chaos* (Macon, GA: Stroud and Hall Publishers, 2005), 49.

3. Catherine Drinker Bowen, *Miracle at Philadelphia* (Boston: Little, Brown, 1966), 126–27.

4. Bowen, 50.

5. Bowen, 53. Excerpts from discussion of De Tocqueville from Matt Kaufman, "Foundation of Freedom," *Citizen Magazine*, March 2004.

6. Bowen, 53–54.

7. National Institute of Mental Health, "The Numbers Count: Mental Disorders in America," NIH Pub. No. 06-4584, 26 December 2006, available from: www.nimh.nih.gov/publicat/numbers.cfm.

8. Quoted in Os Guinness, *The American Hour* (New York: The Free Press, 1993), 286.

9. Dinesh D'Souza, *The Enemy at Home* (New York: Doubleday, 2007).

10. Michael Barone, *Our Country: The Shaping of America from Roosevelt to Reagan* (New York: The Free Press, 1990), 31.

11. Grover Norquist, "Reducing Government by Half," *The Insider*, no. 271 (May 2000), Americans for Tax Reform, www.atr.org./content/pdf/pre2004/05200speech.pdf.

12. Alexander M. Bickel, *The Least Dangerous Branch* (New York: The Bobbs-Merrill Company, 1962), 35.

13. *Engel v. Vitale*, 370 U.S. 421 (1962), available from: http://usinfo.state.gov/usa/infousa/facts/democrac/47.htm.

14. *Trop v. Dulles*, 356 U.S. 86 (1958).

15. Paul Johnson, *A History of the American People* (New York: Harper Collins, 1997), 954.

16. David Brooks, *Bobos in Paradise* (New York: Touchstone Books, 2000), 14.

17. The phrase comes from Theodore Roszak's 1969 book that claimed that "technocratic" social organization and a pervasive managerial ethos had created a "myth of objective consciousness" that impoverished human relations and made life lonely and frightening at any income level. Theodore Roszak, *The Making of a Counter Culture*, 2nd edition (Berkeley: University of California Press, 1995).

18. Michel Foucault, *The Order of Things* (New York: Vintage, 1994), xviii.

19. Douglas E. Litowitz, *Postmodern Philosophy and Law* (Lawrence: University Press of Kansas, 2000).

20. Michael M. Uhlmann, "The Supreme Court Rules," *First Things* 136 (November 2003), 27.

21. Richard A. Pride and J. David Woodard, *The Burden of Busing* (Knoxville: University of Tennessee Press, 1985).

22. *Griswold v. Connecticut*, 381 U.S. 479 (1965).

23. The Beatles, "Nowhere Man," from *Rubber Soul*, 1965.

24. Bill O'Reilly, *Culture Warrior* (New York: Broadway Books, 2006), 1.

CHAPTER 4   THE CULTURE DEVELOPMENT CYCLE: SHAPING AMERICAN VALUES

1. Thomas G. West, "Religious Liberty," January 1, 1997, p. 3, available from: www.claremont.org/writings/970101west.html.

2. West, 15.

3. West, 15.

4. West, 2.

5. West, 4. This is a clear example of the social contract.

6. "Suicide Lite," *TV Guide* 51 (October 11–17, 2003).

7. M. E. Bradford, *Founding Fathers* (Lawrence: University Press of Kansas, 1994).

8. Wilfred E. Binkley, *American Political Parties: Their Natural History* (New York: Alfred A. Knopf, 1949), 16–17.

9. Matthew F. Rose, *John Witherspoon* (Washington, DC: Family Research Council, 2001), 23.

10. John Adams, "Letter to Samuel Adams (1790)," in *Political Thought in America*, ed. Michael B. Levy (Prospect Heights, IL: Waveland Press, 1992), 104.

11. West, 4.

12. J. M. Juran, *Juran on Quality by Design: The New Steps for Planning Quality into Goods and Services* (New York: The Free Press, 1992), 9.

13. W. Edwards Deming, *Out of the Crisis* (Cambridge, MA: MIT Press, 1982), 5–6.

14. Juran, 14.

15. *Imprimis*, April 1983.

16. Mark Bergin, "Junk Science," *World* magazine, February 25, 2006.

17. "Pregnant Cheerleaders Are Allowed to Return," *Cleveland Plain Dealer*, November 3, 1993.

CHAPTER 5   POWER TO INTIMIDATE: THE SLAPP FACTOR

1. The ACLU receives funding from a number of sources, including tax-exempt foundations (Ford, Rockefeller, Carnegie, Field, etc.) and court-awarded legal fees. Recovery of legal fees by nonprofit legal advocacy groups is a common practice, and since 1976 federal law leaves the government liable in some civil cases. Planned Parenthood receives over $50 million annually through Title X funding of the U.S. Department of Health and Human Services, and over $50 million annually through the Medicaid program. Available from: www.stopthcaclu.org; Office of Population Affairs, Department of Health and Human Services, http://opa.osophs.dhhs.gov/titlex.

2. Thomas L. Krannawitter and Daniel C. Palm, *A Nation Under God?* (Lanham, MD: Rowman & Littlefield, 2005), 111.

3. Alan Sears and Craig Osten, *The ACLU vs. America* (Nashville, TN: The Alliance Defense Fund, 2005), 2.

4. Dennis Prager, "The Left Thinks Legally, The Right Thinks Morally," *Creators Syndicate*, 21 September, 2004, excerpted in Sears and Osten, *The ACLU vs. America*, 30–31.

5. "Darrow Argues Law Is Unconstitutional," available from: http://www.law.umkc.edu/faculty/projects/ftrials/scopes/day2.htm.

6. George W. Pring and Penelope Canan, *SLAPPS* (Philadelphia, PA: Temple University Press, 1996).

7. Jennifer E. Sills, "SLAPPS (Strategic Lawsuits Against Public Participation): How Can the Legal System Eliminate Their Appeal?" *Connecticut Law Review*, Winter, 1993.

8. "Historical Perspectives on Religion, Government and Social Welfare in America," available from: www.trincoll.edu/depts/csrpl/Charitable%20Choice%20book/Hall.pdf.

9. Pring and Canan.

10. "SLAPP Happy: Corporations That Sue to Shut You Up," available from: www.prwatch.org/prwissues/1997Q2/slapp.html.

11. Book review: *SLAPPS*, Pring and Canan, available from: www.amazon.com/Slapps-Getting-Sued-Speaking-Out/dp/1566393698/ref=dp_return_1/103-2858498-4055813?ie=UTF8&n=283155&s=books&qid=1180527158&sr=1-1. These are the comments of L. Kline Cappelle, a law student who worked with Pring and Canan.

12. Gallup Poll, May 2003 Galluppoll.com.

13. Gallup Poll, April, May, and June 1970.

14. "Where two or more students are gathered together . . . there is controversy," *The Oregonian*, March 9, 2007.

15. "A Brief Background of Scouting in the United States, 1910 to Today," available from: www.troop97.net/bsahist1.htm.

16. www.tributetoscouts.com.

17. From The Scout Law of 1912 and original 1908 edition of Baden-Powell's *Scouting for Boys*. Available from: www.inquiry.net/ideals/b-p/law.htm.

18. "Schools Face New Scout Suit," *Oregonian*, April 6, 2001.

19. "Equal, Private: High Court Should Strike Down Texas Sodomy Law," *Lansing State Journal*, March 27, 2003. The information on the number of states came from a map available at Image: U.S. Sodomy Laws.org, Wikepedia; see also www.sodomylaws.org.

20. *Lawrence v. Texas* (01-102) 539 U.S. 558 (2003).

21. Available from: www.bsalegal.org/litigation-222.asp .

22. Available from: www.bsalegal.org/litigation-222.asp.

23. "The Case Scouts Had to Win," *New York Times*, June 30, 2000.

24. "Companies Here Ponder Scout Ruling," *Seattle Times*, July 6, 2000.

25. *Boy Scouts of America et al. v. Dale*, 530 U.S. 640 (2000).

26. Available from: www.ScoutsAlumni.com; see "court rulings."

Articles on this website include: "Deputy in youth program charged in child sex," (11/01/03); "Former Explorers Post Leader Admits to Sex Abuse," (10/14/03); "Ex-Teacher Convicted of Abusing Boy Scouts," (10/10/03).

27. "Fact Sheet on Sexual Orientation and Child Abuse," available from: www.wearemichigan.com/reference/childabuse.htm.

28. K. Freund et al., "Pedophilia and Heterosexuality vs. Homosexuality," *Journal of Sex and Marital Therapy* 10, no. 3 (1984): 193–200.

29. David Kupelian, "'Pedophile Priests' and the Boy Scouts," May 8, 2002, available from: www.worldnetdaily.com/news/article.asp?ARTICLE_ID=27539.

30. Leslie Carbone, "Hypocrites on Homosexuality," *National Review*, June 19, 2002.

31. "Guide to Safe Scouting: Youth Protection and Adult Leadership," www.scouting.org/pubs/gss/fss01.html.

32. Donald B. Cozzens, *The Changing Face of the Priesthood* (Collegeville, MN: The Liturgical Press, 2000), 110.

33. Philip Jenkins, *Pedophiles and Priests* (New York: Oxford Press, 1996); Thomas G. Plante, *Bless Me Father for I Have Sinned* (Westport, CT: Praeger, 1999).

34. Reported by the Associated Press, March 8, 2006, in *The Irish Times*, and available from: http://www.ireland.com/newspaper/front/2006/0308.

35. "Spielberg Quits Scout Post," *San Diego Union-Tribune*, April 17, 2001.

36. "Wells Fargo and PGE to Direct funds From Scouts," *The Oregonian*, December 11, 2000.

37. "Boy Scout Troops Lose Funds, Meeting Places," *USA Today*, October 10, 2000.

38. Available from: www.cwa-union.org/issues/civil-rights.

39. "Scouts Successful Ban on Gays Is Followed by Loss of Support," *New York Times*, August 29, 2000.

40. *Las Vegas Sun*, January 7, 2001.

41. "Scouts Ban on Gays Is Prompting School to Reconsider Ties," *Education Week*, October 25, 2000.

42. "City Settles Boy Scouts Lease Suit," *San Diego Union-Tribune*, January 9, 2004.

43. "Senate Backs Scouts Use of Bases," *Omaha World-Herald*, July 27, 2005.

44. "ACLU Threat Causes Boy Scouts to drop public school ties," available from: http://groups.google.com/rec.scoutingissues.

45. Gallup Poll, June 22–25, 2000, Galluppoll.com.

46. "Scouts Use of Schools Under Attack," *Washington Post*, October 4, 2000.

CHAPTER 6 PUBLIC SCHOOLS: DECONSTRUCTING AMERICAN VALUES

1. Jeff Jacoby, "Public Schools vs. Parent Values," available from: www.townhall.com/columnists/JeffJacoby/2006/04/28.

2. Linda de Haan and Stern Nijland, *King and King* (Berkeley, CA: Tricycle Press, 2002).

3. Michael Foust, "Massachusetts 2nd-grade Teacher Reads Class 'Gay Marriage' Book; Administrator Backs Her," Baptist Press, available from: www.bpnews.net/bpnews.asp?ID=23077.

4. Foust.

5. Foust.

6. Daniel J. Boorstin, *The Creators* (New York: Random House, 1992), 5, 41.

7. "Louis Pasteur," from Wikipedia, available from: http://en.wikipedia.org/wiki/Louis_Pasteur.

8. Michael H. Hart, *Religious Affiliation of History's 100 Most Influential People*, summary available from: www.adherents.com/adh_influ.html.

9. "Television & Health," in *The Sourcebook for Teaching Science*, available from: www.csun.edu/~vceed002/health/docs/tv&health.html.

10. "Television & Health."

11. "Students Lagging in American History," *Boston Globe*, July 1, 2005.

12. Martin L. Gross, *The Conspiracy of Ignorance*, (New York: Harper Collins, 1999), 23.

13. "Preparing College Students for College and Work," *The Seattle Times*, November 29, 2006, H18.

14. "Students Lagging in American History," *Boston Globe*, July 1, 2005.

15. Francis A. Schaeffer, *How Should We Then Live?* (Old Tappan, NJ: Fleming H. Revell Company, 1976), 224.

16. Alan Sears and Craig Osten, *The ACLU vs. America* (Nashville, TN: The Alliance Defense Fund, 2005), 22–23.

17. Sears and Osten, 23.

18. "Religious Clothing & Jewelry in Schools," available from: www.religioustolerance.org/sch_clot1.htm.

19. "CA: ACLU Sues School District for Discrimination Against Pregnant Students," *Feminist Daily*, September 7, 2004, available from: www.feminist.org/news/newsbyte/uswirestory.asp?id=8625.

20. Virginia I. Postrel, "Persecution Complex—Religion in the Workplace," *Reason*, August-September, 1994, available from: http://www.findarticles.com/p/articles/mi_m1568/is_n4_v26/ai_15630153.

21. Postrel.

22. Scott LaFee, "Legally Bound: Who Are the Real Losers in School Lawsuits?" 2005 California School Board Association, available from: www.csba.org/csmag/fall05/csMagStoryTemplate.cfm?id=75.

23. *The Daily Tokoyo Yomiuri*. February 5, 2005.

24. Monisha Bansal, "School Board, Conservatives Clash Over Sex-Ed Curriculum," available from: www.cnsnews.com/Culture/Archive/200702/CUL20070226a.html.

25. "Wide Berth Allowed on Teaching About Homosexuality," *Washington Post*, January 16, 2007.

26. "School Board Reverses Ban on Pregnant Cheerleaders," *Houston Chronicle*, November 2, 1993.

27. Bansal, "School Board, Conservatives Clash.

28. Available from: www.reclaimamerica.org/Pages/NEWS/news.aspx?story=2744; www.reclaimamerica.org/Pages/NEWS/news.aspx?story=2671; www.reclaimamerica.org/PAGES/NEWS/news.aspx?story=2403; www.reclaimamerica.org/PAGES/NEWS/news.aspx?story=1809.

29. Sears and Osten, 203–9.

CHAPTER 7　　AMERICA'S SECULAR CATHEDRALS: HIGHER ED OR A LOWER WAY?

1. *San Diego Union-Tribune*, April 23, 2006, available from: http://sll.stanford.edu/projects/tomprof/newtonprof.

2. James Shannon, "Books and Politics: Truth & Beauty Under Fire," *The Beat*, July 25, 2006, available from: www.metrobeat.net/gbase/Expedite/Content?oid=oid%3A3944.

3. Shannon.

4. Shannon.

5. "Truth and Beauty: Part Deux," *Swamp Fox Insights*, August 26, 2006, available from: http://swampfoxinsights.blogspot.com/2006/08/truth-and-beauty-part-deux.html.

6. The procedure to avoid the "freshmen reading project" was so obscure that none of them could make arrangements beforehand to opt out of the assignment.

7. Mike S. Adams, *Welcome to the Ivory Tower of Babel* (Boyne City, MI: Harbor House, 2004).

8. Available from: http://challenge.visualessence.nl/C514241107/E200509/index.html

9. Charles Miller quoted in Kelly Field, "A Texas Millionaire Plots the Future of Higher Education," *Chronicle of Higher Education*, June 2, 2006, A18.

10. Stephen Prothero, *Religious Literacy* (San Francisco: Harper, 2007).

11. Address by Stephen H. Balch, President of the National Association of Scholars, to the Select Committee of the Pennsylvania House of Representatives, November 9, 2005.

12. *Gratz v. Bollinger*, 539 U.S. 244 (2003).

13. Balch, address.

14. Mike S. Adams, "University Officials Buggered by Gay Unicorn," March 27, 2007, www.Townhall.com; Mike S. Adams, "College Republicans Banned from Campus," November 19, 2003, www.Townhall.com.

15. "First Do Harm, " *The Weekly Standard*, February 5, 2007, 35.

16. Anonymous, *Unprotected* (New York: Sentinel, Harper-Collins, 2007).

17. Alexander Hamilton, James Madison, and John Jay, *The Federalist Papers*, ed. Clinton Rossiter (New York: Penguin Publishers, 1961), 342.

18. Plato, *The Republic*, Book VI, in *Classics of Moral and Political Theory*, 4th edition, ed. Michael Morgan, (Indianapolis, IN: Hackett Publishing Company, 2005), 172.

19. Allan Bloom, *The Closing of the American Mind* (New York: Simon & Schuster, 1987), 27.

20. George Washington, "First Inaugural Address," available from: www.bartleby.com/124/pres13.html.

21. Saul Padover, *Thomas Jefferson on Democracy* (New York: Appleton-Century Co., Inc. 1939), 89.

22. Thomas Jefferson, et al., "Report of the Commissioners for the University of Virginia, August 4, 1818," Richmond, Va., Printed by Thomas Ritchie, Virginia General Assembly, House of Delegates.

23. Woodrow Wilson, "What Is Progress?" in *The New Freedom* (New York: Doubleday, Page and Co., 1918), 42.

24. Charles Edward Merriam, *A History of American Political Theories* (New York. The Macmillan Co., 1903), 308–9.

25. "The Rich—Poor Gap Widens for Colleges and Students," *The Chronicle*, April 7, 2006.

26. Daniel B. Klein and Charlotta Stern, "How Politically Diverse Are the Social Sciences and Humanities?" available from: www.ratio.se/pdf/wp/dk_ls_diverse.pdf.

27. Everett Carl Ladd Jr. and Seymour M. Lipset, *The Divided Academy* (New York: McGraw Hill, 1975).

28. Lynn Vincent, "Shedding the Intellectual Straightjacket," *World* magazine, April 29, 2006.

29. David Stoll, *Rigoberta Menchú and the Story of All Poor Guatemalans* (Boulder, CO: Westview Press, 1999).

30. "Guatemalan Laureate Defends 'My Truth.'" *New York Times*, January 21, 1999.

31. "Must People Lie?" *New York Times*, August 18, 2001.

32. *Grutter v. Bollinger* and *Gratz v. Bollinger*, 539 U.S. 306 (2003).

33. Bloom, 344.

34. E. D. Hirsch, *Cultural Literacy* (New York: Vintage Books, 1988), 2.

35. "The Dissolution of General Education: 1914–1993," National Association of Scholars, available from: www.nas.org/reports/disogened/disogened_full.pdf.

36. American Council of Trustees and Alumni and The Institute for Effective Governance, "Becoming an Educated Person: Toward a Core Curriculum for College Students," July 2003, available from: www.goacta.org/publications/Reports/BEPFinal.pdf.

37. American Council of Trustees and Alumni, "The Hollow Core: The Failure of the General Education Curriculum," available from: www.goacta.org/publications/Reports/TheHollowCore.pdf.

38. "Liberal to the Core," *Wall Street Journal*, May 14, 2004.

39. Balch, address.

40. National Association of Scholars, "Today's College Students and Yesteryear's High School Grads: A Comparison of General Cultural Knowledge," available from: www.nas.org/reports/senior_poll/senior_poll_report.pdf.

41. American Council of Trustees and Alumni, "Losing America's Memory: Historical Illiteracy in the 21st Century," available from: www.goacta.org/publications/Reports/acta_american_memory.pdf.

42. Garrison Keillor, *Lake Wobegon Days* (New York: Penguin, 1990).

43. American Council of Trustees and Alumni, "Degraded Currency: The Problem of Grade Inflation," October, 2003, available from: www.goacta.org/publications/reports.html.

44. Martin Anderson, *Imposters in the Temple* (New York: Simon and Schuster, 1992), 95.

45. Southwestern Social Science Association, April 13–17, 2006, San Antonio, TX.

46. Personal communication to Dr. J. David Woodard.

47. Anderson, 98.

48. "Perspectives 2006," from The American Association of State Colleges and Universities, available from: http://aascu.org/perspectives_06/conclusion.htm.

49. Derek Bok, "Are Colleges Failing? Higher Ed Needs New Lesson Plans," *Boston Globe*, December 18, 2005, available from: www.boston.com/news/education/higher/articles/2005/12/18/are_colleges_failing?m.

50. Derek Bok, *Our Underachieving Colleges: A Candid Look at How Much Students Learn and Why They Should Be Learning More*, excerpted on Princeton University Press website, available from: www.pupress.princeton.edu/chapters/i8125.html.

51. Bok, "Are Colleges Failing?"

52. Betsy Stevens, "How Satisfied Are Employers with Graduates' Business Communications Skills? A Survey of Silicon Valley Employers," 2004, available from: www.westga.edu/~bquest/2004/graduates.htm.

53. Richard M. Freeland, "How Practical Experience Can Help Revitalize Our Tired Model of Undergraduate Education," *Chronicle of Higher Education*, February 19, 1999, available from: http://chronicle.com/weekly/v45/i24/24b00601.htm.

54. Bok, "Are Colleges Failing?"

CHAPTER 8   WAR OF THE WORLDVIEWS: ATTACKS AND COUNTERATTACKS

1. "General's Remarks Bring Pentagon Homophobia Out of the Closet," *Baltimore Sun*, March 19, 2007.

2. Editorial, "General Pace and Gay Soldiers," *New York Times*, March 15, 2007.

3. Benjamin Dowling-Sendor, "A Prayer by Any Name," *American School Board Journal* 188, no. 11 (November 2001).

4. Dowling-Sendor.

5. Dowling-Sendor.

6. Antonio Planas, "District Pulls Plug on Speech," *Las Vegas Review-Journal*, June 17, 2006, available from: www.reviewjournal.com/lvrj_home/2006/Jun-17-Sat-2006/news/8014416.html.

7. Planas.

8. Planas.

9. Antonio Planas, "Group Files Lawsuit, Alleges School Officials Violated Teen's Rights," *Las Vegas Review-Journal*, June 14, 2006, available from: www.reviewjournal.com/lvrj_home/2006/Jun-14-Sat-2006/news/8491786.html.

10. Alan Sears and Craig Osten, *The ACLU vs. America*, (Nashville, TN: Broadman & Holman Publishers, 2005), 57.

11. Sears and Osten, 57.

12. Thomas L. Krannawitter and Daniel C. Palm, *A Nation Under God?* (Lanham, MD: Rowman & Littlefield, 2005), 115.

13. Krannawitter and Palm, 57.

14. Krannawitter and Palm, 56.

15. Krannawitter and Palm, 59–60.

16. Krannawitter and Palm, 61.

17. Krannawitter and Palm, 58–59.

18. Krannawitter and Palm, 65.

19. David Greenberg, "The Pledge of Allegiance: Why We're Not One Nation 'Under God'" *Slate*, June 28, 2002, available from: www.slate.com/?id=2067499.

20. Patrick Haynes and Jeremy Lott, "Left, Right and Religious," *USA Today*, October 16, 2006; Nancy Brodertscher, "Legislature 2006," *Atlanta Journal-Constitution*, Janaury 28, 2006; James Salzer, "Legislature 2006," *Atlanta Journal-Constituton*, February 5, 2006.

21. Rutherford Institute, "The Rights of Churches and Political Involvement," available from: www.rutherford.org/PDF/rightsofchurches.pdf.

22. Martin A. Larson and C. Stanley Lowell, *Praise the Lord for Tax Exemption* (New York: Robert B. Luce, 1969). The $300 billion estimate is based on inflation, projected from 1976.

23. Cassandra Niemczyk, "Little-Known or Remarkable Facts about Christianity and the American Revolution," *Christian History* 15, no. 2, issue 50, p. 2.

24. Rutherford Institute, "The Rights of Churches and Political Involvement."

25. Daryl L. Wiesen, "Following the Lead of Defamation: A Definitional Approach to Religious Torts," *Yale Law Journal* 105 (1995).

26. John Leo, "Church Takes Pause at Teacher's Pregnancy," *USNews.com*, December 10, 2005.

27. "State Orders Wal-Mart to Sell Morning After Pill," *Boston Globe*, February 15, 2006.

28. Virginia I. Postrel, "Persecution Complex—Religion in the Workplace," *Reason*, August–September, 1994, available from: www.findarticles.com/p/articles/mi_m1568/is_n4_v26/ai_15630153.

29. Postrel.

CHAPTER 9   AMERICA'S SECULAR CULTURE: THE COST IN DOLLARS AND SENSE

1. Alan Wolfe, *Moral Freedom* (New York: W.W. Norton and Co., 2001), 223.

2. Gary S. Becker and Kevin M. Murphy, *Social Economics: Market Behavior in a Social Environment* (Cambridge, MA: The Belknap Press, 2000), 29.

3. Gallup Poll, July 7–10, 2005, Galluppoll.com.

4. Gallup Poll, July 7–10, 2005

5. American Cancer Society, available from: www.cancer.org/docroot/PED/content/PED_10_2x_cigarette_Smoking.asp.

6. Some still contest the validity of studies that prove the dangers of second-hand smoke. We are not advocating the merits of the research. Instead, we are using the smoking debate to illustrate how government decisions regarding specific behavior are magnified throughout our culture.

7. Patrick F. Fagan, Robert E. Rector, and Lauren R. Noyes, "Why Congress Should Ignore Radical Feminist Opposition to Marriage," *The Heritage Foundation Backgrounder*, no. 1662 (June 2003): 11.

8. Rick Santorum, *It Takes a Family* (Wilmington, DE: ISI Books, 2005), 15.

9. Robert P. George and Jean Bethke Elshtain, *The Meaning of Marriage* (Dallas, TX: Spence Publishing Co., 2006), 19.

10. Kimberley Strasset et al., *Leaving Women Behind* (Lanham, MD: Rowman and Littlefield, 2006).

11. Gallup Poll, May 10–14, 2001, Galluppoll.com.

12. "First comes sex, then comes marriage," *Newark Star Ledger*, December 20, 2006.

13. Edward O. Laumann et al., *The Social Organization of Sexuality* (Chicago: University of Chicago Press, 1994), 214.

14. "The Problem of Cohabitation," available from: http://members.aol.com/cohabiting/intro.htm, 5.

15. Maggie Gallagher, *The Abolition of Marriage* (Washington, DC: Regnery Publishing, Inc., 1996), 7.

16. David T. Ellwood and Christopher Jencks, "The Spread of Single-Parent Families in the United States since 1960," (John F. Kennedy School of Government, Harvard University, October 2002), available from: www.ksg.harvard.edu/inequality/Seminar/Papers/ElwdJnck.pdf.

17. Centers for Disease Control and Prevention, "Trends in Reportable Sexually Transmitted Diseases in the United States, 2003—National Data on Chlamydia, Gonorrhea and Syphilis," available from: http://www.region8ipp.com/articles/2003%20STD%20Surveillance%20Summary.pdf.

18. "Sexually Transmitted Diseases in the US: New Numbers from the CDC," *Healthlink*, Medical University of Wisconsin, available from: http://healthlink .mcw.edu/article/976735469.html.

19. NIAID, "Sexually Transmitted Diseases Statistics, NIAID Fact Sheet: NI-AID," National Institute of Allergy and Infectious Diseases, National Institutes of Health, available from: www.wrongdiagnosis.com/artic/sexually_transmitted_diseases_ niaid_fact_sheet_niaid.htm.

20. American Social Health Association, "STD/STI Statistics," 1998, available from: www.ashastd.org/learn/learn_statistics.cfm.

21. Centers for Disease Control and Prevention, "HIV/AIDS among Men Who Have Sex with Men," 1993, available from: www.cdc.gov/hiv/pubs/facts/msm.htm.

22. Harrell W. Chesson et al., "The Estimated Direct Medical Cost of Sexually Transmitted Diseases among American Youth, 2000," Center for Disease Control and Prevention publication 36, no. 1 (January/February 2004). Note: this conclusion is reached by projecting data provided for youth ages 15–24.

23. "Homosexual Men Boost Increase in Syphilis Rate," *Washington Times*, Friday, March 17, 2006. This information was taken from a study by Centers for Disease Control and Prevention's National Center for HIV, STD, and TB Prevention.

24. James Dobson, "HPV Epidemic Plagues Young People" *Greenville Journal*, January 6, 2006. Syndicated article.

25. Dobson.

26. "Behavioral Risk Factor Surveillance System, (BRFSS) 2004 Survey," available from: www.cdc.org/HPV.

27. Chesson et al.

28. "Tracking the Hidden Epidemics: Trends in STDs in the United States, 2000," Centers for Disease Control and Prevention (CDC), available from: www.cdc.gov/ std/Trends2000/.

29. U.S. Bureau of the Census data, cited in "The Problem of Cohabitation."

30. Alfred DeMaris and K. Vaninadha Rao, "Premarital Cohabitation and Subsequent Marital Stability in the United States: A Reassessment," *Journal of Marriage and the Family* 54 (February 1992): 178–90; Susan L. Brown, "The Effect of Union Type on Psychological Well-Being: Depression Among Cohabitors Versus Marrieds," *Journal of Health and Social Behavior* 41 (September 2000): 241–55; Steven L. Nock, "A Comparison of Marriage and Cohabiting Relationships," *Journal of Family Issues* 16 (January 1995): 53–76.

31. Sonia Milner Salari and Bret M. Baldwin, "Verbal, Physical and Injurious Aggression among Intimate Couples over Time," *Journal of Family Issues* 23 (May 2002): 523–50; Allan V. Horowitz et al., "The Relationship of Cohabitation and Mental Health: A Study of a Young Adult Cohort," *Journal of Marriage and Family* 60 (May 1998): 505–14; Susan L. Brown and Alan Booth, "Cohabitation Versus Marriage: A Comparison of Relationship Quality," *Journal of Marriage and the Family* 58 (August 1996): 668–78; Renata Foste and Koray Tanfer, "Sexual Exclusivity among Dating, Cohabitating and Married Women," *Journal of Marriage and the Family* 58 (February 1996): 33–47; Judith Treas and Deidre Giesen, "Sexual Infidelity among Married and Cohabitating Americans," *Journal of Marriage and the Family* 62 (February 2000): 48–60.

32. Brad Lewis, "Living Together Not Such a Good Idea After All," *Living Together*, available from: www.troubledwith.com/LoveandSex/A000000340.cfm?topic=love%20and%20sex%3A%20living%20together.

33. Roland H. Johnson III, "Cohabitation (Good for Him, Not for Her)," available from: http://personalwevs.myriad.net/Roland/cohab1.htm.

34. Elizabeth Thomason et al., "Family Structure and Child Well-Being: Economic Resources vs. Parental Behaviors," *Social Forces* 73 (September 1994): 221–42.

35. "The Problem with Cohabitation."

36. Alison Bethel, "Unwed Culture Stirs Backlash," *Detroit News*, Sunday, May 15, 2005.

37. Anne K. Driscoll et al., "Nonmarital Childbearing among Adult Women," *Journal of Marriage and the Family* 61 (February 1999): 178–87.

38. Robert Rector, "Out of Wedlock Childbearing and Paternal Absence: Trends and Social Effects," www.catholicculture.org/library/view.cfm?ecnum+1446.

39. Neil G. Bennett et al., "The Influence of Nonmarital Childbearing on the Formation of First Marriages," *Demography* 32 (1995): 47–62.

40. Suzette Fromm, "Total Estimated Cost of Child Abuse and Neglect in the United States," a Prevent Child Abuse America study funded by The Edna McConnell Clark Foundation, 2001, available from: http://member.parentchildabuse.org/site/DocServer/cost_analysis.pdf?docID=144.

41. Fromm.

42. Fromm.

43. Patrick Fagan et al., "The Positive Effects of Marriage: A Book of Charts," *The Heritage Foundation*, April 2002, 13.

44. Patrick Fagan, Robert Rector, and Lauren Noyes, "Why Congress Should Ignore Radical Feminist Opposition to Marriage," *The Heritage Foundation Backgrounder*, no. 1662 (June 2003), available from: www.heritage.org/research/family/bg1662.cfm.

45. Kerby Anderson, "Broken Homes, Broken Hearts," Probe Ministries, 1994, available from: www.leaderu.com/orgs/probe/docs/broken.html.

46. Bill Clinton, "State of the Union Address," January 25, 1994, available from: http://thisnation.com/library/sotu/1994bc.html.

47. Jeffrey M. Jones, research fellow at the Hoover Institution, "The Cost of Care," *Hoover Digest*, no. 4, (1994), available from: http://thisnation.com/library/sotu/1994bc.html.

48. Ellwood and Jencks.

49. Paul A. Nakonezny and Robert D. Shull, "The Effect of No-Fault Divorce Laws on the Divorce Rate Across the 50 States and Its Relation to Income, Education, and Religiosity," *Journal of Marriage and the Family* 57 (May 1995): 477–88; Leora Friedburg, "Did Unilateral Divorce Raise Rates? Evidence from Panel Data," *American Economic Review* 88 (June 1998): 608–27.

50. Pranay Gupte, "It's Personal for a Top NYC Divorce Lawyer," *New York Sun*, May 17, 2005, available from: www.nysun.com/article/13956.

51. B. Whitehead and D. Popenoe, "The State of Our Unions," available from: http://marriage.rutgers.edu/Publications/SOOU/TEXTSOOU2004.htm.

52. Judith S. Wallerstein et al., *The Unexpected Legacy of Divorce* (New York: Hyperion, 2000), xxv.

53. Fagan et al., "Positive Effects of Marriage: A Book of Charts."

54. Steven D. Levitt and Stephen J. Dubner, *Freakonomics* (New York: William Morrow, 2005), 138–43.

55. Dennis M. Howard, "Why the Tide Is Turning," January 27, 2003, available from: www.yourcatholicvoice.org/print.php?print=news&ID=157.

56. Kelly Hollowell, *Struggling for Life: How Your Tax Dollars and Twisted Science Target the Unborn*, Center for Reclaiming America for Christ, an outreach of Coral Ridge Ministries Media, Inc., 2006.

57. "Study Links Abortion, Suicide, Depression," *CWNews*, August 22, 2001.

58. Dr. and Mrs. J. C. Willke, *Why Can't We Love Them Both* (Ch. 23), *Breast Cancer*, available from: www.abortionfacts.com/online_books/love_them_both/why_cant_we_love_them_both.asp.

59. *Miller v. California*, Supreme Court decision 413 U.S. 15, June 21, 1973, established minimum standards for obscene material.

60. D. Zillmann and J. Bryant, "Pornography's Impact on Sexual Satisfaction," *Journal of Applied Social Psychology* 18, no. 5 (1998): 435–53, cited in Victor B. Cline, "Pornography's Effect on Adult and Child," available from: http://mentalhealthlibrary.info/library/porn/pornlds/pornldsauthor/links/victorcline/porneffect.htm.

61. Cline.

62. Larry Baron and Murray Strauss, "Legitimate Violence and Rape: A Test of the Cultural Spillover Theory," *Social Problems* 34 (December 1985), cited in Kerby Anderson, "The Pornography Plague," available from: www.leaderu.com/orgs/probe/docs/pornplag.html.

63. David Alexander Scott, "How Pornography Changes Attitudes," in *Pornography: The Human Tragedy*, ed. Tom Minnery (Wheaton, IL: Tyndale House Publishers), cited in Anderson, "The Pornography Plague."

64. "U.S. 'Worst for Online Child Abuse,'" *BBC News*, July 20, 2006, available from: http://news.bbc.co.uk/2/hi/technology/5195460.stm.

65. Judith Mackey, "How Does the U.S. Compare with the Rest of the World in Human Sexual Behavior," *Western Journal of Medicine* 6, no. 174 (June 2001): 429–33.

66. Ryan Singel, "Internet Porn: Worse Than Crack?" November 19, 2004, available from: www.wired.com/news/technology/0,1282,65772,00.html.

67. Singel.

68. "Porn in the U.S.A." *60 Minutes*, available from: www.cbsnews.com/stories/2003/11/21/60minutes/main585049.shtml?source=search_story.

69. Stanley Kurtz, "The End of Marriage in Scandinavia," *Weekly Standard*, February 2, 2004.

70. Cited in Traditional Values Coalition, "Dutch Study Exposes Infidelity Among Homosexual Partners," available from: www.traditionalvalues.org/modules.php?sid=1059.

71. Lynn C. Wardle, "The Potential Impact of Homosexual Parenting on Children," *The University of Illinois Law Review* 1997, no. 3.

72. John R. Diggs, Jr., "The Health Risks of Gay Sex," Corporate Resource Council, 2002, available from: www.catholiceducation.org/articles/homosexuality/ho0075.html.

73. Diggs.

74. Diggs.

75. Diggs.

76. Diggs. Study referenced: "Netherlands Ends Discrimination in Civil Marriage: Gays to Wed," Lambda Legal Defense and Education Fund press Release, March 30, 2001.

77. Diggs.

78. Diggs.

79. Diggs.

80. Timothy Dailey, "The Negative Health Effects of Homosexuality," November 22, 2006, available from: www.frc.org/get.cfm?i=IS01B1.

81. Dailey.

82. Dailey.

83. Dailey.

84. William Ahern, "Spending on Lotteries in U.S. Tops Spending on Books and Movies," *Budget & Tax News*, February 1, 2005, available from: www.heartland.org/Article.cfm?artId=16332.

85. Cynthia R. Janower, "Gambling on the Internet," from Christensen Capital Advisors Global Internet Gambling Revenue Estimates and Projections (2001–2010).

86. Carl G. Bechtold, "Tide of Gambling Yields Backwash of Addiction," National Coalition Against Legalized Gambling, August 21, 2004.

87. Bechtold.

88. Bechtold.

89. Bechtold.

90. American Gaming Association, State of the States survey, 2003, 3.

91. Janower.

92. "What Really Mattered?" *Time*, October 5, 1983.

CHAPTER 10   CONTRASTING WORLDVIEWS: INTOLERANCE OR COMPASSION?

1. John Kenneth White, *The Values Divide* (New York: Chatham House Publishers, 2003), 63.

2. Richard John Neuhaus, *The Naked Public Square* (Grand Rapids, MI: Eerdmans, 1984), 259.

3. "Fix It, Brother," *Washington Post*, May 22, 2004.

4. Star Parker address, "Reclaiming America for Christ," Conference, April 27–28, 2001, Newport Beach, California.

5. The Opportunity Agenda, "The State of Opportunity in America, African Americans and Opportunity," The Opportunity Agenda, 2005, available from:

http://www.opportunityagenda.org/site/c.minL5kkNOLvH/b.1419965/k.3C7B/African_
Americans_and_Opportunity.htm.

6. Marvin Olasky, *The Tragedy of American Compassion* (Washington, DC: Regnery Press, 1992).

7. The Opportunity Agenda.

8. Juan Williams, *Enough* (New York: Crown Publishers, 2006).

9. U.S. Department of Labor, "The Negro Family: A Case for National Action," March, 1965.

10. Lee Rainwater and William L. Yancey, *The Moynihan Report and the Politics of Controversy* (Cambridge, MA: MIT Press, 1967).

11. Charles Murray, *Losing Ground* (New York: Basic Books, 1994), 128.

12. Charles Murray, "The Coming White Underclass," *The Wall Street Journal*, October 29, 1993.13. Fagan.

13. Patrick Fagan, "Encouraging Marriage and Discouraging Divorce," *Heritage Foundation, Backgrounder*, no. 1421 (March 2001).

14. Fagan.

15. Fagan.

16. U.S. Department of Health and Human Services, "Temporary Assistance for Needy Families Information Memorandum" (Washington, DC, September 30, 2004).

17. U.S. Department of Health and Human Services.

18. U.S. Department of Health and Human Services; Fagan.

19. U.S. Department of Health and Human Services; Fagan.

20. Gertrude Himmelfarb, *The Moral Imagination* (Chicago: Ivan R. Dee, 2007), 6.

21. Available from: www.marriagesavers.org.

22. Fagan.

23. Fagan.

24. "Health Experts Criticize Changes in STD Panel," *Washington Post*, May 9, 2006.

25. "Health Experts Criticize."

26. "Health Experts Criticize."

27. Robert Rector, *Heritage Foundation, Backgrounder*, no. 1533 (April 2002).

28. Rector.

29. Available from: http://plannedparenthood.org/los-angeles/abstinence-only-sex-education.htm.

30. Edmund Burke, "Reflections on the Revolution in France," Terence Ball and Richard Dagger, eds., *Ideals and Ideologies*. (New York: Longman, 2002), 140.

31. Robert N. Bellah, *The Broken Covenant* (New York: Seabury, 1975).

32. Fritz Stern, *The Politics of Cultural Despair* (Berkeley, CA: University of California Press, 1960), 44.

33. Bill O'Reilly, *Culture Warrior* (New York: Broadway, 2006).

34. O'Reilly, 23.

35. Gallup Poll, May 23–26, 2005; Gallup Poll, September 8–11, 2005, Galluppoll.com.

36. Mother Teresa, "Speech at the National Prayer Breakfast, 1994," available from: www.orthodoxytoday.org/articles4/MotherTeresaAbortion.php.

37. Stephen L. Carter, *The Culture of Disbelief* (New York: Basic Books, 1993).

38. Os Guinness, *The American Hour* (New York: The Free Press, 1993), 173.

39. "The 2004 Political Landscape," Pew Research Center, November 5, 2003.

40. Joe Klein, "Beware of Bloggers' Bile," *Time*, May 29, 2007.

CHAPTER 11   OVERCOMING OUR SELF-IMPOSED SILENCE, REGAINING OUR VOICES, AND WINNING THE CULTURE WAR

1. David Frum, *How We Got Here: The 70's* (New York: Basic Books, 2000), xvi.

2. George F. Will, *Statecraft as Soulcraft* (New York: Simon and Schuster, 1983), 20.

3. Pew Research Center, "A Barometer of Modern Morals," February 2006 study, available from: http://pewresearch.org/pubs/307/a-barometer-of-modern-morals.

4. 2004 WirthlinWorldwide study, available from: www.friedmanfoundation.org .quorum.pdf.

5. U.S. Department of Education, press release June 27, 2002, available from: www.ed.gov/news/pressreleases/2002/06/06272002d.html.

6. *Boy Scouts of America et al. v. Dale*, 530 U.S. 640 (2000).

7. Quoted in Keith Jones, *Northern's Exposure: All Male Clubs and the United States Supreme Court*, Journal of the DuPage County Bar Association, DCBA Brief Online, available from: www.dcba.org/brief/sepissue/2005/northern0905.htm.

8. Jones.

9. Jones.

10. "Prostitution Clause in AIDS Policy Ruled Illegal," *Washington Post*, May 19, 2006.

11. "Prostitution Clause," 539 U.S. 558(2003).

12. David Hudson, "California Library Faces New Challenges in Internet Filtering Lawsuit," First Amendment Center, available from: www.firstamendmentcenter.org// news.aspx?id=9286&SearchString=david_hudson_california_library.

13. *Lawrence v. Texas*.

14. Patrick Fagan, "Encouraging Marriage and Discouraging Divorce," *Heritage Foundation Backgrounder*, no. 1421 (March 2001).

15. Matthew Spaulding, "A Defining Moment: Marriage, the Courts and the Constitution," May 17, 2004, Heritage Foundation Backgrounder, #1759.

16. Robert P. George, "What's Sex Got to Do with It?" in *The Meaning of Marriage*, eds. Robert P. George and Jean Bethke Elshtain (Dallas, TX: Spence Publishing Company, 2006), 156.

17. Wikipedia, available from: http://en.wikipedia.org/wiki/Defense_of_marriage_ amendment.

18. Fagan.

19. Taken from the testimony of Ron Haskins to the Committee on Appropriations Subcommittee on the District of Columbia, May 3, 2006. Haskins is a senior fellow at the Brookings Institution.

20. Fagan.

21. Rebecca Cook, "Laws May Reduce Unwed Fathers," *Washington Post*, June 19, 2005.

22. James Dobson, "The Dangers of Gambling," Focus on the Family, January 6, 2006.

23. "America Culturally Divided; Blue vs. Red States, Democrats vs. Republicans—Two Separate Nations, New O'Leary Report/Zogby Poll Reveals," January 6, 2004, available from: www.zogby.com/News/ReadNews.dbm?ID=775.

24. Pew Global Attitudes Project, "U.S. Image up Slightly, but Still Negative," June 23, 2005, available from: http://pewglobal.org/reports/pdf/247.pdf.

25. Pew Global Attitudes Project.

Bibliography

Adams, John. "Letter to Samuel Adams (1790)." In *Political Thought in America*, edited by Michael B. Levy. Prospect Heights, IL: Waveland Press, 1992.

Adams, Mike S. "College Republicans Banned from Campus." November 19, 2003. www.Townhall.com.

———. "University Officials Buggered by Gay Unicorn." March 27, 2007. www.Townhall.com.

———. *Welcome to the Ivory Tower of Babel*. Boyne City, MI: Harbor House, 2004.

Ahern, William. "Spending on Lotteries in U.S. Tops Spending on Books and Movies." *Budget & Tax News* (February 1, 2005), www.heartland.org/Article.cfm?artId=16332.

Alliance Defense Fund Database, "ADF Attorneys Help Secure Equal Access for Church Evicted from Local Community Room." www.alliancedefensefund.org/news/story.aspx?cid=3949.

"America Culturally Divided; Blue vs. Red States, Democrats vs. Republicans—Two Separate Nations, New O'Leary Report/Zogby Poll Reveals." January 6, 2004. www.zogby.com/News/ReadNews.dbm?ID=775.

American Association of State Colleges and Universities. "Perspectives 2006." http://aascu.org/perspectives_06/conclusion.htm.

American Cancer Society. www.cancer.org/docroot/PED/content/PED_10_2x_cigarette_Smoking.asp.

American Council of Trustees and Alumni. "Degraded Currency: The Problem of Grade Inflation" (October 2003). www.goacta.org/publications/reports.html.

———. "The Hollow Core: The Failure of the General Education Curriculum." www.goacta.org/publications/Reports/TheHollowCore.pdf.

———. "Losing America's Memory: Historical Illiteracy in the 21st Century." www.goacta.org/publications/Reports/acta_american_memory.pdf.

American Council of Trustees and Alumni and The Institute for Effective Governance. "Becoming an Educated Person: Toward a Core Curriculum for College Students" (July 2003). www.goacta.org/publications/Reports/BEPFinal.pdf.

American Social Health Association. "STD/STI Statistics" (1998). www.ashastd .org/learn/learn_statistics.cfm.

Anderson, Kerby. "Broken Homes, Broken Hearts." Probe Ministries, 1994. www.leaderu.com/orgs/probe/docs/broken.html.

Anderson, Martin. *Imposters in the Temple*. New York: Simon and Schuster, 1992.

Anonymous. *Unprotected*. New York: Sentinel, Harper-Collins, 2007.

Aquinas, Thomas. "Summa Theologica." In *Classics of Moral and Political Theory*, 4th ed. edited by Michael Morgan. Indianapolis, IN: Hackett Publishing, 2005.

Balch, Stephen H., President of the National Association of Scholars. Personal Address to the Select Committee of the Pennsylvania House of Representatives. November 9, 2005.

Baron, Larry, and Murray Strauss. "Legitimate Violence and Rape: A Test of the Cultural Spillover Theory." *Social Problems* 34 (December 1985).

Barone, Michael. *Our Country: The Shaping of America from Roosevelt to Reagan*. New York: The Free Press, 1990.

Beatles, The. "Nowhere Man." *Rubber Soul*. (1965).

Bechtold, Carl G. "Tide of Gambling Yields Backwash of Addiction." National Coalition Against Legalized Gambling. August 21, 2004.

Becker, Gary S., and Kevin M. Murphy. *Social Economics: Market Behavior in a Social Environment*. Cambridge, MA: The Belknap Press, 2000.

"Behavioral Risk Factor Surveillance System (BRFSS)." 2004 Survey.

Behe, Michael J. *Darwin's Black Box*, 2d ed. New York: The Free Press, 2006.

Bellah, Robert N. *The Broken Covenant*. New York: Seabury, 1975.

Bellah, Robert N., et al. *Habits of the Heart: Individualism and Commitment in American Life*. Berkeley: University of California Press, 1985.

Bennett, Neil G., et al., "The Influence of Nonmarital Childbearing on the Formation of First Marriages." *Demography* 32 (1995).

Bennett, William J. *The Index of Leading Cultural Indicators*. New York: Simon and Schuster, 1994.

———. *The Index of Leading Cultural Indicators: American Society at the End of the Twentieth Century*. rev. and exp. New York: Broadway, 1999.

Bergin, Mark. "Junk Science." *World* magazine, February 25, 2006.

Bickel, Alexander M. *The Least Dangerous Branch*. New York: The Bobbs-Merrill Company, 1962.

Binkley, Wilfred E. *American Political Parties: Their Natural History*. New York: Alfred A. Knopf, 1949.

Blanton, Dana. "More Believe in God Than Heaven." FOX News.com.

Bloom, Allan. *The Closing of the American Mind*. New York: Simon & Schuster, 1987.

Boorstin, Daniel J. *The Creators*. New York: Random House, 1992.

Bok, Derek. Our Underachieving Colleges: A Candid Look at How Much Students Learn and Why They Should Be Learning More. www.pupress.princeton.edu/chapters/i8125.html.

Bork, Robert H. *Slouching Toward Gomorrah*. New York: Regan Books, 1996.

Bowen, Catherine Drinker. *Miracle at Philadelphia*. Boston: Little, Brown, 1966.

Boy Scouts of America et al. v. Dale, 530 U.S. 640 (2000).

Bradford, M. E. *Founding Fathers*. Laurence: University Press of Kansas, 1994.

Brooks, David. *Bobos in Paradise*. New York: Touchstone Books, 2000.

Brown, Susan L. "The Effect of Union Type on Psychological Well-Being: Depression Among Cohabitors Versus Marrieds." *Journal of Health and Social Behavior* 41 (September 2000).

Brown, Susan L., and Alan Booth. "Cohabitation versus Marriage: A Comparison of Relationship Quality." *Journal of Marriage and the Family* 58 (August 1996).

Burke, Edmund. "Reflections on the Revolution in France." In *Ideals and Ideologies*. Edited by Terrence Bell and Richard Dagger. New York: Longman, 2002.

"CA: ACLU Sues School District for Discrimination Against Pregnant Students." *Feminist Daily*. www.feminist.org/news/newsbyte/uswirestory.asp?id=8625.

Carbone, Leslie. "Hypocrites on Homosexuality." *National Review*. June 19, 2002.

Carter, Stephen L. *The Culture of Disbelief*. New York: Basic Books, 1993.

Centers for Disease Control and Prevention. "HIV/AIDS among Men Who Have Sex with Men" (1993). www.cdc.gov/hiv/pubs/facts/msm.htm.

——. "Tracking the Hidden Epidemics: Trends in STDs in the United States" (2000). www.cdc.gov/std/Trends2000/.

——. "Trends in Reportable Sexually Transmitted Diseases in the United States—National Data on Chlamydia, Gonorrhea and Syphilis" (2003). www.region8ipp.com/articles/2003%20STD%20Surveillance%20Summary.pdf.

Chesson, Harrell W., et al., "The Estimated Direct Medical Cost of Sexually Transmitted Diseases Among American Youth, 2000." Center for Disease Control and Prevention 36, no. 1 (January/February 2004).

Cline, Victor B. "Pornography's Effect on Adult and Child." http://mentalhealthlibrary.info/library/porn/pornlds/pornldsauthor/links/victorcline/porneffect.htm.

Clinton, Bill. "State of the Union Address," January 25, 1994. http://thisnation.com/library/sotu/1994bc.html.

Cozzens, Donald B. *The Changing Face of the Priesthood*. Collegeville, MN: The Liturgical Press, 2000.

Dailey, Timothy. *The Negative Health Effects of Homosexuality*. November 22, 2006. www.frc.org/get.cfm?i=IS01B1.

de Haan, Linda, and Stern Nijland. *King & King*. Berkeley, CA: Tricycle Press, 2002.

DeMaris, Alfred, and K. Vaninadha Rao. "Premarital Cohabitation and Subsequent Marital Stability in the United States: A Reassessment." *Journal of Marriage and the Family* 54 (February 1992).

Deming, W. Edwards. *Out of the Crisis*. Cambridge, MA: MIT Press, 1982.

Diggs, John R. *"The Health Risks of Gay Sex."* Corporate Resource Council. (2002) www.catholiceducation.org/articles/homosexuality/ho0075.html.

Dobson, James. "The Dangers of Gambling." Focus on the Family. January 6, 2006.

Dowling-Sendor, Benjamin. "A Prayer by Any Name." *American School Board Journal* 188, no. 11 (November 2001).

Driscoll, Anne K., et al., "Nonmarital Childbearing Among Adult Women." *Journal of Marriage and the Family* 61 (February 1999).

D'Souza, Dinesh. *The Enemy at Home*. New York: Doubleday, 2007.

Ellwood, David T., and Christopher Jencks. "The Spread of Single-Parent Families in the United States since 1960." www.ksg.harvard.edu/inequality/Seminar/Papers/ElwdJnck.pdf.

Engel v. Vitale, 370 U.S. 421 (1962).

Fagan, Patrick. "Encouraging Marriage and Discouraging Divorce." *The Heritage Foundation Backgrounder* 1421 (March 2001).

Fagan, Patrick F., Robert E. Rector, and Lauren R. Noyes. "Why Congress Should Ignore Radical Feminist Opposition to Marriage." *The Heritage Foundation Backgrounder* 1662 (June 2003).

Fagan, Patrick et al., "The Positive Effects of Marriage: A Book of Charts," *The Heritage Foundation*, April 2002.

Foste, Renata, and Koray Tanfer. "Sexual Exclusivity Among Dating, Cohabiting and Married Women." *Journal of Marriage and the Family* 58 (February 1996).

Foucault, Michel. *The Order of Things*. New York: Vintage, 1994.

Foust, Michael. "Massachusetts 2nd-grade Teacher Reads Class 'Gay Marriage' Book; Administrator Backs Her." Baptist Press. www.bpnews.net/bpnews.asp?ID=23077.

Freund, K. et al., "Pedophilia and Heterosexuality vs. Homosexuality." *Journal of Sex and Marital Therapy* 10, no. 3 (1984).

Friedburg, Leora. "Did Unilateral Divorce Raise Rates? Evidence from Panel Data." *American Economic Review* 88 (June 1998).

Fromm, Suzette. "Total Estimated Cost of Child Abuse and Neglect in the United States." Prevent Child Abuse America, 2001.

Frum, David. *How We Got Here: The 70's*. New York: Basic Books, 2000.

Gallagher, Maggie. *The Abolition of Marriage*. Washington, DC: Regnery Publishing, Inc., 1996.

Gallup, George Jr. and D. Michael Lindsey. *The Gallup Guide: Reality Check for 21st Century Churches*. Loveland, CO: Group Publishing, 2002.

Gallup Poll. April–June 1970; 22–25 June 2000; 10–14 May 2001; May 2003; 23–26 May 2005; 7–10 July 2005; 8–11 September 2005.

George, Robert P., and Jean Bethke Elshtain. *The Meaning of Marriage*. Dallas, TX: Spence Publishing Co., 2006.

Gratz v. Bollinger, 539 U.S. 244 (2003).

Greenberg, David. "The Pledge of Allegiance: Why We're Not One Nation 'Under God.'" *Slate*, June 28, 2002. www.slate.com/?id=2067499.

Griswold v. Connecticut, 381 U.S. 479 (1965).

Gross, Martin L. *The Conspiracy of Ignorance*. New York: Harper Collins, 1999.

"Guide to Safe Scouting: Youth Protection and Adult Leadership." www.scouting.org/pubs/gss/fss01.html.

Guinness, Os. *The American Hour*. New York: The Free Press, 1993.

Hamilton, Alexander, James Madison, and John Jay. *The Federalist Papers*. Edited by Clinton Rossiter. New York: Penguin Publishers, 1961.

Harris, Sam. *Letter to a Christian Nation*. New York: Alfred A. Knopf, 2006.

Hart, Michael H. *Religious Affiliation of History's 100 Most Influential People*. www.adherents.com/adh_influ.html.

Hedges, Chris. *American Fascists: The Christian Right and the War on America*. New York: The Free Press, 2007.

Himmelfarb, Gertrude. *The Moral Imagination*. Chicago: Ivan R. Dee, 2007.

Hirsch, E. D. *Cultural Literacy*. New York: Vintage Books, 1988.

Horowitz, Allan V. et al., "The Relationship of Cohabitation and Mental Health: A Study of a Young Adult Cohort." *Journal of Marriage and Family* 60 (May 1998).

Howard, Dennis M. "Why the Tide Is Turning." (January 2003), www.yourcatholicvoice .org/print.php?print=news&ID=157.

Hudson, David. "California Library Faces New Challenges in Internet Filtering Lawsuit." First Amendment Center. www.firstamendmentcenter.org//news.aspx?id= 9286&SearchString=david_hudson_california_library.

Hunter, James Davidson. *Culture Wars: The Struggle to Define America*. New York: Basic Books, 1991.

Imprimis. (April 1983).

Jacoby, Jeff. "Public Schools vs. Parent Values." www.townhall.com/columnists/ JeffJacoby/2006/04/28.

Janower, Cynthia R. "Gambling on the Internet." Christensen Capital Advisors Global Internet Gambling Revenue Estimates and Projections (2001–2010).

Jefferson, Thomas et al. "Report of the Commissioners for the University of Virginia, August 4, 1818." (Richmond, VA: Virginia General Assembly, House of Delegates).

Jenkins, Philip. *Pedophiles and Priests*. New York: Oxford Press, 1996.

Johnson, Paul. *A History of the American People*. New York: Harper Collins, 1997.

Johnson, Roland H., III. "Cohabitation (Good for Him, Not for Her)." http://personalwevs .myriad.net/Roland/cohab1.htm.

Jones, Keith. "Northern's Exposure: All Male Clubs and the United States Supreme Court, Journal of the DuPage County Bar Association." DCBA Brief Online. www.dcba.org/brief/sepissue/2005/northern0905.htm.

Juran, J. M. *Juran on Quality by Design: The New Steps for Planning Quality into Goods and Services*. New York: The Free Press, 1992.

Kaufman, Matt. "Foundation of Freedom." *Citizen Magazine*, March 2004.

Keillor, Garrison. *Lake Wobegon Days*. New York: Penguin, 1990.

Klein, Daniel B., and Charlotta Stern. "How Politically Diverse Are the Social Sciences and Humanities?" www.ratio.se/pdf/wp/dk_ls_diverse.pdf.

Krannawitter, Thomas L., and Daniel C. Palm. *A Nation Under God?* Lanham, MD: Rowman & Littlefield, 2005.

Kristol, Irving. *Reflections of a Neoconservative: Looking Back, Looking Ahead*. New York: Basic Books, 1983.

Kupelian, David. "'Pedophile Priests' and the Boy Scouts." May 8, 2002. www.worldnetdaily.com/news/article.asp?ARTICLE_ID=27539.

Ladd, Everett Carl Jr., and Seymour M. Lipset. *The Divided Academy*. New York: McGraw Hill, 1975.

LaFee, Scott. "Legally Bound, Who Are the Real Losers in School Lawsuits?" CA School Board Association (2005). www.csba.org/csmag/fall05/csMagStoryTemplate .cfm?id=75.

Larson, Martin A., and C. Stanley Lowell. *Praise the Lord for Tax Exemption*. New York: Robert B. Luce, 1969.

Laumann, Edward O. et al., *The Social Organization of Sexuality*. Chicago: University of Chicago Press, 1994.

Lawrence v. Texas (01-102) 539 U.S. 558 (2003).

Layman, Geoffrey. *The Great Divide: Religious and Cultural Conflict in American Party Politics*. New York: Columbia University Press, 2001.

Leo, John. "Church Takes Pause at Teacher's Pregnancy." *USNews.com*. December 10, 2005.

Lewis, Brad. "Living Together Not Such a Good Idea After All." *Living Together*. www.troubledwith.com/LoveandSex/A000000340.cfm?topic=love%20and%20 sex%3A%20living%20together.

"Liberal to the Core." *Wall Street Journal*, (May 14, 2004).

Litowitz, Douglas E. *Postmodern Philosophy and Law*. Lawrence: University Press of Kansas, 2000.

"Louis Pasteur." *Wikipedia*. http://en.wikipedia.org/wiki/Louis_Pasteur.

Mackey, Judith. "How Does the U.S. Compare with the Rest of the World in Human Sexual Behavior." *Western Journal of Medicine* 6, no. 174 (June 2001).

Marsden, George. *The Soul of the American University*. New York: Oxford University Press, 1994.

——. *Understanding Fundamentalism and Evangelicalism*. Grand Rapids, MI: Eerdmans, 1991.

McCullough, David. *John Adams*. New York: Simon and Schuster, 2001.

Merriam, Charles Edward. *A History of American Political Theories*. New York: The Macmillan Co., 1903.

Mill, John Stuart. "On Liberty." In *Classics of Moral and Political Theory*. 4th ed., edited by Michael L. Morgan. Indianapolis, IN: Hackett Publishing, 2005.

Murray, Charles. *Losing Ground*. New York: Basic Books, 1994.

Nakonezny, Paul A., and Robert D. Shull. "The Effect of No-Fault Divorce Laws on the Divorce Rate Across the 50 States and Its Relation to Income, Education, and Religiosity." *Journal of Marriage and the Family* 57 (May 1995).

National Association of Scholars. "The Dissolution of General Education: 1914–1993." www.nas.org/reports/disogened/disogened_full.pdf.

——. "Today's College Students and Yesteryear's High School Grads: A Comparison of General Cultural Knowledge." www.nas.org/reports/senior_poll/senior_poll_report.pdf.

National Institute of Allergy and Infectious Diseases, National Institutes of Health. "Sexually Transmitted Diseases Statistics, NIAID Fact Sheet: NIAID." www.wrongdiagnosis.com/artic/sexually_transmitted_diseases_niaid_fact_sheet_niaid.htm.

National Institute of Mental Health. "The Numbers Count: Mental Disorders in America," NIH Pub No. 06-4584. www.nimh.nih.gov/publicat/numbers.cfm.

Neuhaus, Richard John. *The Naked Public Square*. Grand Rapids, MI: Eerdmans, 1984.

Niemczyk, Cassandra. "Little Known or Remarkable Facts about Christianity and the American Revolution." *Christian History* 15, no. 2.

Nock, Steven L. "A Comparison of Marriage and Cohabiting Relationships." *Journal of Family Issues* 16 (January 1995).

Norquist, Grover. "Reducing Government by Half." *The Insider*, no. 271 (May 2000). Americans for Tax Reform, www.atr.org./content/pdf/pre2004/05200speech.pdf.

Office of Population Affairs. Department of Health and Human Services. http://opa.osophs.dhhs.gov/titlex.Olasky, Marvin. *The Tragedy of American Compassion*. Washington, DC: Regnery Press, 1992.

Opportunity Agenda, The. "The State of Opportunity in America, African Americans and Opportunity" (2005). http://www.opportunityagenda.org/site/c.minL5kkNOLvH/b.1419965/k.3C7B/African_Americans_and_Opportunity.htm.

O'Reilly, Bill. *Culture Warrior.* New York: Broadway Books, 2006.

Padover, Saul. *Thomas Jefferson on Democracy.* New York: Appleton-Century Co., Inc. 1939.

Parker, Star. "Reclaiming America for Christ." Address at conference, April 27–28, 2001, Newport Beach, California.Pew Global Attitudes Project. "U.S. Image up Slightly, but Still Negative" (June 23, 2005). http://pewglobal.org/reports/pdf/247.pdf.

Pew Research Center. The 2004 Political Landscape." November 5, 2003.

Pickering, Charles. *Supreme Chaos*. Macon, GA: Stroud & Hall Publishers, 2005.

Planas, Antonio. "District Pulls Plug on Speech." *Las Vegas Review-Journal*, June 17, 2006). www.reviewjournal.com/lvrj_home/2006/Jun-17-Sat-2006/news/8014416.html.

———. "Group Files Lawsuit, Alleges School Officials Violated Teen's Rights." *Las Vegas Review-Journal*, (June 14, 2006). www.reviewjournal.com/lvrj_home/2006/Jun-14-Sat-2006/news/8491786.html.

Plante, Thomas G. *Bless Me Father for I Have Sinned*. Westport, CT: Praeger, 1999.

Plato. *The Republic.* Book VI. In *Classics of Moral and Political Theory*, 4th ed., edited by Michael L. Morgan. Indianapolis, IN: Hackett Publishing Company, 2005.

"Porn In The U.S.A." CBS News *60 Minutes.* www.cbsnews.com/stories/2003/11/21/60minutes/main585049.shtml?source=search_story.

Postrel, Virginia I. "Persecution Complex—Religion in the Workplace." *Reason.* (August–September 1994) www.findarticles.com/p/articles/mi_m1568/is_n4_v26/ai_15630153.

Prager, Dennis. "The Left Thinks Legally, The Right Thinks Morally." *Creators Syndicate*, September 21, 2004.

Pride, Richard A., and J. David Woodard. *The Burden of Busing*. Knoxville: University of Tennessee Press, 1985.

Pring, George W., and Penelope Canan. *SLAPPS*. Philadelphia, PA: Temple University Press, 1996.

Prothero, Stephen. *Religious Literacy*. San Francisco: Harper, 2007.

Rainwater, Lee, and William L. Yancey. *The Moynihan Report and the Politics of Controversy*. Cambridge, MA: MIT Press, 1967.

Reagan, Ronald. "Inaugural Address," January 21, 1985. Ronald Reagan Presidential Library.

Rector, Robert. *The Heritage Foundation Backgrounder* 1533 (April 2002).

———. "Out of Wedlock Childbearing and Paternal Absence: Trends and Social Effects." www.catholicculture.org/library/view.cfm?ecnum+1446.Rose, Matthew F. *John Witherspoon*. Washington, DC: Family Research Council, 2001.

Roszak, Theodore. *The Making of a Counter Culture*. 2nd ed. Berkeley: University of California Press, 1995.

Sabine, George H. *A History of Political Theory*. 4th ed. Hinsdale, IL: Dryden Press, 1973.

Salari, Sonia Milner, and Bret M. Baldwin. "Verbal, Physical and Injurious Aggression among Intimate Couples over Time." *Journal of Family Issues* 23 (May 2002).

Santorum, Rick. *It Takes a Family*. Wilmington, DE: ISI Books, 2005.

Schaeffer, Francis A. *How Should We Then Live?* Old Tappan, NJ: Fleming H. Revell Company, 1976.

Scott, David Alexander. "How Pornography Changes Attitudes." *Pornography: The Human Tragedy*, Edited by Tom Minnery. Wheaton, IL: Tyndale House Publishers. www.leaderu.com/orgs/probe/docs/pornplag.html.

"Scouts Ban on Gays Is Prompting School to Reconsider Ties." *Education Week*. October 25, 2000.Sears, Alan, and Craig Osten. *The ACLU vs. America*. Nashville, TN: Broadman & Holman Publishers, 2005.

"Sexually Transmitted Diseases in the US: New Numbers from the CDC." *Healthlink*. Medical University of Wisconsin. http://healthlink.mcw.edu/article/976735469.html.

Shannon, James. "Books and Politics: Truth & Beauty Under Fire." *The Beat* (July 25, 2006). www.metrobeat.net/gbase/Expedite/Content?oid=oid%3A3944.

"Shedding the Intellectual Straightjacket." *World*, April 29, 2006.

Sills, Jennifer E. "SLAPPS (Strategic Lawsuits Against Public Participation): How Can the Legal System Eliminate Their Appeal?" *Connecticut Law Review* (Winter 1993).

Singel, Ryan. "Internet Porn: Worse Than Crack?" November 2004. www.wired.com/news/technology/0,1282,65772,00.html.

Smith, Christian, ed. *The Secular Revolution: Power, Interests and Conflict in the Secularization of American Public Life*. Berkeley: University of California Press, 2003.

Southwestern Social Science Association. San Antonio, TX. (April 13–17, 2006).

Spaulding, Matthew. "A Defining Moment: Marriage, the Courts and the Constitution." May 17, 2004, Heritage Foundation Backgrounder, #1759.

Stern, Fritz. *The Politics of Cultural Despair*. Berkley, CA: University of California Press, 1960.

Stevens, Betsy. "How Satisfied are Employers with Graduates' Business Communications Skills? A Survey of Silicon Valley Employers" (2004). www.westga.edu/~bquest/2004/graduates.htm.

Stoll, David. *Rigoberta Menchú and the Story of All Poor Guatemalans*. Boulder, CO: Westview Press, 1999.

Strasset, Kimberly, et al. *Leaving Women Behind*. Lanham, MD: Rowman and Little-field, 2006.

Sweetman, Brendan. *Why Politics Needs Religion*. Downers Grove, IL: InterVarsity Press, 2006.

"Television & Health." In *The Sourcebook for Teaching Science*. www.csun.edu/~vceed002/health/docs/tv&health.html.

Teresa, Mother. "Speech at the National Prayer Breakfast" (1994). www.orthodoxytoday.org/articles4/MotherTeresaAbortion.php.

"The Problem of Cohabitation." http://members.aol.com/cohabiting/intro.htm.

Thomason, Elizabeth, et al. "Family Structure and Child Well-Being: Economic Resources vs. Parental Behaviors." *Social Forces* 73 (September 1994).

Treas, Judith, and Deidre Giesen. "Sexual Infidelity among Married and Cohabitating Americans." *Journal of Marriage and the Family* 62 (February 2000).

Trop v. Dulles, 356 U.S. 86 (1958).

"Truth and Beauty: Part Deux." Swamp Fox Insights (August 26, 2006). http://swampfoxinsights.blogspot.com/2006/08/truth-and-beauty-part-deux.html.

TV Guide. (October 11–17, 2003).

Uhlmann, Michael M. "The Supreme Court Rules," *First Things* 136 (November 2003).

U.S. Department of Education. press release 27 June 2002. www.ed.gov/news/press releases/2002/06/06272002d.html.

U.S. Department of Health and Human Services. "Temporary Assistance for Needy Families Information Memorandum" (September 30, 2004).

U.S. Department of Labor. "The Negro Family: A Case for National Action." March, 1965.

Vincent, Lynn. "Shedding the Intellectual Straightjacket." *World* magazine. April 29, 2006.

Wallerstein, Judith S., et al. *The Unexpected Legacy of Divorce*. New York: Hyperion, 2000.

Wardle, Lynn C. "The Potential Impact of Homosexual Parenting on Children." *The University of Illinois Law Review* (1997).

Washington, George. "First Inaugural Address." www.bartleby.com/124/pres13.html.

West, Thomas G. "Religious Liberty." www.charemont.org/writings/970101west .html.

"What Really Mattered?" *Time*, October 5, 1983.

White, John Kenneth. *The Values Divide*. New York: Chatham House Publishers, 2003.

Whitehead, B., and D. Popenoe. "The State of Our Unions." http://marriage .rutgers.edu/Publications/SOOU/TEXTSOOU2004.htm.

Wiesen, Daryl L. "Following the Lead of Defamation: A Definitional Approach to Religious Torts." *Yale Law Journal* 105 (1995).

Will, George F. *Statecraft as Soulcraft*. New York: Simon and Schuster, 1983.

Williams, Juan. *Enough*. New York: Crown Publishers, 2006.

Willke, J. C. *Why Can't We Love Them Both. Breast Cancer*. www.abortionfacts.com/online_books/love_them_both/why_cant_we_love_them_both.asp.

Wilson, Woodrow. "What is Progress?" In *The New Freedom*. New York: Doubleday, Page and Co., 1918.

WirthlinWorldwide. 2004 study. www.friedmanfoundation.org.quorum.pdf.

Wolfe, Alan. *Moral Freedom*. New York: W.W. Norton and Co., 2001.

Zillmann, D., and J. Bryant. "Pornography's Impact on Sexual Satisfaction." *Journal of Applied Social Psychology* 18, no. 5 (1998).

NEWSPAPERS

Atlanta Journal-Constitution
Brodertscher, Nancy. "Legislature 2006." Janaury 28, 2006.
Salzer, James. "Legislature 2006." February 5, 2006.

Baltimore Sun
"General's Remarks Bring Pentagon Homophobia Out of the Closet." March 19, 2007.

BBC News
"U.S. Worst for Online Child Abuse." July 20, 2006.

Boston Globe
Bok, Derek. "Are Colleges Failing? Higher Ed Needs New Lesson Plans." December 18, 2005.
"Students Lagging in American History." July 1, 2005.
"State Orders Wal-Mart to Sell Morning After Pill." February 15, 2006.

Charleston Post & Courier
Bass, Jack. October 13, 2004.
Kropf, Schuyler. "Neck & Neck." October 24, 2004.

Chronicle
"The Rich–Poor Gap Widens for Colleges and Students." April 7, 2006.

Chronicle of Higher Education
Freeland, Richard M. "How Practical Experience Can Help Revitalize Our Tired Model of Undergraduate Education." February 19, 1999.
Field, Kelly. "A Texas Millionaire Plots the Future of Higher Education." June 2, 2006.

Cleveland Plain Dealer
"Pregnant Cheerleaders Are Allowed to Return." November 3, 1993.

CWNews
"Study Links Abortion, Suicide, Depression." August 22, 2001.

Daily Tokoyo Yomiuri
  February 5, 2005.

Detroit News
  Bethel, Allison. "Unwed Culture Stirs Backlash." May 15, 2005.

Greenville Journal
  "HPV Epidemic Plagues Young People." January 6, 2006.

Greenville News
  Hoover, Dan. "DeMint Offers an Apology." October 7, 2004.

Houston Chronicle
  "School Board Reverses Ban on Pregnant Cheerleaders." November 2, 1993.

Knoxville News Sentinel
  October 25, 2001.

Lansing State Journal
  "Equal, Private: High Court Should Strike Down Texas Sodomy Law." March 27, 2003.

Las Vegas Sun
  January 7, 2001.
New York Times
  "Guatemalan Laureate Defends 'My Truth.'" January 21, 1999.
  "Must People Lie?" August 18, 2001.
  "The Case Scouts Had to Win." June 30, 2000.
  "Scouts Successful Ban on Gays Is Followed By Loss of Support." August 29, 2000.
  Editorial. "General Pace and Gay Soldiers." March 15, 2007.

New York Sun
  Gupte, Pranay. "It's Personal for a Top NYC Divorce Lawyer." May 17, 2005.

Newark Star Ledger
  "First comes sex, then comes marriage." December 20, 2006.

Omaha World-Herald
  "Senate Backs Scouts Use of Bases." July 27, 2005.

Oregonian
  "Schools Face New Scout Suit." April 6, 2001.
  "Wells Fargo and PGE to Direct funds from Scouts." December 11, 2000.
  March 9, 2007.

San Diego Union-Tribune
   "City Settles Boy Scouts Lease Suit." January 9, 2004.
   "Spielberg Quits Scout Post." April 17, 2001.
   April 23, 2006.

Seattle Times
   "Companies Here Ponder Scout Ruling." July 6, 2000.
   "Preparing College Students for College and Work." November 29, 2006.

State
   Bandy, Lee. "DeMint's Missteps Give Boost to Tennebaum." October 10, 2004.
   Bauerlein, Valerie. "A Contest of Contrasting Styles." June 17, 2004.
   Markoe, et al., "DeMint Apologizes for Remark." October 7, 2004.
   Sheinin, Aaron G. "DeMint Says Gays Can't Teach In Schools." October 4, 2004.

Sun
   Martin, Sandra. October 7, 2004.
   Miner, Barbara. "Antigay Stance Fits Party Platform." October 21, 2004.

Time
   Joe Klein. "Beware of Bloggers' Bile." May 29, 2007.

USA Today
   "Boy Scout Troops Lose Funds, Meeting Places." October 10, 2000.
   Haynes, Patrick and Jeremy Lott. "Left, Right and Religious." October 16, 2006.
   December 19, 2006.

The Wall Street Journal
   Charles Murray. "The Coming White Underclass." October 29, 1993.

Washington Post
   "Fix It Brother." May 22, 2004.
   Cook, Rebecca. "Laws May Reduce Unwed Fathers." June 19, 2005.
   "Health Experts Criticize Changes in STD Panel." May 9, 2006.
   "Prostitution Clause in AIDS Policy Ruled Illegal." May 19, 2006.
   "Scouts Use of Schools Under Attack." October 4, 2000.
   "Wide Berth Allowed on Teaching About Homosexuality." January 16, 2007.

Washington Times
   "Homosexual Men Boost Increase in Syphilis Rate." March 17, 2006.

Weekly Standard
   Kurtz, Stanley. "The End of Marriage in Scandinavia." February 2, 2004.
   "First Do Harm." February 5, 2007.

Index

40-Year Old Virgin, The, 165
60 Minutes, 140
1964 Civil Rights Act, 9
1992 Presidential election, 8, 10
1996 Welfare Reform Act, 156, 194
1996 Welfare Reform Law, 158, 179

AAUP. *See* American Association of
    University Professors
Abortion: as an issue, 16, 24, 29;
    government intervention, 45, 54, 61;
    late-term, 49, 69; morality of, 58–59;
    privacy, 42
Abramoff, Jack, 148
Academic freedom, 94
ACE. *See* American Council on
    Education
ACLU. *See* American Civil Liberties
    Union
Acquired Immune Deficiency Syndrome
    (AIDS), 180, 187
Adams, John, 30, 53–53, 173
Adams, Mike, 96
Adams, Samuel, 53
Aiken Standard, 6
AFDC. *See* Aid to Families with
    Dependent Children
African-American studies, 101

Aid to Families with Dependent
    Children (AFDC), 157
AIDS. *See* Acquired Immune
    Deficiency Syndrome
Alliance Defense Fund, 57, 89, 117
American Association of State Colleges
    and Universities, 109
American Association of University
    Professors (AAUP), 95
American Civil Liberties Union
    (ACLU): and religion, 50, 64–65, 85,
    115; lawsuits, 55–56, 58–59, 66–67,
    70, 86, 100, 116–18, 166, 183, 196;
    para-government group, 37–38, 40,
    57, 63, 77, 159, 181; values, 120;
American College Health Association,
    96
American Council of Trustees and
    Alumni, 104
American Council on Education (ACE),
    95
American Economic Review, 108
American Family Therapy Academy, 192
American Political Science Review, 108
American political system, 18
American Revolution, 30, 32, 54, 96
American Sexually Transmitted
    Diseases Association, 163

American spirit, viii
Americans United for the Separation of
    Church and State, 22, 26, 193
Anderson, Martin, 108
Aquinas, Thomas, 18
Arizona State University, 101
Atheism, 48–49

"Baby mama," 133
Baron, Larry, 140
Barrett, Gresham, 13
Barrino, Fantasia, 133
Bass, Jack, 5
Beasley, Governor David, 1–2
Bellah, Robert, 167
Bennett, William, x
Bible: and science, 81; as an authority:
    16–17, 20, 22; influence on the
    Constitution, 31; in schools, 42, 45,
    69, 94, 168
Bickel, Alexander, 36
Bill of Rights, 41
Births outside of marriage, 12, 60
Births out of wedlock, 54, 61, 69
Black, Justice Hugo, 37
Block, Don, 192
Bloom, Allen, 97, 103, 190
Bob Jones University v. United States
    (1983), 119
Bok, Derek, 109
Bork, Robert, ix, 41
Bowers v. Hardwick (1986), 188
Boy Scouts of America: 38, 66–67, 70,
    72–78, 114; oath, 72; traditional law,
    71; *v. Dale* (2000), 185
Brennan, William, 99
Breyer, Stephen, 99
British Broadcasting System, 140
Brown v. Board of Education (1954),
    38–41, 155
Brown, Heywood, 113
Burke, Edmund, 60, 166
Bush, George W., 22
"Bush-haters," 170
Burgos, Elizabeth, 102
Butler, Octavia, 104

California Women's Law Center, 86
Carter, President Jimmy, 38
Carter, Stephen L., 169
Carville, James, 7
Castro, Fidel, 95
Catholic Church, 74–75
Catholic Diocese of Brooklyn, 122
Cathy, Dan, 123
Center for Disease Control (CDC), 131,
    162
CDC. *See* Center for Disease Control
CFV. *See* Colorado for Family Values
Charleston Post and Courier, 7
Chavez, Hugo, 95
Chaucer, Geoffrey, 104
Chelmsford, Massachusetts, 117
Chick-Fil-A, 123
Child support laws, xi
Children's Defense Fund, 157
Christianity, ix, 21
Christians, 16, 18
Cicero, x
Cigarette smoking, 126
"Civil religion," 167
Civil rights groups, 37
Civil rights movement: American, viii;
    of the 1960s, 8
Civil War, viii
Clemson University, 91–92
Clinton, Bill, 8, 10, 135, 169
Closing of the American Mind, The
    (Bloom), 97, 103
Colorado for Family Values (CFV),
    9–10
Columbia University, 195
Columbine High School, 52
Commission on the Future of Higher
    Education, 93
Community Marriage Covenants, 161
Condon, Charlie, 1
Constitution of the United States:
    interpretation of, 36–38, 40–42; on
    freedom of expression, 17; on
    freedom of speech, viii; on religion,
    30–31, 72; preamble, xii; protection
    under, 7; separation of powers, 18

Constitutional Convention of 1787, 31
Cooke, Miriam, 105
Core curriculum, 106
Cornell University, 104
Cosby, Bill, 155–156
Creationism, 21
Crossfire, 7
Culture development cycle, 55, 67, 175
Culture of Unbelief, The (Carter), 169
Culture war, vii, 8, 16–17, 25, 39, 59, 61
Culture Warrior (O'Reilly), 25, 46, 168
Culture Wars (Hunter), 15

Dale, James, 73
Darrow, Clarence, 64
Darwin, Charles, 23
Davis, Orly, 1
De Tocqueville, Alexis, 31
Declaration of Independence, 38, 47–48, 84, 98
"Deconstruction," 98
Deming, Edward, 54
Democracy, viii, ix, 31, 52–53, 59
Democratic Party, 100, 196
Denmark, 190
Detroit News, 133
Diggs, John R. Jr., 142
Diversity, 94, 101, 103
Divorce: and children, 60; family structure, 16; government sanction of, 45, 61; no-fault, 24, 136; rates, x, 12, 135
Dobson, James, 195
Dubner, Stephen J., 137
Duval County, 114

Educational choice, 6
Employment Non-Discrimination Act, 123
Engel v. Vitale (1962), 37, 85
Enloe, Cynthia, 105
Enough (Williams), 156
Epperson v. Arkansas (1968), 85
European Union, 138
Everson v. Board of Education, 137, 184

Fagan, Patrick, 189, 191
Federal income tax, 3
Federal Marriage Protection Amendment, 189
Federalist Papers, viii
Few, William, 31
Field, Joe, 170
First Amendment: clauses, 37, 115; on religion, 118; rights protected, viii, 17, 25, 65–66, 73, 85, 114, 187; separation of church and state, 72, 93, 184; violation of, 177
Foucault, Michael, 39
Franklin, Benjamin, 31, 52
Free Exercise Clause, 121
"Free speech," 188
Freedom of speech, viii, ix, xi, 22, 25–26, 42–43
Frum, David, 173

Gallagher, Maggie, 129
Gallup Poll, 126
Gambling, 145
Gay rights, 11
Gender studies, 105
General Motors, 141
Georgetown University, 104
Glenn, Narval D., 133
Golden rule, 17
Government regulation, ix
Graham, Reverend Franklin, 22
Graham, Lindsey, 13
Gratz v. Bollinger (2003), 95
Great Depression, 152
Great Society, 156
Greenville News, The, 6
Gross national product, x, 35
Guinn v. Church of Christ of Collinsville (1980), 121

Hamilton, David, 109
Harvard, 93
Havel, Vaclav, 33
Health care, 4
Health insurance reform, 6
Health Risks of Gay Sex, The (Diggs), 142

Hempstead High School, 58
Heritage Foundation, 164
Heterosexual, 10, 73
Heterosexuality, 63
Heterotopia, 39
Hill, 6
Hirsch, E. D., 103
HIV. *See* Human Immunodeficiency Virus
Homosexual, 4–5, 7–11, 15–16, 72–74, 76; groups, 8–11; rights, 8
Homosexuality: and the government, 4, 45, 63; as a lifestyle, 11; discussion of in schools, 79, 83; in lawsuits, 73, 75; opposition to 12;
Horowitz, David, 100
HPV. *See* Human Papillomavirus
Huckabee, Mike, 160
Hull, Jane Dee, 160
Human Immunodeficiency Virus (HIV), 141
Human Papillomavirus (HPV), 130–132
Human Rights Campaign Fund, 10
Humanism, 48
Hunter, James Davidson, 15, 17

I, Rigoberta Menchú (Burgos), 102
Identity politics, 100
Illegal immigrants, 45, 54
Immutable trait, 10
"In God We Trust," 118
Indian Gaming Regulatory Act of 1988, 147
Inglis, Bob, 13
InnerChange Freedom Institute, 193
Internal Revenue Code, 119
Internet gambling, 147
Internet Watch Foundation, 140
"Invisible force," 115
Iranian mullahs, 152

Jefferson, Thomas, 97, 106
Jim Crow laws, 40, 44
Jones, Walter, 193
Joseph Eastbrook Elementary School, 79

Judeo-Christian: bias, 49; context, 44; cultural values, 59, 64, 83, 86, 98; ethics, 17, 152; religious adherents, 18; tradition, 22, 24; worldview, 21, 29, 42, 57, 64, 111
Juran, Jin, 54

Kane, Judge John, 151
Kansas City, Kansas 161
Kansas City, Missouri, 161
Kansas City Star, The, 161
Kennedy, Anthony, 99
Kennedy, Ted, 157
"Kerry-haters," 170
Kierkegaard, Soren, 152
King, Martin Luther Jr., 95, 154, 169

Labor unions, 37
Ladd, Everett Carol Jr., 100
Lake Wobegon, 106
Layden, Mary Anne, 140
Leaving Women Behind (Strassel et al.), 128
Lee v. Weisman (1992), 85, 114
Legion of Honor, 102
Leo, John, 122
Lerner, Gerda, 105
Levitt, Steven D., 137
Lewis, John, *157*
Lincoln-Douglas debates, viii
Lipset, Seymour Martin Jr., 100
Locke, John, 98
"Love Child," 133
Lynn, Barry, 193

Machiavelli, 54
Madison, James, 53–54, 97
Male and Female Homosexuality (Saghir and Robins), 144
Male Couple, The (McWhiter and Mattison), 144
Marriage: 4, 12, 16, 18; gay marriage, 11; homosexual marriage, 12; same-sex marriage, 24; savers, 161

Marriott, 141
Marshall, Thurgood, 99
Marx, Karl, 98
Massachusetts Family Institute, 80
Mattison, Andrew M., 144
McBride, Mark, 1
McCartney, Bill, 9–10
McComb, Brittany, 115
McWhirter, David P., 144
Medicaid, 192, 195, 199
Medicare, 138, 199
Meet the Press, 7
Men's Resource Center, 93
Merriam, Charles, 99
Mill, John Stuart, ix
Miller, Charles, 93
Miller v. California (1973), 139
Milton, John, 104
Miss America Pageant, 151
"Moment of silence," 114
Moral: absolutes, 18; authority, 16;
    relativism, ix, 17, 20, 45, 48;
    relativists, xii
Moral Freedom (Wolfe), 125
Moses, 30
Mother Teresa, 169
Moynihan, Senator Daniel Patrick, 52,
    156
Multiculturalism, 94, 100, 101
Murdoch, Jan, 92
Murray, Charles, 156
Murray v. Curlett (1963), 167

NARAL. *See* National Abortion Rights
    Action League
National Abortion Rights Action League
    (NARAL), 123, 159
National Association for Research and
    Therapy of Homosexuality, 74
National Association of Scholars, 103,
    105
National Gambling Impact Study
    Commission, 147
National Institute of Mental Health
    (NIMH), 32

National Longitudinal Study of
    Adolescent Health, 165
National Organization of Women
    (NOW), 65, 77, 159
Natural laws, 18
Neuhaus, Richard John, 153
New Deal, 158
New Hampshire, 145; Constitution of
    1784, 50
New York Times, The, 8, 73, 102, 113
NIMH. *See* National Institute of Mental
    Health
Nobel Peace Prize, 102
Norway, 190
NOW. *See* National Organization of
    Women

O'Connor, Sandra Day, 99
O'Reilly, Bill, 25, 46, 168
Oklahoma Marriage Initiative, 160
On Liberty (Mill), ix
Operation "keepsake," 165
Orthodox traditionalism, 16–17
Our Underachieving Colleges (Bok), 109

Pace, General, 113
Paige, Ron, 185
Patchett, Ann, 91
Pell Grants, 94
People's Republic of China, 200
Pew Research Study, 176
Pickering, Judge Charles, 30–31
Planned Parenthood: funding of, 166;
    lawsuits, 41; para-government group,
    56, 63, 65, 120, 159, 165; political
    influence of, 138
Plato, 97, 174
Playboy, 92
Pledge of Allegiance, 18, 38
Pluralism, 39
"Political correctness," 103
"Politically correct," 107
Pope Paul II, 102
Pornography: cost of, 139; court
    decision on, 57; government stance

on 29, 45, 63; in the media, 75; lawsuits, 67; public opinion of, 16, 69

Postmodernism, 100

Prager, Dennis, 64

"Praxis," 105

Prayer in public schools, 16

Premarital sex, 24, 42, 69, 83

Prevent Child Abuse America, 134

Prison Fellowship, 193

Pro-Choice Massachusetts, 123

Progressive, 20; modernism, 16–17; worldview, 39, 82

Protected class, 11

Promise Keepers, 9

Radical: egalitarianism, 19; feminism, 100–1; individualism, 19

Ravenel, Thomas, 1–2

Readings, Bill, 110

Reagan, Ronald, vii

Rector, Robert, 164

Rehnquist, William H., 186

Revolutionary War. *See* American Revolution

"Right to privacy," 188

Roberts v. United States Jaycees, 186

Roe v. Wade (1973), 137, 167, 188

Roosevelt, Franklin, 98

Roosevelt, Francis Delano, 158

Roosevelt, Theodore, 91

Rounds, Mike, 138

Rugged individualism, 32

Russert, Tim, 7

Rutherford Institute, 116, 120

Same-sex marriage, 24, 49, 80

Santorum, Rick, 128

School choice, 184

School District of Abington Township v. Schempp (1963), 85

School prayer decision, 153

Science, 109

Secular worldview, 113

Secularism, 19–21, 23, 26–27, 41, 49

Sexual promiscuity, 132

Sexual Trauma and Psychopathology Program, 140

Sexually transmitted diseases (STDs), 129–131, 141, 163, 180, 191

Shakespeare, William, 100, 104

Silicon Valley, 110

Single-parent homes, x, 24

SLAPP. *See* Strategic Lawsuits against Public Participation

Smith, William, 163

Social Security, 4, 35, 138; reform, 6

Socrates, 95

South Carolina, 1–3, 7–8, 12; Department of Education, 5

Soviet Union, x, 33

Sprinkle, Anne, 104

Stare decisis, 38

State, The, 2–3, 5–7

State Library Board, 138

STDs. *See* Sexually transmitted diseases

Stein, Arlene, 104

Stem cell: debate, 22; research, 21

Stern, Fritz, 168

Stern, Howard, 92

Stewart, Potter, 139

Stoics, 95

Strategic Lawsuits against Public Participation (SLAPP), 65–70, 76, 86, 88, 181, 183

Strauss, Murray, 140

Strengthening Families Initiative, 160

Supreme Court: justices, 40; nominations, 41; on prayer, 72; on religion, 31, 38; rulings, 5, 10, 37, 39, 47, 76–77;

Supremes, 133

Suspect class, 11

Sweetman, Brendan, 26

Taliban, 152

TANF. *See* Temporary Assistance for Needy Families

Tax: code, 3; reform, 3, 6

Teenage suicide rate, x

Temple University, 104
Temporary Assistance for Needy Families (TANF), 134
Ten Commandments, 21, 30, 153, 168, 179
Tennebaum, Inez, 2–7
Texas Department of Criminal Justice, 193
Thomas, Clarence, 41, 189
Time (magazine), 148
Time Warner, 141
Traditionalists: 25–26, 63; speech, 20; worldview, 32, 38
Trigg, Bruce, 163
Trop v. Dulles (1958), 38
Truth and Beauty: A Friendship (Patchett), 91–92

United States Census, 134
United States Department of Defense, 77
United States Department of Health and Human Services, 134, 192
United States Department of Housing and Urban Development, 65
United States House of Representatives, 30, 84
University of California at Berkeley, 131
University of Illinois Law Review, 142
University of Michigan, 103
University of New Hampshire, 140
University of Texas at Austin, 133
University of Virginia, 97
University of Washington, 195

"Vagina Monologues," 95
"Victimless crimes," xi
"Victimology," 101
Vietnam War, 33
Violent crime, x, 61

Virginia's Right Choices for Youth, 160
Virginity Pledge Programs, 164

Wal-Mart, 123
"Wall of separation," 72, 98, 111
Wall Street Journal, 156
Wallerstein, Judith, 136
Wallace v. Jaffree (1985), 85
Walter, Marina, 105
Waltz v. Tax Commission of the City of New York (1970), 119
War on terror, 4
Wardle, Lynn D., 142
Washington, George, 52, 97, 125
Washington Post, 162, 187
Washington Times, 117
Weber, Max, 178
Webster v. New Lenox (1990), 85
Websters New World Dictionary, 95
Welcome to the Ivory Tower of Babel, 93
Welfare reform, xi
West, Thomas, 47–49
« Whisper Zone, The , » 183
Whitehead, Michael K., 123
Wiesen, Daryl L., 121
Will, George F., 174
Williams, Juan, 156
Wilson, Woodrow, 99
Wisconsin v. Yoder (1972), 116
Witherspoon, John, 53
Wolfe, Alan, 125, 148
World War I, 98
World War II, 34, 44, 152
Worldview, 16–22, 24, 29, 32, 64, 83

Xiridou, Dr. Maria, 141

Zelman v. Simmons-Harris (2002), 49, 184
Zenilman, Jonathan, 163
Zogby poll, 197

About the Authors

Senator **Jim DeMint** was born and raised in Greenville, South Carolina. He earned his bachelor's degree from the University of Tennessee and received his master's in business administration from Clemson University. Before winning election to Congress in 1998, he founded a successful Greenville-based market research firm. This work made him an expert in positioning products in a crowded marketplace, a skill that helped him become an effective representative in Washington's crowded noise of ideas. When first elected to the House of Representatives, his colleagues recognized this unique attribute and elected him president of the Republican freshman class.

In 2004, Jim DeMint became South Carolina's fifty-fifth U.S. Senator. He quickly established himself as one of the most effective conservative leaders in Washington as a fighter for smaller government, individual liberty, a strong national defense, and traditional values. He was recently elected as chairman of the Senate Steering Committee, a body of active Republican senators who work to advance conservative legislation.

He and his wife, Debbie, live in Greenville and are the parents of four children and have one grandchild.

J. David Woodard holds the Strom Thurmond Chair of Government at Clemson University, where he has taught political science since 1983. His bachelor's degree is from Abilene Christian University and his Ph.D. was earned at Vanderbilt University. Professor Woodard's research interests are in the field of American government, especially in political theory and voting behavior. He is the author or coauthor of five books, including *The Conservative Tradition in America*, *The New Southern Politics*, and *The America That Reagan Built*.

In addition to his academic responsibilities, he works as a political consultant and has managed political campaigns for Senator Lindsey Graham, then Representative Jim DeMint, Representative Bob Inglis and Representative Gresham Barrett. J. David Woodard is also codirector of the Palmetto Poll, sponsored by Clemson University.

He is interested in the interaction of political ideas and public policy, especially the effect postmodern thinking has had on American education, politics, and social life. He and his wife, Judy, live in Clemson and are the parents of two sons.